T0332842

The Strangers

The Strangers

Five Extraordinary Black Men and
the Worlds That Made Them

Ekow Eshun

HAMISH HAMILTON
an imprint of
PENGUIN BOOKS

HAMISH HAMILTON

UK | USA | Canada | Ireland | Australia
India | New Zealand | South Africa

Hamish Hamilton is part of the Penguin Random House group of companies
whose addresses can be found at global.penguinrandomhouse.com.

First published 2024
001

Copyright © Ekow Eshun, 2024

The moral right of the author has been asserted

Set in 12.5/16pt Fournier MT Std
Typeset by Jouve (UK), Milton Keynes
Printed and bound in Great Britain by Clays Ltd, Elcograf S.p.A.

The authorized representative in the EEA is Penguin Random House Ireland,
Morrison Chambers, 32 Nassau Street, Dublin D02 YH68

A CIP catalogue record for this book is available from the British Library

ISBN: 978-0-241-47202-6

www.greenpenguin.co.uk

MIX
Paper | Supporting
responsible forestry
FSC® C018179

Penguin Random House is committed to a
sustainable future for our business, our readers
and our planet. This book is made from Forest
Stewardship Council® certified paper.

For Jenny

People are trapped in history and history is trapped in them.

James Baldwin

Contents

Author's Note

The Strangers is a book about the lives of five remarkable Black men: Ira Aldridge, Matthew Henson, Frantz Fanon, Malcolm X and Justin Fashanu. Five men of varied character and outlook who lived in different places, at different times. Some of them are well known today, their legacies closely studied; others have been largely overlooked by history. Famous or forgotten, a thread runs between them. Each was, in his own way, a pioneer, embodying and enacting striking change in his respective field and in society at large. Each was a traveller and, at one point or another, an exile: a figure in motion through a world that regarded him as alien. Each strove to reach beyond the constraints of race to assert himself as fully human, fully alive.

In telling the stories of these men, I have not attempted to give a complete account of their lives. Instead I have focused on a period in time when each figure stands at a crossroads, grappling with the signal anxieties and ambitions of his era alongside his own personal dilemmas. In some cases that period runs over decades. In others it spans no more than a handful of months, or even days. The structure of my narrative has been guided by the factual details of each man's biography but I have also given myself licence to conjure what the often limited archive cannot supply: the tone and texture of their inner lives. Toni Morrison said that Black people are 'spoken of and written about as objects of history, not subjects within it'. In *The Strangers*, I seek to do the opposite: to move from looking at the Black male figure to seeing as him. Through storytelling that intertwines the documentary and the imaginary, I aim to reach a deeper emotional truth than fact alone can offer in order to create an intimate, affective portrait of each man.

I realized very early in the literary process that, to achieve this goal, I would need to speak through the men's own voices. This idea of direct voicing became the second-person-narrative approach which predominates through the book, and via which I have attempted to stand in my subjects' shoes, and to invite my reader to do the same. To do justice to these individual stories, it also felt important to evoke the dense web of Black diasporic history, culture and politics within which they stand. So the book also features a second strand: a series of short but expansive essays that counterpoint the character-driven main chapters. These essays range much more widely across place and era than the character chapters, introducing a broad cast of artists and writers, travellers and tricksters, and through them tracing the development of my own thinking on Blackness and masculinity.

This densely constellated and more-than-factual approach to personal histories seems especially fitting given that the enterprise of simply being a Black man moving through a white world frequently takes the individual beyond the everyday into a charged space of performance, fantasy and myth. The stories and stereotypes that frequently categorize Black men as brutish or lawless are as well worn and persistent as the fantastical idea of race itself – a socially constructed fiction without any basis in scientific fact, but one which nevertheless shapes how we see the world. Each Black man is the heir to this legacy of caricature, which renders him simultaneously invisible and hypervisible. His existence is inextricably entangled with his representations in popular culture and the white imaginary. To live in such a state involves sustained impositions on one's personhood, from minor daily slights to heightened threats to your freedom and your life itself. It constitutes a feat of self-authorship under intensely hostile conditions which remains, to my mind, inherently heroic.

But Black men are also denizens of what the poet Elizabeth Alexander calls the black interior: 'our abstract space, our space of the real/not-real . . . Far, far beyond the limited expectations and definitions of what black is, isn't, or should be.' In writing this book, I hope to speak also to that zone of possibility: approaching each of my subjects from a position of not-knowing, and moving freely across time and place, memory and imagination, to encounter Black masculinity not as a fixed state but as an open proposition.

I

Ira Aldridge

Five Points, Manhattan, 1821

To white eyes every black man is Othello. A creature of ungovernable desires, lusting after white women and liable to murder. This is why you stay silent in the presence of white folks. When the trustees pay their annual visit to the African Free School, you're not one of the boys who stick up their hands to recite the scripture passages your teachers have made you memorize. Rather than put yourself on display, you prefer to watch the white men enact their own performance. Puffed up and red-faced, quoting Latin mottos whose only purpose is to remind you: know your place.

Philip Bell

We spent our schooldays together but we weren't close. I always had the impression of him holding back. Ira rarely shouted or wrestled with the rest of us and sometimes, when I was walking down the road with him, I would hear him sigh to himself. You couldn't pick his face out in a crowd and that seemed to be how he preferred it. The peculiar thing was that we were each of us supposed to stand out.

The trustees called us the future leaders of our race, the first black generation in New York born to freedom. But our school was a sorry thing. Five hundred children crammed into dilapidated buildings. Teachers coming and going so often you hardly knew their names. And the pupils themselves turning up in ragged clothes, going back to squalid homes at the end of each day. The trustees said they'd make us into 'men of distinction'. They lined us up at our public examinations and gave out prizes for the best Bible recitation. We offered 'our feelings of warmest gratitude and tenderness' – that was the phrase – to the trustees, as they sat looking on. Receiving a prize was a great honour and there was plenty of vying for the right to speak. I never once saw Ira volunteer. Looking back now, I think he had a better idea than the rest of us.

What was our future to be, as leaders of our race? Boys were taught to be tailors or carpenters, shoemakers or blacksmiths. Girls learned to sew and knit. Or else they said, go and work the land so that our nation may be cultivated by intelligent and industrious coloured persons. In the year of our graduation, the best of our class, aged fifteen, long-limbed and light-skinned, stood before us to give his valedictorian's address. The trustees sat in a row behind the stage, wearing smiles of expectation. But the boy failed to strike the anticipated note of optimism. 'What are my prospects?' he said. 'To what shall I turn my hand? Shall I be a mechanic? No one will employ me; white boys won't work with me. Shall I be a merchant? No one will have me in his office; white clerks won't associate with me. Drudgery and servitude, then, are my prospective portion.' Across the hall I spotted Ira, face blank, shoulders bowed, and I thought of him then as flotsam, about to be swept out into the tumult of the city, once the doors shut behind him for the last time. As we all were.

—

At dawn. Your father asleep on the other side of the basement room. Your brother beside you in the bed. The winter morning is so cold that you can't bear to move, so you lie still trying to preserve the pocket of heat beneath the blanket while the city grumbles to life outside. Carriages rattle over rutted streets. The cries of the baker's boy with his basket of spiced gingerbread and fresh-baked tea rusk.

Then two pedlars pushing a wheelbarrow and a Dutch churn, calling out, *Sour buttermilk*. A scratching sound inside the room shakes you out of your reverie. In the half-light, a mouse explores the wooden floor. Torn between lassitude and revulsion, you watch its staccato movements, nosing the ground for scraps of food wedged between the floorboards. Your disgust flares at the temerity of the creature. Its interloper presence. Its thin, flickering tail.

You spring out of bed, fetching the broom from the corner and, raising the handle, slam its brush head down in the direction of the mouse, which goes skittering behind a wooden chest. Joshua jolts awake and across the room Father sits up. By the time they are on their feet you've pushed the chest aside but the mouse has disappeared into a knothole in the floorboards. It's the third time this week. The endless repetition of the morning, waking to the same four walls, hemmed in between Joshua's sleeping body and the noise of the street outside, the vermin indistinguishable one from the next. You long to be someplace else. At least Joshua is free to come and go as he pleases. He, being five years older than you and employed as a labourer, regards himself as a man of the world, departing the basement at night dressed up in his coat and long watch chain, leaving you alone with Father, who sits reading scripture aloud by candlelight at the end of every day.

Father is a lay preacher at Old Zion, on the corner of Frankfort and William, and carries himself stiff-backed like he's ready to deliver a sermon, even though every day except Sunday he's out on the streets as a straw vendor. It's his white, broad-brimmed hat you see first, coming down the road as he sits mounted on his cart, the skinny horse pulling his wares and him required to shout, *Here's straw*, like every other Negro jostling for attention in Five Points. You can tell the time in this neighbourhood, day or night, by the sounds of the street. The later the hour, the more raucous the cries. Women parade the sidewalk, banging tin pails and shouting, *Come-get-your-lily-white-hot-corn-just-out-of-the-boiling-pot.* Oystermen steer horse-drawn carts down the street. Stalls materialize along the sidewalk for vendors selling Rockaway clams until the early hours. After dark, an army of tubmen emerges. They work in pairs, bawling back and forth to each other, as they push their carts down to the wharves to dump the waste from the city's privies in the Hudson. The men spend their earnings from each cartload on rum to help them endure the night's labour, and thus the commotion gets worse as the hours progress. They take to singing or shouting abuse, the contents of their carts splattering on to the streets as they become more careless, and the houses along their route filling with the reek of their passing.

But inside the apartment itself, the nights are terribly quiet compared to the nocturnal hubbub outside. Once Father has finished reading there's little you have to say to each other. When you and Joshua were small, Mother would sing in the evenings. You remember sitting, one on either side of her, while she recited an exquisitely sad hymn that was only bearable because it gave you an excuse to squeeze close to her in the candlelight. You can recall her voice lilting the words to 'Leaning on the Everlasting Arms', more readily than you do her face now. Five years after her passing, the time you spend with Joshua and Father is a daily reminder of her absence.

It is viciously cold when you climb the steps to the street. A layer of ice coats the sidewalk. Carriage wheels have shaped the horse muck on the cobblestones into grooves frozen hard as iron. You are apprenticed to your father's brother, a shoemaker. Already you've spent more time at the foul-smelling tannery than you think you can stomach for the rest of your life. You're early this morning so, before

6

you submit to another day in the over-hot workshop, you turn in the opposite direction and begin walking through the streets without destination.

New Yorkers say Five Points is the city at its most fetid. Its red-brick tenements harbour every kind of wickedness and degradation. Mr Foster calls the neighbourhood 'a sad, an awful sight – a sight to make the blood slowly congeal and the heart grow fearful and cease its beatings'. You read his book in school and were angry that some-one could dismiss your home so ungraciously. 'The very type and physical semblance of hell itself.' To your mind Five Points is not much different to any other poor, rough district of New York City. Its benighted reputation is more to do with white folks' disdain for a neighbourhood where black people have gathered together in num-bers. A place where they walk free from the shadow of slavery.

Despite what is said about it, Five Points is not all whorehouses and gambling dens. You pass Old Zion, where every Sunday the whole neighbourhood comes together, and, walking west through the cold streets, you think of how the cooks and domestics and day labourers in the congregation transform themselves weekly into creatures of marvellous plumage. And the way that, in the evening, after church is done, Negroes gather from all across lower Manhattan to parade along Broadway, the ladies in hats abundant with ribbons and flowers, the gentlemen wearing striped trousers and kid gloves, swinging gold-headed canes, extravagant lengths of watch chain in their waist-coat pockets. Negroes are barred from the city's pleasure gardens, and many of its finer establishments, but during the Sunday promenade you would think New York City belonged to them.

Not that the white folks will have it that way. The newspapers carry letter after letter protesting that the 'black dandies and dandi-zettes' have taken over the streets. They complain about black folk

7

walking in groups, arm-in-arm, and not stepping off the sidewalk to let white folk pass. The lot of black people in this country is so abysmal that you revel in the complaints. Each anecdote is a small victory. Sometimes you pick up old newspapers from the street and scour them for stories of outraged white people. On Broadway, reported the *National Advocate*, a black woman was heard to say 'she wished the yellow fever would kill all the whites, that the blacks might have the sidewalks to themselves.' In another edition of the same publication, a black man was quoted exclaiming, in a peevish tone, as he elbowed a lady out of her way, 'Damn these white people, there's no getting along for them.' The *Gazette and General Advertiser* described one Mr Isaiah Kip assailed by four black women who 'spoke to him in a very vulgar obscene manner, calling him Blue Bollocks'.

You blink against the wind, eyes moistening. Reflected in the window of a hat store you see a thin boy with his head bowed and his collar raised, swimming up the street on this frigid morning. The prospect of another day of paring, rasping, scraping, hammering shoes with only another day and then another of the same after that makes you sigh aloud. You pause at the corner, lifting your face to a shaft of pale sunlight that has broken through the clouds. Once again you wish that you could be Joshua instead. After he's done with work for the day, he's out to the dance cellars, returning home in the early hours wreathed in the scent of tobacco and sweat. You picture the room, packed with bodies, hot and noisy with fiddle, drum and trumpet, and the dancers crossing their feet, stamping their heels, beating their hands against their legs, spinning and dropping to the floor.

Without noticing where you're headed, you have walked to the Hudson River. Your feet often lead you here. You like to stand at the edge of the water, gazing out at the open horizon, the three-masted packet ships gliding out from the docks. Isaac Wright & Son. Jeremiah and Francis Thompson. Goodhue & Co. Sailing out of view, New York to Liverpool in forty days. Do black people live better abroad than here? Can they be much worse off?

The cold is severe enough this morning to have iced over parts of the water, just thinly. Last winter, the whole river set hard like a pavement. The packet ships were stuck in place. Terns and herring gulls paced impatiently across the ice, pecking at its surface. Boys amused themselves by throwing stones across the frozen expanse, and occasionally at the birds too. In your mind, you saw yourself walking out on to the motionless river, walking until you had left New York behind and were quite alone, advancing across the sea, mile after mile over the creaking ice, fragile as it was.

2

The play is *Macbeth*. The actor, Edmund Kean. You watch from the gallery of the Park Theatre, trying to make sense of what you're seeing. There is an elemental vigour to Kean's movements. The unexpected pauses. His mercurial shifting from the mundane to the spectral. Each transition is a shock, a lightning strike in the dark. Joshua has been coming to the Park for years but it's only lately you've joined him. Father regards the theatre as a cesspit of immorality. You come anyway, in secret, choosing the liveliness of the playhouse over another night with him and his verses.

But until now you've never seen anything like Kean. He is an Englishman and the finest Shakespearean actor of his generation. Where other classical performers are grandiose and declamatory, Kean is alarmingly naturalistic. He hardly looks as if he belongs onstage. He is small, dark, with a grating voice and, it's widely known, a heavy drinking habit. His characters are dishevelled and mumbling, as if they've wandered in off the street. Yet his presence throws the rest of the production into shade. Even the raucous atmosphere in the gallery is not enough to distract you from his performance.

All around you, bodies are crushed in close, talking loudly, coughing and spitting, drinking gin. Cigar fumes sting your eyes and cloud the view below. A man next to you is trying to eat a steaming meat pie, balancing the hot pastry on the tips of his fingers as, with each bite, its soft base collapses further, and chunks of meat and gravy slide on to his pants. Behaviour in the third-tier gallery is absent the illusion of refinement. Up here whites and blacks mix together and the idea that the former are members of a superior race is readily contradicted by the boorish conduct on display from all parties.

In the interval, the musical numbers are met with hooting and loud jeers. Apples and roast chestnuts are hurled on to the stage. You squeeze back through the crowd, past a whore and her client rutting in a half-lit corner near the bar, and down the stairway to the alley. No Joshua with you this evening. As you lean against the wall, trying to ignore the stink of piss, you wonder how it is that the rest of the audience aren't lined up beside you, so dazzled by Kean's performance that they also need to breathe in the night air and recover themselves.

Unprompted yet fully formed, the thought comes: you want to stand in his place, on the stage, to know the fullness of that alchemy, the mystery of his performance. The notion is as unlikely as it is compelling. You, who have always hidden away and refused attention. Yet it seizes you so hard you lose your bearings for a moment, dazed, standing out in the noxious alley, as a white man pushes past you through the narrow doorway and up the stairs.

On the African Theatre

Before he founded the African Theatre, William Brown was a ship's steward, working aboard the transatlantic passenger packets between Manhattan and Liverpool. A steward was one of the most important figures on the ship. He was the solicitous attendant to the passengers' needs, the ship's discreet go-between and fixer, who saw all and knew all. Brown, charming and self-assured, born a free man in the Caribbean, earned enough from his salary and generous tips to quit the sea and settle in New York.

In August 1821, he launched a venture in the yard behind his house, which stood on Thomas Street at the dividing line between Manhattan's affluent West Side and the raucous Five Points. The African Grove was a tea garden, catering to black gentlemen and ladies who were unwelcome in the city's other fashionable ice-cream parlours and cafes, and the tone was firmly refined. Visitors were entertained with vocal recitals and a string quartet. Gentlemen dressed in wide pantaloons and shining boots. Ladies wore pink kid gloves, silk parasols hooked on their arms. There were cakes and roast meats to eat and a bar offering brandy and gin toddies, strong ale and mulled wine.

The African Grove was a victim of its own success. Less than a month after opening, it was shut down by the patrolmen of the watch after Brown's West Side neighbours complained about the excessive noise. By September, Brown was back with a new business. Opening the upstairs of his house to the public, he launched the country's first black drama company: the African Theatre.

The company debuted with *Richard III*. It was a production of variable quality. The actors were amateurs who worked by day as servants and tradesmen; each member of the small cast played several roles. On the frequent occasions they forgot their lines they resorted to ad-libbing. Props and costumes were rudimentary: Richard III wore a robe fashioned from a red velvet curtain. But many of the company had previously been enslaved and the mere fact of their being onstage, performing Shakespeare, was a powerful refutation of the idea of black benightedness.

From among the cast, James Hewlett, a Caribbean ship's steward like Brown, emerged as the troupe's star performer. In *The Drama of King Shotaway*, an original play written by Brown, he performed several songs and danced in a ballet, in addition to taking the title role. Led by Hewlett, the company was popular enough with black New Yorkers for Brown to make an audacious move in January 1822 to new premises at the Hampton Hotel on Park Row, next door to the Park Theatre, one of the city's foremost venues. From there, Brown, the impresario, and Hewlett, the virtuoso, set themselves up as a mirror image to their storied neighbour. When the Park announced the American debut of the great English tragedian, Junius Brutus Booth, in *Richard III*, Brown countered with a revival of his own production, starring Hewlett. Where black visitors were confined to the third tier of the Park, white attendees to the African Theatre were likewise seated in the far reaches of the house.

The calculated irreverence of the theatre matched the growing assertiveness of black New Yorkers across the city in the waning days of slavery. Newspaper court reports echoed the same irritation with impudent blacks as the readers that wrote in complaining about haughty dandies and dandizettes on Broadway. The *Courier and Enquirer* reported that Diana Dixon, a young black woman, responded with derision when given six months in prison for stealing two teaspoons and a fan. 'Six months is nothing,' she told the judge. 'I would not care if you added ten more to it.' Eliza Hazard, a mulatto given fifteen months hard labour for theft, uttered 'an audacious laugh' and told the judge to 'go to hell'. A young black man sentenced to six months 'burst into a loud laugh, and remarked that six months to him was only a breakfast spell'. From the 'boisterousness of their manners' to 'the disgusting indecency of their language', wrote the *New York Enquirer*, free black people were 'impudent and offensive beyond all precedent', and 'a nuisance incomparably greater than would be a million slaves'.

Leasing a space right next door to the Park signalled the level of Brown's ambition. But it also brought him into direct conflict with the Park's intimidating manager, Stephen Price, the most powerful figure in the New York theatre world. Price was also known as King Stephen, a title that inevitably brought to mind the English tyrants America had fought so hard to escape only decades earlier. Plainly put, he was not someone you wanted for an enemy. In May 1816, Price's youngest brother, Benjamin, was killed in a duel with a British army officer, who subsequently fled to England. A few years later, an army captain from the same regiment visited New York and boasted of being 'instrumental in goading' his fellow officer into the duel. Price, who was confined to his bed with gout, forced himself up, hobbled to the Washington Hotel and issued a challenge to the visiting captain. They duelled on Bedloe's Island, where Price shot his opponent dead with a single bullet.

By relocating to Park Row, Brown made himself Price's latest adversary. For years New York theatres had been entertaining audiences with plays featuring an array of simple-minded blacks. The Park itself had presented *The Disappointment; or, The Force of Credulity*, in which a black man named Raccoon – inevitably shortened to Coony – was the ready target of swindlers. At the City Theatre, *Triumph of Love; or, Happy Reconciliation* featured Sambo, a doltish former plantation slave, followed by *The Irishman in London; or, The Happy African*, pairing a black man and a 'wild' Irishman, two races united in their subhuman nature. Brown's company had given the lie to that popular notion of black people as overgrown children. Mounting productions of Shakespeare, and even directly competing with the Park to stage the same play, suggested a parity between black and white – Hewlett and Booth, Brown and Price – that Price could not stand for.

He sent hecklers to join the white theatregoers at the back of the African Theatre. They talked over every performance and threw chestnuts and apple cores at the actors. When Brown persisted in staging his performances, airily observing that 'whites do not know how to conduct themselves at entertainments for ladies and gentlemen of color', Price went further. At his instigation, a dozen members of the watch raided a performance of *Richard III*, storming the stage midway through a soliloquy by Hewlett, who was hauled off, along with the rest of the cast, and locked up at the watchhouse. The actors were released only after swearing to the magistrate never to perform Shakespeare again.

Little Africa, January 1823

You learn the history of the African Theatre belatedly, when you finally become a member of its troupe. This is after you quit the tannery, to the anger and disappointment of Father, who hoped you'd eventually follow him into preaching instead of taking up the sinful business of acting. After Hewlett decides the rest of the company is holding him back from fame and leaves to star in his own one-man shows. And after you, at no one's invitation, have made yourself an inconspicuous but constant presence backstage, sweeping up, carrying costumes, running errands. The company has moved to a new home, out of town, a roughly built wooden playhouse on a vacant lot on the corner of Bleecker and Mercer, in the free black community known as Little Africa. Brown is casting around for a leading man and you are ready.

You are sixteen when you perform Shakespeare for the first time: an earnest Romeo, smooth-cheeked and slender. When you speak blushingly to Juliet it sounds as natural as any adolescent fumbling with grown-up words of desire. Where Hewlett would dominate the stage, bullying his way through a part, you are softer, more sinuous. You take your cue from Kean. His Macbeth felt like an inevitable presence, as if the play would fall apart without him. There was no thundering or stomping about but rather a stillness so that, once he began to speak, there was nowhere you wanted to be but listening, rapt before him. Maybe acting is not like winning a prize at school for declaiming the loudest. Perhaps it is more like silencing the room with your whispering voice.

This, more than any school, is your true education. You discover how to twist and transform yourself for the night, becoming a nobleman in Verona, a rebel chief defying British rule in the Caribbean or a Native Indian on the plains of Chippewa. Sometimes you think it is too great a pleasure to be permissible. But once you have known this feeling, it is impossible to let go of the idea that the whole of life is a performance. Watching the well-dressed black patrons take their seats with such a show of dignity, heads high, looking neither left or right, it seems to you that they must know they're taking part in a masque. No less than the white folks with their feigned superiority, which reveals itself so easily as an illusion when you see how they behave at close quarters.

On the inimitable mimic

The Englishman Charles Mathews is known as the 'inimitable mimic'. His one-person *At Home* shows are a cavalcade of impersonations, ventriloquism, facial and physical contortions, character sketches and comic songs lampooning his English countrymen and figures from further afield, such as the Scots, French and Flemish. Everyone is fair game in a Charles Mathews entertainment.

At the invitation of Stephen Price, Mathews has been touring theatres in North America while developing material for a new production. He is fascinated by the accents and customs and the 'broken English' of black America. A visit to a black church in Boston was particularly enlightening. 'The pranks that are played in the "nigger meetings", as they are called, are beyond belief. Yelling, screeching, and groaning, resembling a fox-chase much more than a place of worship.' The new show will be based on his research. It will be 'rich in black fun'.

True to his pledge, Mathews's *Trip to America* opens in May and features an array of comic characters. These include Colonel Hiram Peglar, a Kentucky shoemaker; Jonathan W. Doubikin, a slow-witted Yankee; 'a runaway Negro' named Agamemnon who is played in blackface as 'a fat, unwieldy fellow'; and, most strikingly, Caesar Alexander Hannibal, a 'Black Tragedian' who Mathews claims to have seen at 'the Niggers Theatre' engaged in the 'preposterous' act of performing Hamlet.

The Hannibal sketch opens with the tragedian delivering a soliloquy. 'To be, or not to be, dat is him question; whether him nobler in de mind to suffer or tak up arms against a sea of trouble and by opossum end 'em.' Then Mathews breaks character to explain to the audience the extraordinary response he witnessed when Hannibal accidentally substituted 'opossum' for 'oppose them': 'At the word opossum, the whole audience burst forth into one general cry of "opossum, opossum, opossum". On enquiring why, I was informed that "Opossum up a Gum Tree" was the national air, or sort of God Save the King of the Negroes, and that being reminded of it by Hamlet, there was no doubt but that they would have it sung. The cries increasing, the sable tragedian comes forward and sings their favourite melody to great cheers before proceeding with the play.'

The target of Mathews's mockery is the African Theatre, with the character of Hannibal based crudely on Hewlett. The show is supported by Price, sending a clear message to Brown, who he still has in his sights. A warning in the *National Advocate*, written by an ally of Price, is yet more explicit. 'It is rather hazardous for Mr Brown to continue with his theatrical experiment this summer. The thermometer is at 85 and the mercury is rising.'

August 1823

It is nine o'clock and you are backstage when the commotion starts. You are not performing tonight but you hear men shouting and the tumble of furniture. The screams of ladies. You rush front of house to see a mob of fifteen white men charging through the theatre. Black patrons are scrambling out of their way. A woman in a peach-coloured dress is shoved to the floor. The white men break up the benches, turning them into clubs with which they smash the lamps. Some of them climb into the boxes, others on to the stage. They cut the cord holding up a circular frame of candles and send it crashing downwards. They slash the scenery and rip down the curtain. They tear the costumes off the struggling bodies of the actors.

And even as you watch, paralysed in horror, someone punches you, catching the side of your face, and you collapse to the ground. An overweight man with ginger hair stands over you. From the floorboards you briefly consider the flapping sole of the man's boot as he launches a kick at your head. You shut your eyes and you can hear the man exhaling with the effort of each kick, and further away, running feet, cries, a burst of guttural laughter.

Later, as you sit amid the wreckage of the theatre, William Brown, his face bruised and swollen, his white shirt torn, is adamant that he recognized the thugs. Price's men. Brown rises stiffly and goes to the watchhouse to bring action against them. He insists you come with him. But it is a forlorn endeavour and you both know it. The men are charged with assault and battery but the case is dismissed before arriving in court. Brown's patrons are too frightened to come back to the theatre. His venture is thoroughly broken.

3

London, 1825

George Davidge

The boy turned up at my door knowing no one in London and barely able to look me in the eye. Even before he spoke I'd decided to put him on the stage. You just had to look at him. His movements languid like he was swimming. Eyes blinking so slowly he might

18

have been dreaming. And the colour of him. Skin that caught the light and held it. Actors, they come to you hungry to please, like panting dogs. He gave you nothing and you couldn't get enough of it.

Our theatre, the Royal Coburg, is a handsome one, with gilt cherubs watching from the ceiling and a 36-foot-high curtain. But it is Lambeth, the wrong side of the Thames. Hazlitt was unjust to compare us to a 'brothel filled with Jew-boys, prostitutes and mountebanks'. But all the same, the better class of patron is reluctant to pay the toll to cross Waterloo Bridge for the privilege of being robbed by the pickpockets of the Marshes.

As manager this past year I have tried to raise our sights. There's less of the regular fare, the farces and melodramas. Dr Preston and his demonstration of nitrous oxide will not be booked for this season. Instead we have *King Lear* and *Hamlet*, albeit abridged and with musical interludes. And now, *The Revolt of Surinam; or, A Slave's Revenge*, 'a most faithful Portrait of the horrors that arise out of the dreadful traffic of slavery, as depicted in its principal role by A Man of Colour'.

—

The wonders of the London stage are various and magical. Every day is a chance to see the greatest performers of their generation. To be an actor yourself in their midst is like inhabiting a dream within a dream. You watch Macready as Lear, G. F. Cooke in *Richard III* and Sarah Siddons's mesmerizing portrayal of the sleepwalking Lady Macbeth. Then, once the curtain is down, you're a witness to the complicated drama of their personal lives in the private clubs of Soho and Covent Garden, where actors gather after hours. Cooke, drunk one night and slumped in a corner, descending so fully from exuberance to melancholy that he's unaware of the wet patch blossoming at his crotch and spreading down his breeches. Master Bailey, despondent enough at losing a part at the Covent Garden Theatre that he tries to cut his own throat. And Kean himself, notorious for arriving late onstage because he's too busy making love to an actress in his dressing room, eventually sued by the husband of Charlotte Cox, another performer who he's having an affair with.

Theatre managers know their stars are made of volatile matter. Cooke is sometimes too inebriated to leave his dressing room when the curtain goes up. Worse yet are the occasions when he does arrive onstage but is unable to recall which character he's playing — declaiming 'Tomorrow and tomorrow and tomorrow' while the rest of the cast bravely tries to make it through the first act of *Lear*. An audience, scenting disarray, will be pitiless, hurling fruit and storming the stage.

To ameliorate the threat of a riot from an unsatiated crowd, London plays are spectacular affairs. For the Battle of Waterloo at the Royal Garden, the Vauxhall promises 'A Grand Military Fete; Ballets, minuets, quadrilles, fireworks and an American aerialist enveloped in fire'. There are shipwrecks, earthquakes, volcanoes, burning houses, aquatic dramas, and animals of all kinds. Lions, tigers, elephants. A horse cast as the lead in a production of *Richard III*. A dog so versatile it plays the cat in *Dick Whittington*.

One night, at the Westminster Pit, you see a fighting monkey called Jacco Macacco pitted against Puss, the favourite bull terrier bitch of the prizefighter Tom Cribb. You stand in the swaying crowd of sweeps, lamplighters, dog-meat men and drunken sons of nobility pushing and jostling to stay on your feet as the animals claw and bite each other until the dog's carotid artery is severed and Jacco's jaw has been torn away and they both lie, twitching and bleeding and whining for it to end. To your shame, you allow yourself to be carried onwards with the crowd, roaring in search of the night's next distraction.

There are times when you wake with a pounding head and puke-spattered pantaloons, clawed creatures and shapeless debaucheries swimming monstrous in the dark of your memory. It is too easy to be swept along in the lurid entertainments of this city at night. Better perhaps to stand apart, as you learned to do at school, than follow the pack. From two o'clock to five o'clock every afternoon, the city's fashionable people show themselves on Bond Street. Fancy shops and splendid equipages and the self-conscious haut-ton desperate to give the impression that they do not care whether or not heads turn at their passing. Sometimes you join that throng, enjoying the effervescent novelty of the spectacle. You are watching an unfolding performance. The city, both backdrop and leading character. London, playing itself. You could never tire of it. There is a kind of splendour in every detail, even in the flight of a pigeon. Watch it glide. Hollow bones and a grey body against a grey sky. A flash of iridescence, green and purple, as it turns and catches a shaft of sunlight on its wing.

—

It is five months since you first arrived in London and here you are rushing through the streets of Lambeth with a script stuffed in your jacket pocket, on your way to play the lead at the Coburg. Heads turn as you hurry by and you like to imagine that the barrow boys and shopkeepers recognize you from the stage, that they shout eager greetings in your wake. And if they are simply staring at the novelty of a black man not dressed in livery or pulling a cart, well, you will still accept that.

The playbills for the Coburg announce you as Mr Keene, the name you've adopted in homage to the great actor. Its familiarity is intended to catch the eye of theatregoers. Maybe it will also silence some of the sceptics in the press who say a black man doesn't belong onstage. 'We have endured the spectacle of theatrical dogs, horses, and elephants before,' said the *Sunday Monitor* in response to the bills. 'And now, for a more monstrous exhibition than all the rest, we are to be treated with a Black Actor, a right earnest African Tragedian.'

The idea that your presence onstage is inherently ridiculous has been shaped in part by Charles Mathews's return to London. His show, *A Trip to America*, has proved wildly popular here, and the conjunction of his performance with your recent arrival from New York has convinced many theatregoers that you must be the real Caesar Alexander Hannibal. In advance of your debut the English press hasn't troubled to hide its preconceptions. 'Mr Mathews gave us a man who looked like a devil and danced like a baboon, whose language was *eew* massa, and me *kill* him Brute, and whose voice was like the bellowing of a townbull. We confess, Mr Mathews's description has prejudiced our minds and we expect to see a mere burlesque on acting, by some sooty child of ignorance.'

October 10th. Standing in the wings on opening night, there's a ringing in your head, a jangling through your body. From beyond comes the sound of chattering voices, coughing and laughter, as the audience settles in place. You are nervous and excited and afraid. You close your eyes, breathe deeply, and try to still time. Then, as the curtain rises, you step out on to the wide stage.

The Revolt of Surinam calls itself 'a Grand West Indian Melodrama' and an actor might be tempted to wail and smite his breast in the role of Oroonoko, a noble prince tricked into slavery. You forgo bombast for sorrow. In your interpretation, Oroonoko clings to dignity despite his subjugation. His choice of suicide over slavery at the climax of the play is a symbolic act of liberation. When you finally take your bow, you are met by the experience – unimaginable in America – of the all-white crowd joined in applause for you. The morning after, you arrive at George Davidge's office to find his desk already scattered with newspapers. The manager watches you with an arch smile as you leaf through them, afraid to see the critics' verdict, and already berating yourself at the foolhardiness of standing on a stage exposed to the judgement of strangers.

'This is, we believe, the only case in which one of "Afric's swarthy sons" has in Europe aspired to the honours of the buskin,' reports the *Globe*. 'The part of Oroonoko, which Mr Keene performed last night, is so characterised by rant and affectation, that it is almost impossible for a performer to avoid falling into these defects. However, on the whole, his conception of the character was very judicious and he rarely overstepped the modesty of nature.' Your heart gives a little jump as you read. London is so large, its theatregoers so opinionated, that you'd feared only a cold response to your debut. But here instead is pure happiness. A vindication of the temerity of your decision to cross the ocean. 'His conception of his part is decidedly good, his action rather graceful, his step firm, and his attitudes dignified,' says the *British Press*. 'He has evidently studied the tricks, the starts, and the hems and ha's of his namesake but he is by no means deficient in original talent. We do not hesitate to express our opinion that his acting will gratify many and astonish all.'

Davidge, keenly attuned to the power of novelty, extends your stay at the Coburg from a fortnight to seven weeks. In addition to Oroonoko you take on an array of dark-skinned roles, from a fierce Moor in *The Castle Spectre* and a rebellious slave in *The Death of*

Christophe to an imperious soldier in *The Divan of Blood!* The parts all share the broken speech and supposedly brutish demeanour of a black man as imagined by a white playwright, but you strive to surmount the flimsiness of the characters as they're written and bring them to nuanced life. Sometimes you think of those abolitionist medallions illustrated with a kneeling slave: whenever you see one, you want to break the man out of those chains and pull him up to his feet. But you have no quarrel with the legend beneath the image: 'Am I not a man and a brother?' You pose the same question to the audience every night you perform.

On slavery

The humanity of a black man is a timely and controversial subject in the Britain of 1825. After two hundred years during which the trafficking, bondage and barbaric treatment of millions of Africans was accepted as the price of sugar and cotton, the public is finally sickening of slavery. Parliament abolished the trade in 1807 but it is still legal in the colonies, with more than 700,000 enslaved Africans labouring on plantations in the West Indies. But William Wilberforce, hero of the 1807 abolition bill, is ailing. The emancipation cause is now led by more cautious figures, like Thomas Fowell Buxton of the Society for the Mitigation and Gradual Abolition of Slavery. Nevertheless, a grassroots movement is building. Campaigners circulate pamphlets throughout the country describing how, in the Caribbean, 'the most disgusting sights that any part of the world can produce' are to be witnessed daily. Dozens of ladies' anti-slavery associations are formed across the nation. In Leicester, the radical Quaker Elizabeth Heyrick is calling for a boycott of 'the deadly bane' of Caribbean sugar.

Pitted against the abolitionists are the powerful interests of the pro-slavery lobby. The aristocrats and men of business that run this country. Among them are dozens of MPs with financial ties to the colonies. In the House of Lords, Prince William, third in line to the throne, calls himself 'an attentive observer of the state of the Negroes', by which he means he is a frequent visitor to the Caribbean, where he is a friend to plantation owners and is known to have contracted a sexual disease at a mulatto whorehouse.

In the West End, the hit of the summer season is *Presumption; or, The Fate of Frankenstein*, an adaptation of Mary Shelley's novel staged at the English Opera House. T. P. Cooke plays the monster as hulking and baleful, his hair lank and skin coloured an unnatural blue, the bestial antithesis to the cool and rational Victor Frankenstein. Hisses sound from the audience at his presence. A lady has to be helped out of the theatre after becoming faint at the sight of him.

There are significant differences between the play and the novel. Notably, the monster onstage is a mute creature whereas the book derives its pathos from the fact that he speaks more eloquently than his creator and is able to narrate the horror of his condition with moving sincerity. Did Mary Shelley have in mind the plight of the enslaved, yearning to free themselves from a life that is not their own? In *Presumption*, the monster's reflection on his suffering is missing. He is reduced to a childlike brute. A caricature of a black man as a simple-minded savage.

In Parliament, soon after the production opens, Foreign Secretary George Canning, a wily and influential supporter of pro-slavery interests, reaches for this version of the monster to press the case against abolition. 'In dealing with the Negro,' Canning tells MPs, 'we are dealing with a being possessing the form and strength of a man, but the intellect only of a child. To turn him loose in the manhood of his physical strength, but in the infancy of his uninstructed reason, would be to raise up a creature resembling the splendid fiction of a recent romance.'

—

You'd think that after seven weeks headlining the Coburg, the theatre world would take note. But the Adelphi will not book you. Nor the Pantheon, the Globe or the Egyptian Hall. Even that dust hole of a playhouse, the Prince of Wales, turns you down when you go begging for work. You crossed the Atlantic to escape New York's bigotry but it seems the sentiment travels with you. Even Stephen Price is here, now running the Drury Lane in Covent Garden. As he did at the Park in New York, he still seems to regard the idea of a black thespian as an affront to social dignity. What you realize following a raft of fruitless meetings is that no theatre manager in London will hire you for fear of offending him.

Neither does it help that although much of the press has supported you, *The Times*, the most influential national publication, remains hostile. Just last week, the paper ran a supposedly humorous sketch devoted to 'theatrical novelties'. 'At the Surrey Theatre there's a man who plays a monkey in the most natural manner possible and at the Coburg they've brought out a genuine nigger.' On other occasions the paper has derided your 'woolly' hair and your lips which are apparently so thick theatregoers can't follow your words. They even complain that your skin is not the authentic shade of a real African, your complexion being 'but little darker than a dun cow'. Perhaps Mr Keene should be replaced by the 'blackamoor who sweeps the crossings at Fleet Street', quips the paper. Or else the problem could be easily solved with a generous application of Day and Martin boot polish.

In honour of your talents, the paper sneers, you should be known as the African Roscius, recalling the great Garrick who used to be called the English Roscius. These days the title is more cliché than tribute. There is a Hibernian Roscius, a Manchester Roscia (the female honorific), the occasional Infant Roscius and even, by way of a performing horse called Buttermilk, an Equestrian Roscius. 'African Roscius' is another way of telling you you're not welcome in this city among these people. Maybe then, as you've done before, it's time to move on.

Exeter, February 1826

You are hungry each night as you fall asleep and cold every morning when you wake. You travelled here by carriage, across the raw Wiltshire Downs, past groups of women dressed in rags and pale as ashes, bent over, working fields strewn with flint. There is employment for an actor in the provinces but it is thin fare. You've played Brighton, Portsmouth and Chichester in the past weeks. Devizes, Devonport and Penzance are still to come. At each town, there's a draughty room in a boarding house, no money for coal and your breath visible in the room's chill air. In the streets, you try to ignore the gawking locals and their predictable jokes about how you've left your greasepaint on.

At these local theatres you're expected to do two or three plays a night, plus songs in between, and to supply your own costumes to boot. The bill changes every day and there are never enough copies of the script to go round, so that you're often looking at the part for the first time during rehearsal on the day of the performance. Even with a *Macbeth* or a *Hamlet*, actors are liable to resort to mugging and pratfalling to cover forgotten lines. It's like going back to the early days of the African Theatre.

Maybe the stress of living in this piecemeal fashion explains why last month in Brighton, midway through playing Rolla in a production of *Pizarro*, the stage began to feel like it was rocking beneath you and you crumpled to the floor. For a while, the other actors continued oblivious, perhaps imagining that you'd also strayed into a temporary spell of improvisation. You could move your eyes to watch them but your limbs would not obey your commands, instead jerking strangely of their own accord. Eventually someone realized you were convulsing and dragged you into the wings. The following week in Portsmouth the same thing happened, although you were able to escape offstage before collapsing. Nothing like it has occurred since, but the uncanny nature of the experience has left you wretched.

You haven't mentioned these fainting spells to anyone in Exeter, but bad news travels fast. Before you take your leave of the city, you read a gloating review in the *Theatrical Observer*. 'It is with regret that we acquaint our readers that the celebrated Mr Keene, who arrived in England a year ago, on a theatrical speculation, has so completely failed in his object, as to be now in the greatest distress. The public are now most respectfully appealed to for aid to free him from immediate want, and to supply him with the funds to return to his native country.'

Liverpool, 1826

The laughter starts as soon as they see you in the costume and that's how it should be. In his red-and-white-striped silk suit, Mungo is the charismatic centre point of Bickerstaff's comedy, *The Padlock*.

The play is sixty years old but the character still feels fresh. Mungo is a type of black man otherwise unknown on the English stage; a sly trickster of an enslaved man who plays his master for a fool. The proposition is so novel that the character has taken on a life of his own. In stores, you can buy Mungo prints and Mungo tea caddies. He's even made it into the *Oxford English Dictionary*: Mungo, meaning 'a Negro'. And also, 'a person of position, a swell'.

To your knowledge, you are the first black person ever to play the character. You stage *The Padlock* as a double bill: in the first half of the show, you demonstrate your range as a serious actor with scenes from *Othello* or *The Revolt of Surinam*, then you lift the mood after the interval by bounding onstage as Mungo. It's a role you've become increasingly associated with, especially since you decided to try your luck in the north of England. They like you better up here and much of that is due to Mungo. Sometimes you can't get through the first half without the crowd shouting for him. They call his name out to you in the street and occasionally you'll catch a person doing a double take, as if to say, what's Mungo doing at large without his striped suit?

Sometimes, though, a heaviness seizes your body as the second half approaches. For all that Mungo is smarter and more self-possessed than any of the white characters in *The Padlock*, he will never be their equal because he is black and enslaved. In the end he's just a fool, confined to performing songs that the audience demands: 'Negro Boy' or even 'Opossum up a Gum Tree'. You know there's a queasy parallel here with your own life. By playing the tragic and the comic in succession, you want the audience to recognize your versatility as a performer. Maybe they might also see that neither of the two roles is your real identity – Othello and Mungo both are the fictions of white men, not the thing itself. Or perhaps this is simply your attempt to explain away the cul-de-sac you now face as a performer. To eat, you must act. Perhaps it's inevitable, then, that you must act the fool.

All blacks in this country are condemned to be performers. The maid, the footman, the dutiful cook – each is playing a role. But if you eschew household service, or the part of day labourer, you face the much more precarious challenge of living by your wits. As singers, trapeze artists, French horn players, lion tamers and bare-knuckle boxers, the blacks here survive by clinging to a threadbare and treacherous fame. Pablo Fanque – acrobat, rope-walker, circus master – is known for his ability as the loftiest jumper in England. Watch and wonder as he leaps lengthwise over a carriage with a pair of horses between the shafts. The bare-knuckle boxer James Wharton, 'Jemmy the Black', is feted for sinews of steel and the punch of a hammer. He is undefeated against all opponents, including his infamous fight with Tom Britton of Liverpool, which went to two hundred rounds over four hours.

Back in your London days, your route to the Coburg sometimes took you through Seven Dials, where the street-sweeper Billy Waters, 'King of the Beggars', and his fellow blackbirds roost. The blackbirds are black men and women, most of them former sailors or servants, who cluster together in the warren of overcrowded houses at St Giles Rookery. Among them are a dustman known as Nasty Bob, and African Sal, who gets about legless on a wheeled trolley. Billy has a peg leg and a military-style bicorn hat festooned with ribbons and feathers. He cleans the crossing outside the Adelphi Theatre in the Strand, clowning and singing and playing the fiddle as he does so. At the height of a song – usually his signature tune, 'Kitty, Will You Marry Me' – he is liable to kick away his wooden leg and spin round on the spot, to the great amusement of onlookers.

This is the life that waits for you if you leave the stage.

1829

The African Roscius was a title meant to shame but you have made it your own. It is another character to play and you have created an entire biography for him. The African Roscius was born in Senegal, the son of a Fullah prince who converted to Christianity and tried unsuccessfully to end his people's involvement in the Atlantic slave trade. Usurped as leader, the prince and his family escaped into exile in America, from whence he came to Britain. This story of royal birth, and the noble father who fought against heathenism and slavery, enables you to make a contrast between the enslaved figures you play onstage and your own distinguished background. With Britain divided on the subject of slavery, it casts you as a noble outsider, a moral force as much as an accomplished performer. Not a person to be compared to Caesar Alexander Hannibal.

John Cole

On Friday evening, the African Roscius visited our theatre in Scarborough. I closed up my bookshop and arrived early to my seat because in truth we do not often have the cream of the acting profession here in our town. To see a man of colour, onstage, in Shakespeare's *Othello* no less, is a spectacle we're rarely accorded.

The African Roscius has a complexion deeply tinctured by the sun. His figure is tall, manly and muscular. His Moor was imposing, sublime. What struck me was the elegance of his gestures. The strange and affecting tone of his voice, by turns impassioned and then dropping to a melancholy cadence at what he imagines to be Desdemona's betrayal. He is only twenty-five years old, in the very vigour of manhood. He is a performer enriched with the brilliancy of genius.

Afterwards, my daughter, who sat beside me through the performance, showed me the poem she wrote in her notebook. It is a poem about the evils of slavery inspired by the nobility of the African Roscius. Mrs Cole and I read it through twice and shed tears on both occasions.

—

Sheffield, Halifax, Newcastle, Glasgow, Edinburgh, Hull, Swansea – many are the towns you have toured since being shut out of London. You are no longer a stranger in the provinces. They call you 'radiant' in Nottingham. Sheffield hails you as 'a genius in his profession'.

As Othello in Dublin, there are cheers through the last three acts. When the play is over the audience rises to its feet and won't sit down till you come back out. The curtain call is a contentious innovation, derided by traditionalists, but to be celebrated by a crowd this way is an overwhelming feeling. To cap the night, you are met backstage by Edmund Kean himself, who is in Dublin to play Richard III. Kean is expansive. Throwing his arm around your shoulders, he declares to the clustered cast members that 'this man is one of the finest performers on the British stage.'

When news of this meeting spreads, a petition is got up among Dublin's theatre-lovers for the two of you to appear together in *Othello*. But when Kean embraced you, you smelled the brandy fumes on the man's breath. Years of unruly living have left him with bloodshot eyes and a fragile constitution. He can barely get through his own dates, let alone add extra nights.

—

In Manchester, you are invited to sit for a portrait by James North-cote, who, at eighty years old, is one of the truly venerable figures in British art. A butler leads you through dark, panelled passageways to a large studio at the back of the house with a glass skylight. Paintings are propped against the walls, five or six deep, all of them facing inwards so it's impossible to tell whether they're still in progress or Northcote has simply lost interest in them.

Above the skylight, clouds pass in front of the sun, the light bright then muted. A slight corruption in the window glass lends the view a provisional quality, like it too is waiting to be finished by the artist. Northcote stays seated when you enter. There's a walking stick beside his chair, so maybe the effort to stand is too great. He already has a canvas set up and he points with his brush for you to take the stool opposite him. Muscular hands, you observe, the veins standing out in them thick and green, even while the rest of him is bent over in the chair. He peers at you from behind his easel without speaking, and then swaps the brush for a stick of charcoal and starts to sketch in long, elegant strokes, barely lifting his hand from the canvas.

The sable prince. The man of colour. A child of the tropical sun. You wonder what hoary fantasy Northcote will conjure. Perhaps the African Roscius holding a spear or dressed in a turban and silk coat like a Moorish prince.

When you return to his house a fortnight later to view it, the por-trait is a shock. Northcote has caught something unexpected of you. He has dressed you in white, against a darkening sky. Your eyes glance to the left, out of the frame, with a wariness that you've never seen before, even in a mirror. But you know the painting shows the truth. Somewhere in this face is the five-year-old boy mourning his mother. The fifteen-year-old fearful for his future. It's the face you thought you'd masked beneath the antic Mungo and the noble Roscius, stripped bare, looking back at you. As you gaze at it, the painting blurs, and it takes you a moment to realize your eyes are wet with tears.

Leeds, 1830

You are in Leeds for *The Revolt of Surinam*, the story of a tragic and dignified enslaved man. The second play on the bill is, inevitably, *The Padlock*, and after the audience has hooted its way through Mungo's jesting and you've taken your bow, you visit the private box of your friend, John Henry Alexander, the Scottish actor-manager.

Alexander has been watching the play with a half-dozen guests but he's so boisterous that he takes up practically all the space in the box himself. This is a man who has the startling habit of scolding his own audiences in the middle of his performances. You've seen him break off during *Rob Roy* and call out beyond the footlights, 'Madam, will you please stop that wean's crying.' Alexander talks as much as ever tonight, and you hardly have a chance to speak to the woman called Margaret Gill who he introduces as one of his guests. But you are conscious of her at the edge of your vision. A jade evening dress, with a low-cut bodice and bouffant sleeves. The black pupils at the centre of her pale blue eyes give her gaze a particular intensity. You can feel her watching you and how, in response, you talk and laugh too loudly at Alexander's jokes, as if you're still onstage.

The following day you call on Margaret and the two of you sit in the front parlour at her guest house, making stilted conversation while the tea cools in your cup. Six weeks later you're married.

It's a small wedding breakfast, just Alexander, Davidge, a few other friends from the theatre. On an impulse you send an invitation to Kean, who replies with his apologies and his compliments to Mrs Aldridge. Margaret has no one present. She is ten years your senior, reserved in public, but when you're alone she becomes playful and mischievous. Her family comes from Northallerton, Yorkshire. Her father is a stocking weaver. Her mother raised Margaret and her seven younger siblings in a dank little house filled with the sound of their bawling and squabbling, the memory of which makes Margaret shudder visibly. She says she wants a future that doesn't look like her parents' past.

You are both aware of what it means for a black man and a white woman to marry. Where you come from, you say, you'd be killed many times over for such a thing: for looking at a white woman, for daring to speak to her, for the mere thought of intimacy with her, let alone performing the act. In this country you've seen the anger and jealousy that follow when you share a stage with one. At the Theatre Royal Dublin, the husband of your co-star, Madame Céleste, refused to let her perform with you. J. B. Howe, a middling actor you once appeared with in Hull, has just published a memoir, scorning 'the repugnant Desdemonas' in the audience excited by your presence in a play. 'It shocks a sensitive nature to see a pure blonde with almost angelic features and form, putting on a most bewitching smile and using every art of feminine blandishment to win the notice of the true bred "African Nigger".'

The impropriety of your union is a thrill that binds you together and inspires you both to further mischief. Margaret is introduced to company as the daughter of a Member of Parliament. Sometimes she elaborates on the story, declaring with an immaculately sober expression that her father is a man of high standing in a northern English county, who successfully opposed Mr Lambton, the present Earl of Durham, in a strongly fought election.

She encourages you to play the African Roscius to the full. Don't hide away, she says. Give them something to really look at. If they don't want you in London, make your mark in every other town until you can't be ignored. So now, as you travel with her, you do so in style, with a top hat, frock coat and servants, hired for the occasion, both of you delighting in the scandalized looks you draw. A letter from Dingwall, Scotland, to the *British Press* is outraged but also grudgingly admiring. 'He arrived here (would you believe it) – in a hired Carriage, a smart Chariot & pair, mounted Postilion, flashy Livery, Black Velvet Hunting Cap trimm'd with Gold Lace & a Lady (White) inside – and his footman in the Rumble – Is that not going it?'

On the Moor

Picture this. A man bestrides the stage. He is brave and proud. A primitive who has found his way into civilization but might yet relapse to barbarism if provoked. This 'lascivious Moor' spellbinds a maiden. In the coupling of his blackness and her fair body only the grossest images come to mind. A girl mounted by a horse. An old black ram fucking a white lamb. Onstage, the couple's marital bed is hidden from view but is never far from thought. The bedchamber is the site of the play's bloody climax. Etchings of the scene linger on its erotic charge. Desdemona lies asleep among the dishevelled bedclothes, lips parted, her head lolled back and a breast exposed outside her nightdress, while the jealous and enraged Othello rears over her, a dagger unsheathed in his hand.

The idea of their congress is 'extremely revolting' writes the author Charles Lamb. The notion is so intolerable that the poet Samuel Taylor Coleridge insists Shakespeare can't have meant Othello to be 'a veritable Negro' from tropical Africa. Rather, he must have imagined 'a gallant Moor, of royal blood, combining a high sense of Spanish and Italian feeling'. Coleridge's view is influential. When Kean debuts his groundbreaking 'tawny' Moor, he wears a toga of vaguely Roman origin, bare arms decorated with bracelets, and a plumed headdress. Backstage, he prepares himself by reciting passages from the Qur'an. Despite these leavening touches, the prospect of a sexual encounter across lines of race can still be distressing for audiences. In a different production, William Macready chooses to poke his head out of the awnings of the bed during the climactic murder scene. The shock of seeing him 'thrust his dark despairing face from between the white curtains' is enough to send at least one lady into a 'hysterical faint'.

John Henry Alexander

Of all the roles I've seen Ira play, it is Othello that most stirs the crowd. For a man who is truly black to play the part, it's something. This is a role that he's performed up and down the country but every time you feel the tension. And I fear that some enraged gentleman will see him up there more as a primate than man, and look to take his revenge on behalf of all respectable ladies in the theatre.

Ira played the Moor for me just these months ago in Leeds. The next morning, I got a letter from a lady who had been watching. 'A full-blooded Negro, incarnating the profoundest creations of Shakespeare's art? One's spirit cannot accept it. The African jungle should have been filled with the cries of this black, powerful, howling flesh, not the Leeds Playhouse. By the very fact that that flesh is so powerful – that it is genuinely black – this natural black Othello, pardon me, causes only revulsion.'

I showed him the letter, I don't mind telling you, with some nervousness. Ira read it carefully and then looked up laughing, as if it was some joke. I think he enjoys stirring a reaction. There's the moment in the play when Othello has to say, 'Your hand, Desdemona.' He makes a great show of placing her palm in his, then holding up their paired hand so you can't escape the sight of white skin on black.

January 1832

In the limbo of some small town, far distant from Margaret at home in London, sometimes you do take another woman. At first it was disorienting the way ladies approached you with such directness. But where, once, you turned away in embarrassment, you've learned to look back at an interested gaze. A night spent with an actress or a woman you meet after a performance feels like a game. At the boarding house in Worksop run by a retired apothecary and his wife, where you stayed after a production of *The Revolt*, you signed the register as 'Mr Aldridge, Comedian'. Madge Kendal, your co-star, wrote beside you, 'Sarah, wife'.

Letters pursue you after you've left a town. 'Oh God, is it possible that you, a stranger, a man I only know at a distance, and that I shall perhaps never see again, can be so dear to me?' writes Emily from Durham. 'Is it not sad and strange?' Anna from Dundee: 'My Ira, my love grows daily deeper and more tender. The longer I do not see you, the clearer I see you are everything to me, and that my love will only end with my death. I have never believed what those who despised you have said. I do not ask what the world says. You are my world.'

It troubles you how readily you betray Margaret. Your excuses are conventional. You are lonely. You are bored. You are only a man. It is only ever for one night or two and nothing to take seriously. It reminds you of how Kean drinks and fucks to excess while insisting that his behaviour is a choice and that he, as an artist, is free to flout the rules of propriety, never mind that his health and good reputation are ruined as a result. You worry that you are seen in a similar light. Rumours already circulate backstage that no white woman is safe around you. Yet you feel no inclination to change your behaviour, especially when you hear them gossiping. In truth, they'd say the same about you whether you had slept with every white woman in England or never laid a hand on a single one.

March 1832

When you look back on it, you wonder if you'll see the whole business with Emma Stothard as an act of sabotage against yourself. Emma is a seamstress. Her husband William fancies himself an actor. He's a utility player who hares around the country taking any role he can get for a guinea a week. They're young and recently married and Emma is already disenchanted by his constant absence. She lodges with her aunt in Sheffield and last year you took a room in the aunt's house while you played Oroonoko at the Sheffield Theatre. A real actor couldn't help but shine in her eyes compared to that feckless husband. For a week you were sneaking into her bed at night while the aunt slumbered in the room next door. And now she writes to say she is pregnant with your child.

You answer, 'My dear Emma – Your letter has just now reached me, and I am very much surprised by its contents. You may be mistaken. You say William has been with you, and is it not likely that his visits have occasioned this mischief? Write me particulars immediately. Write by return, enclosing the same in the envelope I send you. I would rather my wife did not notice any correspondence. If you give me the assurance that the child is "of colour" and that the father is the person you name – you understand me – both you and your child shall not be neglected. Tell me, does your aunt know whose child it is, and is she unkind to you?'

There is no reply.

Birmingham, May 1832

The stage door of the Prince of Wales opens on to an alley. A woman with a shawl wrapped around her head is waiting as you leave the theatre after playing Othello. 'Mr Aldridge, I have come about Emma Stothard.' It is the aunt, who has tracked you down from Sheffield.

'She has had a child,' says the aunt. 'Its name is Frederick and you are the father.'

'Emma is married,' you reply. 'Surely it belongs to the husband.'

She regards you scornfully. 'White men don't beget black children, Mr Aldridge. I have had nine children but I have never had a black one.'

Right there in the alley you make the arrangement. You will pay a weekly sum of five shillings to the aunt. In return there will be no contact from Emma and you won't be obliged to recognize the child as yours. The deal can't be done fast enough as far as you're concerned.

July 1832

A letter from Emma. It is only a few lines long and you'd have thought it brusque if it wasn't for the pain it must have cost her to write it. Frederick is dead. He was sick this past fortnight with dysentery. And now he has passed away.

Your thoughts dissolve into reminiscence. You think of the softness of Emma's skin and your hands moving up through the layers of her nightdress. Your fingers tangled in her hair and her kisses, slow then frantic. Pressing yourself against her, trying to still the creaking of the bed, hushing her moans against the presence of the aunt on the other side of the wall. Now those memories are a prelude to emptiness.

Amid the guilt and regret there is also relief. You have escaped the awkward entanglement. You walk lighter today than you have done these past several months.

August 1832

The reprieve is short-lived. Another letter. This time it is from William Stothard, the husband. He is taking you to court for 'criminal conversation', the legal charge that a cuckolded husband can bring against an adulterer. Stothard is suing you for sleeping with his wife.

Immediately you write to Margaret, declaring the case a lie. William Stothard is embittered by his failing career as an actor and blames you for his lack of success. It is a flimsy story, but as good a one as you can conjure in such straitened circumstances.

Sheffield, January 1833

Margaret doesn't travel with you to the trial. She says she's sure the case will be put right and Stothard exposed as a liar, so why bother attending. But Margaret is no actor. Her voice is brittle and she looks away as you lean down to kiss her goodbye. In return you offer your own wretched performance by pretending to believe her words, all the time burning with shame.

In the courtroom you sit beside your barrister, Mr Serjeant Wilkins. Thankfully there's no sign of Emma but Stothard is at the front shooting you hostile glances, beside his own counsel, Mr Edwin James. You spot the aunt in the gallery, purse-lipped with her shawl over her head. She turns away when she sees you and you feel another stab of guilt at the memory of Margaret making the same expression.

'It has been shown that the plaintiff had not the means of supporting his wife,' begins Mr James for Stothard. 'His career is a most precarious one. Rather than drag his wife about with him to share his miserable poverty, he sent her where he thought she would be safe – to her aunt. She would have been secure there had it not been for the arts of the defendant. He has taken advantage of Mrs Stothard's vulnerability and seduced her.'

Mr James invites his witnesses to swear to the complexion and the untimely passing of the child. 'I had the child when it was three months old,' says Mrs Matthews, wet nurse. 'It was a coloured child. It died with me.'

'The child was brought to my house,' says Dr Smelley, physician. 'It was coloured and had woolly hair. It died of dysentery and I certified the cause of death.'

Mr Wilkins rises slowly. He gazes about himself, savouring the attention of Justice Roberts and the rest of the courtroom. 'My lord, the proof of adultery is very slight. The defendant is not the only man of colour in England. What evidence is there of any seduction? Many things have been stated but little has been proved. Consider this. Othello was a Moor – a handsome man; but the defendant is an African. For a woman to yield to the desires of such a figure would be a curse on her nature. What would they say of a lady who would fall to the arts and devices of a "nigger"? It didn't happen. It is fantasy.'

Finally the judge gives his verdict. Stothard, he says, is more at fault for neglecting his wife than you are for pursuing her affections. Moreover, he agrees with Wilkins that the prosecution case rests on such a bizarre and unnatural proposition that it can't be regarded credibly. You are found guilty of criminal conversation but fined the nominal sum of forty shillings.

Wilkins, looking fantastically pleased with himself, invites you to his chambers for brandy. You make an excuse and leave the court-room behind you, walking hurriedly, with your head down, away from the town centre, away from the shame of a defence and a judgement based on your skin colour. It is one thing to knowingly flout convention by bedding white women and even to court the scandalized reactions. Another to be presented, so starkly, with evidence of these people's contempt. To be designated an abhorrent creature whose presence cannot be countenanced near white flesh.

You are so sunk in your thoughts that you don't notice at first how you've wandered from your lodgings. You are in an unfamiliar neighbourhood of grimy, back-to-back red-brick terraced houses. Two girls, playing in the street, stop their game as you walk by. One of them, in a dirty smock, calls after you, 'Hey, mister.' The girls start to follow you, and other children in the street break off their amusements to join in, until there's a whole gang of them trailing after you shouting, 'Mister, mister.' You walk faster. Today of all days, you have no appetite to be a figure of jeering fun. And then, abruptly, you stop and let them catch up. The children swarm about you, shouting and waving, 'Mister, what's your name? Mister, where you from?' Not mockery but curiosity. So, in turn, you ask their names. And when they've yelled out Alice, Jacob, Martha, Eliza, Harriet, Walter, you strike a dramatic pose, hands raised to the sky, and say that you are the great African Roscius. And then you launch into a routine from *The Padlock*, and here's Mungo, capering in the street with the children, and you carried along by the moment too, a spectator to your own performance.

A letter, pushed under the door by some hasty hand, lies waiting for you on the floor of your boarding room when you return. It is from Pierre Laporte, manager of the Theatre Royal Covent Garden. You have heard of him: a small, anxious man, lately arrived from Paris, another outsider trying to make his mark in London. He is one of the few managers willing to book foreign performers for his plays, for which the press calls him a disgrace and a grasping fraud. Recently, though, Laporte has played a canny hand. He has cast Kean as Othello, with the star's son, Charles, as Iago, and Charles's wife, Ellen Tree, as Desdemona. The family production is a triumph. But the letter carries startling news that has yet to reach you in Sheffield. Two nights ago, midway through the third act, Kean collapsed into his son's arms and had to be carried offstage. He died last night, aged forty-six. And now Laporte writes to you, 'Please, Mr Aldridge, come to the Theatre Royal and take on the part, I beg of you.' After seven years in the provinces, you are finally being called back to London.

Only two playhouses in London have received a royal patent allowing them to stage Shakespeare unabridged and without the usual novelty songs: the Theatre Royal and the Royal Opera House. To perform a full-length *Othello* in front of an audience of two thousand is the chance of a lifetime. It will place you in a line with Garrick, Kemble, Macready, Kean. It means braving the critics and envious fellow actors. But what a prize. You are about to give the most important performance of your life.

4

London, March 1833

London theatregoers are already versed in the notion of a black Shake-spearean. For that you can thank Charles Mathews. After his success with the bumbling Caesar Alexander Hannibal, the comic has brought more 'black fun' to the stage with *Othello, the Moor of Fleet Street*, 'an Historical, Comical, Operatic, Travestical Burletta'. The show is set in the slums of London, with Othello, played by Mathews, as a street-sweeper in the mould of Billy Waters. Like his previous creation, Mathews's character speaks in mangled dialect – 'Now den is de winter of him discontent' – but rather than 'Opossum up a Gum Tree', his signature song is a commentary on his own misguided attempts to master Shakespeare, as set to the tune of the popular ditty, 'Ackee O':

> *When holiday bring nigger joy,*
> *Hack him, oh – hack him, oh!*
> *Roll him eye like any ting,*
> *Den him dance, and den him sing,*
> *Immortal Shakespeare den him hack,*
> *Poor Othelly, hero black!*

Mathews's Othello is described as an African prince who 'left his land, to cut a figure in the Strand'. The show will have closed by the time you arrive at the Theatre Royal, but the public will inevitably make a comparison between his Othello and your version. Already the press are primed. Gilbert Abbott à Beckett, the editor of the new satirical weekly, *Figaro in London*, is especially vituperative. À Beck-ett is twenty-two years old and a descendant of Thomas à Becket.

He fancies himself a dangerous wit. His magazine promises 'spark-ling, sharp-flavoured and high-relished' comment on politics, theatre and the gentry. To protests at the vindictiveness of its prose, à Beckett is consoling. 'We are doing a service to the object of our severity. We wound to heal.' The absurd idea of a black Othello is exactly the kind of folly that the magazine has set itself up to skewer. It is *Figaro*'s duty 'to drive the presumptuous black from the metro-politan boards'.

In the evenings, after rehearsals, you read à Beckett's latest jibes with grim conscientiousness. 'Is it because nature has supplied him with a skin that renders soot and butter superfluous? Is it on the strength of his blackness that this wretched upstart considers him-self competent to enact the part? Unless he is immediately withdrawn from the bill we must inflict on him such a chastisement as must drive him from the stage he has dishonoured. We will jam him into atoms by the relentless power of our critical battering ram. We will force him to find, in the capacity of street-sweeper, that level for which his colour renders him peculiarly qualified.'

On the fight for abolition

The London Ira Aldridge returns to in 1833 is more divided than ever on the subject of slavery. Seven hundred public petitions a month are reaching Parliament from abolitionist groups around the country. The largest such entreaty, organized in just ten days by the London Female Anti-Slavery Society, gathers the signatures of 187,157 women, 'one vast and universal expression of feeling from all the females of the United Kingdom'. The document is so heavy it takes four MPs to carry it into the Commons.

Abolitionist feeling has grown all the fiercer since the so-called

Baptist War in Jamaica. Eighteen months ago, an uprising among enslaved people led by a black Baptist deacon, Samuel Sharpe, spread from a single plantation in the hills above Montego Bay to engulf the island. Up to sixty thousand enslaved men and women rose up to join what became the largest insurrection in Jamaica's history. Hundreds of plantations were set on fire. In response white colonials formed themselves into armed militias and delivered violent summary justice. By the time the revolt was quelled eleven days later, around a thousand black people had been shot, burned, hanged or otherwise lynched.

Many colonials blamed abolitionist missionaries for encouraging the revolt. Baptist chapels were burned down and missionaries arrested and beaten in retaliation. Henry Bleby, a Baptist minister, was held by a colonial gang who threatened to burn him alive and was only released after being tarred and feathered. The brutal aftermath of the Baptist War, with white preachers its victims as well as enslaved blacks, and the increasing number of revolts springing up elsewhere in the colonies, seem proof that the system of Caribbean slavery is collapsing upon itself. The 1832 general election has returned an anti-slavery majority to Parliament for the first time. An Emancipation Bill is already going through the Commons. If it passes in May, it will finally mean victory for the abolition movement and the end of slavery in the colonies.

But freedom is not a foregone conclusion. From the City, where the merchants cluster, to the West India Club in Mayfair, the favourite meeting place of politicians with Caribbean interests, London's pro-slavery lobby still wields huge power. William Gladstone, the son of a plantation-holding dynasty, is one of the new intake of MPs in 1832. He uses his maiden speech to warn against the 'debasement, bloodshed and war' that will surely follow in the event of emancipation. With the vote imminent, supporters of slavery are marshalling their forces. Mobs of dockers and sugar-bakers, whose living is tied to the Caribbean, are hired to barrack public lectures by abolitionists. Favourable coverage of the colonial cause is purchased in *The Times*, the *Chronicle*, *John Bull* and the *English Gentleman*. Other publications weigh in spontaneously in support of slavery. 'It may be all very well to emancipate the nigger,' says *Figaro in London*. 'But the chief use that the niggers have hitherto made of their emancipation is to get very drunk and cut the throats of their former masters. It is better to have plenty to eat and drink and have a little restraint, than to be called free, and starved to death; which will be the case with some of the lazy niggers, who, too indolent to work, will decline all employment, except the commission of depredations on persons and property.'

For opponents and supporters of slavery alike, it's all in the balance: fortunes forged from black labour; individual liberty for millions; Britain's future standing in the world. And Ira Aldridge is returning to the capital to perform a play based on the fault lines of race and power, the same lines that divide the nation.

10 April 1833

Of course, an actor wants to be alone before a performance. But tonight, opening night, your dressing room, with its thick carpet and burgundy damask wallpaper, feels suffocating. In the last minutes before final call, you slip out of the stage door. From the shadows at the side of the theatre you watch the carriages drawing up, disgorging the audience members in their evening wear. A lady in a dress of midnight-blue silk with voluminous leg-o'-mutton sleeves. A woman with a black velvet hat decorated with two long, rose-coloured ostrich feathers walks in on the arm of a gentleman in a black dress coat and a cream silk waistcoat. At the side of the pavement, a vendor sells bags of roast chestnuts hot from his brazier. A pair of boys weave through the crowd begging for pennies, or more likely looking to spirit a pocketbook from the tails of a gentleman's coat.

Watching the crowd churn, your mind conjures an image of Othello arriving in Venice for the first time as a young man. He has been a wanderer since his childhood, an outsider in many cities. It is winter when he first comes here. A grey mist snakes through the narrow streets, shrouding the city's elegant palazzos from view. Footsteps echo in the deserted lanes. A stray dog, a whippet, sniffs at a heap of rubbish and then trots away with the particular loping angularity of its breed. A gondola glides silently beneath him as he stands on the Ponte della Paglia. The water of the canal is green and fronds of seaweed sway beneath its surface. When he closes his eyes, he feels the faint but perceptible sensation of the island itself swaying. In the mazelike streets he passes pilgrims and knife grinders, noblemen in long, stiff gowns and porters carrying wicker baskets loaded with fish. All of them wrapped in cloaks and scarves against the cold. Venice is cosmopolitan. Turks and Greeks and Cypriots who came here to trade carpets and silks for Murano glass have made the city their home. The Jews have their own quarter. But he doesn't pass unseen. Eyes remark his progress as he wanders through alleyways. All those he watches regard him in turn. In this city of foreigners, he remains an outsider.

You gather yourself, walk back inside the theatre and out on to the stage that has been waiting for you all your life.

Later, when you look back on this night, you will remember almost nothing of it. All that you recall is Ellen Tree's hand, resting soft in yours, in the bedchamber. Othello is supposed to be enraged at her betrayal. But you feel only grief. The weight of this man's story bears down on you. Your hand, clutching hers, trembles. You beg that when they come to tell your story, they speak of you as you were, with nothing set down in malice. You close your eyes. Fall into darkness. Into silence. And are resurrected by cheers and clapping. Wave after wave of applause that fills the theatre and brings you to the front of the stage, struck dumb by the sound. As you straighten from bowing, your face is streaked with tears.

11 April 1833

You have breakfast late with Margaret. She tells you again how magnificent you were. Keep it coming, you say. And so she does. 'You were astonishing. Noble, Majestic. Inspiring. Splendid' – until you're both giddy with laughter, as if last night's champagne is still fizzing through your veins.

Spring light washes through the glowing city. You float to the theatre. Although it's early afternoon, Laporte already has a fire going in his small office. The manager looks up from behind a desk stacked with letters, scripts, copies of playbills and newspapers. Last night you parted with loud, affectionate farewells. Today he looks grave. Lips taut, Laporte pushes a stack of the day's newspapers across the desk. You have been holding off on them until reaching him, in anticipation of reading the reviews together. At the sight of his expression the warm feeling inside you begins to dissipate. What strikes you first, as you leaf through the pages, is the attention to your appearance. 'His feet and hands disproportionately large, his lips protruding, and chin underhung, his hair woolly, and his eyes sullenly dark,' says the *Town Journal*. 'His foot is ugly, and he walks upon it with the heavy unelastic tread of a dromedary,' reports the *Morning Chronicle*. By contrast, the *Morning Post* at least calls you 'Noble and somewhat refined' in appearance. And the *Globe and Traveller* probably considers it a compliment to describe your skin colour as 'an oily and expressive mulatto tint' which 'seems to show that he has European blood in his veins'.

You look up, heartened. It's true there are the inevitable mentions of street-sweeps, Day and Martin, and Billy Waters. But overall nothing you haven't heard in the past. If these aren't the accolades you'd hoped for, they are still respectable. The *Age*, which admits it had come prepared to laugh at 'this bit of ebony', concedes that 'for a man of colour it was a very clever piece of acting'. And the *National Omnibus* mounts a defence of you against attackers in the press like à Beckett. 'Mr Aldridge has been the victim of an unmanly, vindictive, and unprincipled persecution, got up by a gang of callous, mischievous ruffians, who took the advantage of an unworthy prejudice, which still lingers in the minds of weak persons, in whose ears the sound of "nigger" conveys less idea of a human being than that of villain, burker or murderer.'

But Laporte's expression hasn't lifted and you realize that this is only the beginning. 'His accent is unpleasantly, and we would say, vulgarly foreign; his manner, generally, drawling and unimpressive,' says *The Times*. 'And when by chance (for chance it is, and not judgement), he rises to a higher strain, we perceive in the transition the elevation of rant, not the fiery dignity of soul-felt passion.'

You dig further through the pile, your fingers numbing. Here of course is *Figaro in London*, declaring you 'quite destitute of talent'. No great surprise there. But the most damning review is from the *Athenaeum*. 'On Wednesday, this establishment aimed another blow at its respectability, by its production of *Othello* – *Othello* forsooth!!!

Othello, almost the master-work of the master-mind – a part which the fire and genius of Kean have, of late years, made his exclusive property; and this be personated in an English national theatre, by one whose pretentions rest upon the grounds of his face being a natural instead of an acquired tint. It is truly monstrous and sufficient to make Shakespeare's indignant bones kick the lid from his coffin. We have no ridiculous prejudice against any fellow creature, because he chances to be of a different colour from ourselves; but we are, on the other hand, altogether above the twaddle of helping the drama to bear an indignity of this nature, while we quote this silly exhibition as a proof of England's being called "the stranger's home". In the name of common sense, we enter our protest against a repetition of this outrage.'

As you read, the numbness seeps through your whole body. The review repeats the same opinion about your proximity to white women as the Stothard verdict did. 'In the name of propriety and decency, we protest against a lady-like girl like Miss Ellen Tree being pawed about by Mr Aldridge. It is truly monstrous.'

You drop the paper on the desk in disgust. It's obvious that any hope of a life in London is futile. These people have not seen you. There is no redemption at the end of this story. You hear Laporte saying that after tonight there will be no further performances.

Othello is the only Shakespearean hero who doesn't receive a funeral oration. He attempts to do it himself, but the words ring hollow. 'I have done the state some service, and they know't.' Once he has killed Desdemona and turned a dagger on himself there's only Cassio to say, 'He was great of heart.' And this in itself is to remember him as a creature of passion, not reason. A figure who must be cast off. Vanished from sight and memory.

Instead of this ignominious finale, you picture Othello again as a young man, this time even before he travels to Venice. See him walking through landscapes of mountain and desert. Upon bare earth. Beneath raw sun. Until he stands with his back to the land, the sea before him, watching the sailing ships cross the water to Sicily, Croatia, the Ottoman Empire. In his head he sees his future take shape. He will fight in foreign wars under unfamiliar flags, learning how to lead men and win battles. In one nation, having achieved great victories, he will captivate a woman with his stories of adventure and her home will become his. Those narrow streets and slender palazzos. The green waters of the canals. The happiness he finds there, forged by love and victory, he imagines will last forever. Perhaps lack of foresight is an inevitable aspect of youth. Fresh-faced Othello cannot yet perceive how happiness fades. Like every other living thing, it dies. There is no resurrection.

You leave Laporte in his rooms and return to the street. Between you and the porters from Covent Garden market pulling carts loaded with turnips and cauliflowers, and the ladies taking up the pavement with their full skirts, there is an impossible gulf. They hurry past in blithe certainty of their role in the world. You move in glacial time, inching through the resistant medium of history. You are chilled to your bones and there's no warmth to be found on this thin spring afternoon. You might be a diver at the bottom of the sea. The depths black and the dappled surface far above. Your feet kick against absence. You are buoyant and you are heavy. You reach up an arm and watch your hand vanish into the infinite volume of the water.

Monstrous Races

In the suffocating heat of summer 2022, I took a train from London to see the Hereford Mappa Mundi, the largest surviving map of the world from the medieval era. In addition to looking at the document, I wanted to escape the increasingly apocalyptic atmosphere brought on by the extreme temperatures in southern England. Overcome by the heat, swifts were falling from the sky, I read in a newspaper, and a thousand-year-old village near East London had caught fire and largely burned to the ground. From Hereford station I walked through a city which was hot and uncannily still, as if its inhabitants were sheltering from an angry god.

The Mappa Mundi was on display in the darkened cool of a small museum in the grounds of Hereford Cathedral. Drawn on vellum in the year 1300, the map is both a record of the world as it was known at the time and a swirling work of imagination teeming with impossible creatures. Unicorns. Griffins. A winged salamander. The Minotaur in his labyrinth. The map is also illustrative of the medieval conviction that the remote edges of the Earth were populated by fantastic human tribes. These included the Blemmyae, a warlike race with no heads and facial features in their chests, and the Sciopods, a tribe of men in Africa with only one leg and a single giant foot, who moved about by hopping. On this and other maps from the period, these tribes, the so-called 'monstrous races', were always to be found in Asia and Africa, on the fringes of the known world.

The further from Christian Europe you ventured, the more exotic became the depictions of foreign peoples. The travel writings of the fictional English knight Sir John Mandeville, widely circulated in mid-fourteenth-century Europe, detailed his encounters with the strange races said to live in 'countries beyond': Ethiopia, India, China, the Middle East. Mandeville describes Cyclopes and hippopotami, creatures that were half-man, half-horse, dwarves who subsist on the aroma of apples and men whose 'ballocks' hang to their knees. The few Europeans who had travelled to Africa in real life spoke of its people in equally lurid terms. They were 'wild men' with 'hideous countenances', reported Friar Jordan Catalani of Sévérac. 'They have big mouths and their noses are so flattened and their lips and eyes so big that they are horrible to look at,' said Marco Polo. 'Anyone who saw them in another country would say that they were devils.'

In medieval thinking, a person's appearance was an indication of how civilized they were. The Tatars of Central Asia were frequently compared to the grotesque, cannibalistic, dog-headed Cynocephali, the one indistinguishable from the other in their barbaric nature. Other travellers echoed similar beliefs. Where white skin symbolized a proximity to the light of God, Africans were, in the words of the poet Paulinus of Nola, 'black with vice, sin giving them the colour of night'. Their dark skin was considered evidence of traffic with the infernal. The Devil himself was referred to as the 'Black Jehovah', 'Black Ethiopian' or simply 'Black Man'.

The fear of racial difference that seemed to characterize the period can only have been exacerbated by medieval Europeans' fragile sense of mortality. In the 1340s, the Black Death spread across the continent, travelling west from Cyprus through to the British Isles. 'We see death coming into our midst like black smoke,' wrote the Welsh poet Jeuan Gethin. 'A plague which cuts off the young, a rootless phantom which has no mercy or fair countenance.' Many took the terror of the plague years as a sign that God had turned His back on them. In Germany, macabre processions of flagellants went from town to town scourging themselves against His displeasure. Prophets and holy men suffered fearsome visions of the future. The Franciscan friar John of Rupescissa predicted the coming of the Antichrist, whose arrival would be met by famine, earthquake and the piling up of cadavers. Following suit, the Carmelite monk William of Blofield announced that the Antichrist had already arrived and was spreading his lies in the form of a beautiful ten-year-old boy. It is the anxieties and impotent superstitions of this age that are visible in the Mappa Mundi, taking shape in the disquieting creatures depicted across its surface.

The day was cooler and Hereford busier when I left the museum. Returning to the present while still mentally absorbed in the medieval era was jarring. The streets seemed too noisy and crowded. The cloying scent of lavender and patchouli wafting from a shop selling thick blocks of handmade soap turned my stomach. The sensation of nausea, which seemed to come from inside and around me at the same time, only began to subside once I took my seat to return to London. As the train retreated out of the station, I realized that, without volition, the name David Oluwale had come into my mind. Years ago, I'd seen a picture of a Victorian iron bridge with the words 'Remember David Oluwale' graffitied on its side. In some way, the invocation had done its work, because his name had now returned to me, enmeshed with the unsettled feeling I'd carried away from the Mappa Mundi.

David Oluwale: the only thing I knew about him was the nature of his untimely passing. On 4 May 1969, Oluwale's body was found floating in the River Aire in Leeds. How he drowned – that is, whether his death was an accident or a murder – had never been conclusively proved. Once I was home, I decided to look further into his life.

———

In August 1949, at the age of nineteen, David Oluwale left his birthplace, Lagos, Nigeria, hoping to become an engineer in Britain. Although as a Commonwealth citizen he was free to work in the UK, he had no money for the sea passage. On an overcast morning, the rainy season coming to an end and the day already humid, he managed to inveigle his way dockside at the crowded Apapa Wharf in Lagos and stow away on the cargo ship *Temple Bar*, which was bound for Hull with a consignment of groundnuts. Shortly after the voyage began he was discovered by a crew member and put to work on the ship, where he laboured in the kitchens and the engine room until the *Temple Bar*'s arrival in Hull. There he was arrested by police and sentenced to twenty-eight days in prison. His incarceration took place at Armley Gaol in Leeds, a forbidding edifice of quarried stone that resembled a medieval fort, where executions, performed by Harry Allen, one of Britain's last official hangmen, were still carried out. This was Oluwale's introduction to the UK.

After his release, the Nigerian took work where he could find it. Employment at a fabric workshop gave way to a job as a hod carrier on a building site, then as a labourer in an abattoir in the Kirkgate meat market, carrying carcasses and hosing viscera off the killing floor. He rented a small room in a red-brick terrace on Camp Road, a neighbourhood of dilapidated Victorian houses where Leeds's small number of Commonwealth immigrants, Jamaicans, Nigerians,

Ghanaians, Pakistanis and others – what the *Yorkshire Evening Post* called the city's 'foreign element' – mostly gathered, after having the doors shut in their faces in the smarter parts of town. Among the young West Africans he made friends with there, Oluwale was known as 'Yankee'. He was a popular figure, boisterous and talkative, a stylish dresser who was only five foot five but carried himself cocksure like a Hollywood hero, and spent more than he could afford on looking good and going out.

See him on a Saturday night at the Mecca dance hall. Yankee in a tailored suit, arm around a local girl, whispering something in her ear that makes her laugh, jiving on the dance floor, never leaving before lights up. Perhaps he clung to those nights as a respite from the otherwise hostile conditions faced by him and his friends. The *Yorkshire Evening Post* blamed the city's immigrants for a rise in prostitution and for public brawls involving 'un-British attacks with knives, pepper and ginger'. In West Africans, the Home Office saw a particular threat to the civil order, describing them as 'arrogant and violent ... with little regard for law and order and other people's property'; 'dirty and lazy'; 'work-shy and content to live on National Insurance'. What did it feel like to know yourself among the tiniest of minorities – there were no more than eighty-two West Africans in a city of half a million – and still find yourself scapegoated as a troublemaker?

On Saturday night, 25 April 1953, a scuffle broke out at the bar of the King Edward Hotel in Leeds city centre, involving Oluwale and some friends who were blamed for an unpaid bill. Police were called and in the melee Oluwale was struck hard on the head with a truncheon.

He was charged with disorderly conduct and sentenced to two months in prison. While jailed he began to act erratically, possibly due to distress at his circumstances or as a result of the severe blow to the head. He was alternately withdrawn and mute, or overactive and aggressive. He suffered hallucinations and described seeing fantastical creatures, such as a lion with a fish's head, which he believed was trying to kill him. A prison psychiatrist reported that he seemed 'apprehensive, noisy and frightened without cause'. He 'wept when talking of his fears'. Oluwale was diagnosed as schizophrenic and transferred to the West Riding Pauper Lunatic Asylum in Menston, Leeds.

The year of Oluwale's incarceration, 1953, coincided with the publication of *The African Mind in Health and Disease*, by the colonial psychiatrist J. C. Carothers, an influential work which may have shaped staff's perceptions of him, as perhaps the first West African patient admitted to the hospital – and done so for the worse. The African, wrote Carothers, was a figure 'lacking in spontaneity, foresight, tenacity, judgement and humility . . . given to fabrication; and in general unstable, impulsive, unreliable, irresponsible and living in the present without reflection or ambition'. He existed in 'that strange no-man's land 'twixt sleep and wakening where fact and fantasy meet on equal terms'.

Oluwale was placed on Ward 8, an area reserved for the hospital's most disturbed patients. He was given electroconvulsive therapy and the antipsychotic drug chlorpromazine. Sometimes he was violent. He bit the face of another patient and the hand of a nurse, his teeth piercing through to the bone. He was isolated and withdrawn. He could be found most of the time sleeping beneath a radiator on the day-room floor with a blanket over his head. His incarceration at Menston lasted for eight years. During that time he lost contact with his African friends. Not a single person came to visit him at the hospital.

By the time of his release in 1961, the gregarious, swaggering Yankee was long gone, replaced by a prematurely aged figure with stained clothes, matted hair and a shuffling gait, given to mumbling and laughing abruptly to himself for no reason.

He worked sporadically and couldn't manage to hold down a job for more than a few days due to his erratic behaviour. He slept in parks and in shop doorways, covered with newspapers. A year on from his release he was convicted of malicious wounding, after biting the finger of a park ranger, and was jailed for another six months. The arresting officer described a 'shortish, thick-built man with deep anthropoid features. Huge teeth, sunken eyes.' More time in and out of prison followed. He was hearing voices and experiencing intense hallucinations. In 1965, Oluwale was returned to the asylum, since renamed High Royds Hospital. He was spoken of there as 'aggressive' and 'overactive', a 'dullard' who was 'somewhat childish'. He was freed in 1967, by which time he had become less agitated and was considered 'quiet and cooperative'. He said he wanted a job and a place to stay.

On 4 May 1969, David Oluwale's dead body was discovered by a group of boys playing by the side of the River Aire, about a mile outside Leeds city centre. 'We all thought at first it was a sack or a Guy Fawkes,' one of the boys told the police. 'But then it rolled over slightly with the current and I realized it was a black man.' A police pathologist estimated the corpse had been in the water for around two weeks. An inquest delivered a blunt, incurious verdict: 'Found drowned'. Oluwale was buried in a common grave. His headstone carried no inscription other than his name and those of the nine other indigents whose coffins lay piled, one on top of the other, in the same resting place.

There he would have remained, unmourned, if a young cadet based at Millgarth police station in Leeds hadn't reported a rumour linking two local officers to the death of Oluwale. An investigation was opened and, the following year, the two police, Sergeant Kenneth Kitching and Inspector Geoffrey Ellerker, were put on trial for manslaughter. Opening the case for the prosecution, John Cobb QC detailed a violent campaign waged against Oluwale by the two men. The officers had taken it upon themselves to purge Leeds city centre of rough sleepers. As the only homeless black man in Leeds, Oluwale was an easy target for them. 'They hounded him, harassed him and assaulted him: they teased him cruelly, and they made a torment of his life.' In the early hours of 18 April 1969, said the prosecution barrister, Kitching and Ellerker had 'unlawfully brought about Oluwale's death by causing him to fall or jump into the River Aire, whence he never emerged, save sixteen days later as a corpse'.

Over the two-week trial, a succession of their colleagues testified that Kitching and Ellerker had made Oluwale their 'plaything'. They put him in a dustbin and rolled him down the street. They set fire to the newspapers he slept under. They were seen standing over him, Ellerker shining a torch, while Kitching urinated on him, the steam rising from his piss in the night air. The men made Oluwale bow before them and bang his head repeatedly on the ground – the officers called it 'doing penance'. One time at the station Kitching kicked him so hard in the genitals he was lifted bodily off the floor. They liked to wake him up while he was asleep in a storefront and drive him out of town then roar away in their panda car. Leaving him stranded in Middleton Woods at 3.30 a.m. once, Kitching had joked that Oluwale would 'feel at home in the jungle'.

According to Cobb, Ellerker and Kitching came upon Oluwale in a furniture shop doorway at about three in the morning on 18 April

1969. They beat him heavily around the body and head and he'd run off towards Leeds Bridge, which spans the River Aire. Around 5 a.m., a bus conductor starting his shift said he saw two policemen chasing a scruffily dressed man down an alley near the bridge. However, the conductor admitted, it had been too dark to identify the officers or to tell if the man they were pursuing was black or white. Oluwale was not seen alive again after that day. When his body was recovered two weeks later, downstream of the bridge, it bore signs of bruising on the head.

Under questioning by Cobb, Kitching confessed he'd struck Oluwale. But any blows were minor. He had 'kicked him gently', given him 'just a slap' and 'tickled him with my boot'. Besides, his actions were only in self-defence. Oluwale was unpredictable and dangerous. He, Kitching, had been bitten, punched, cursed and spat upon by Oluwale. 'He was a wild animal, not a human being.'

Other accounts contradicted Kitching. Oluwale was 'never violent', said Constable Peter Smith. When you asked him to move on, 'he just picked his bag up and went away chuntering'. David Odamo, a Nigerian nurse at High Royds, stated that Oluwale 'was a victim of circumstances, he was not a violent person. He was one of the unlucky ones among us immigrants.'

None of the more benign descriptions of Oluwale's character were heard in court. The judge, Mr Justice Hinchcliffe, ruled them inadmissible. Instead, the impression of him as a monstrous creature was allowed to prevail. 'You would not bend over,' said Gilbert Gray QC for the defence. 'Because as quick as a flash and as lithesome as may be, David Oluwale would leap up like a miniature Mr Universe and have hold of you, scratching and biting with a mouthful of the biggest, dirtiest teeth you had ever seen in your life.'

Hinchcliffe appeared to concur. The dead man was 'a dirty, filthy, violent vagrant', 'a menace to society', 'a frightening apparition to come across at night'. Hinchcliffe told the jury there was insufficient evidence to try Ellerker and Kitching for manslaughter. Summing up, he pointedly cautioned them 'not to let their nausea and outrage at the shocking conduct of Oluwale cloud their judgement'. But the jury rejected his guidance, choosing instead to follow Cobb's lead. The officers were found guilty of assault and sentenced to three years and twenty-seven months respectively in jail. It was the first successful prosecution in British history of police officers for being involved in the death of a Black person. But due to Judge Hinchcliffe's ruling, they could not be convicted of manslaughter, and in all the years since the trial no one has ever been found responsible for the death of Oluwale.

In March 2022 an elegant new footbridge was installed over the River Aire, at the instigation of the David Oluwale Memorial Association, a campaigning group organized to raise awareness of his story. In an act of belated commemoration for a man failed by his adopted home, it was named by Leeds City Council the David Oluwale Bridge.

———

'Remember David Oluwale.'

I think of him now when I recall my own childhood.

An autumn afternoon in the 1980s. I am a teenager, sitting beside my dad in the front of the family car. We are parked outside the Express Dairy in Edgware. The engine is off and we are chatting idly as we wait to pick up my sister from a friend's house nearby. There is a rap on the glass on my dad's side. He rolls down the window and a policeman leans down to address us. What are we doing here? he wants to know. Someone from the dairy has called the station to say there are two suspicious men loitering outside. Who are we? What do we want? He is formal but polite and, as we drive off, my dad chuckles to himself at the idea that anyone could think of us, a middle-aged man and his son in a Volvo estate, as a possible threat.

I laughed too. But it dawned on me later that, for whoever had telephoned the police, the presence of two Black men was no joke. I was sixteen years old and more used to thinking of myself as a kid than an incipient adult. Yet I was also aware of how my no-longer-childlike body seemed to prompt unease around me. Handbags were clutched closer on the Tube. Security guards trailed me through shopping aisles. Another figure, the young Black male of their imagining, walked before me, hulking and miscreant, more physically present in their minds than the boy that followed behind him.

With hindsight, I can hardly blame them. Their attitude only mirrored the prejudices that have been embedded in Western thought since the era of the monstrous races, and reinforced many times since then. 'The Negro can be disciplined and cultivated but is never genuinely civilized,' wrote Immanuel Kant in the eighteenth century. 'He falls of his own accord into savagery.' Kant's statement was an obvious fiction, one belied by prominent Black figures of that era, including the composer Samuel Coleridge-Taylor, abolitionist writers Ottobah Cugoano and Olaudah Equiano, and the French general Thomas-Alexandre Dumas, father of novelist Alexandre Dumas. Not that individual brilliance did much to counter popular prejudice. In the summer of 1896, half a million people visited Vienna's Prater Pleasure Garden to see a group of Africans, from the Ashanti region of present-day Ghana, dressed in animal skins, next to a pair of elephants and a giant salamander. Vienna was also home to Angelo Soliman, a formerly enslaved Nigerian man who climbed to the highest ranks of eighteenth-century Austrian society. Soliman spoke several languages, married into aristocracy and played chess with Emperor Joseph II. And after his death, his corpse was stuffed like the prize from a hunt, dressed in a loincloth and placed on display in Vienna's Natural History Museum.

—

How to count all the slights and misapprehensions, so trivial yet so numerous, that have trailed me into adulthood since that day outside the Express Dairy? At Heathrow, plainclothes security pull me aside for questioning, because I 'fit the description of a criminal'. In Lisbon I'm taken off a flight and questioned on suspicion of smuggling drugs. Arriving in Japan, I'm held in a room for several hours while immigration officers finger each page of my passport suspiciously, as if they think the watermark will rub off on their hands.

Years ago, I was interviewed by a national newspaper for the first time. I was excited at the prospect. I'd been appointed the editor of a prominent magazine and being interviewed seemed like its own thrilling adventure. I met the journalist, the interview went well, and afterwards I called my parents and told them to look out for the paper the following week. The next day, I got a call from the journalist with a query. She was following up a story that, when I was younger, I'd been a track and field athlete and had been banned from competing for failing a drug test. Listening to her, I felt hot, faint, humiliated. My head ached. Even after spending an hour with her, talking about my life and work, the journalist had still mistaken me for another Black person. I told her that whoever the story applied to, it was not me. After I put the phone down, my head continued throbbing. When the article came out it didn't mention the sports story. It was a decently written profile accompanied by a big close-up portrait. My parents called and read parts of it back excitedly down the phone. But looking at the page, the blown-up photo staring out at me, I only felt numb. Once I finished talking to them, I folded up the paper, shoved it in a drawer, and didn't take it out again.

Another time, at a wedding, trading small talk about the food and speeches with the mother of the bride. Abruptly, she asked me if I had spoken to the one other Black man at the wedding, who was standing across the room with his family. I said I didn't know him and had no plans to approach him. A silence fell between us. Then she said with the hint of a smile, 'I'm sorry, was that wrong of me? I find it so hard to know. Please do tell me what's right.' She looked at me keenly, waiting, expecting an answer. I found I could not speak.

Another time, on the subway in New York, two thick-necked white men in vests talking loudly about the 'monkey people' on the train. They wanted to be overheard and they knew they were big enough to fight off anyone who might tell them to be quiet. So we, the Black people in the carriage, rode in silence, not making eye contact. Carrying our indignation out of the station, ripe as it was with the odour of old food and engine oil, and up the stairs into the day above.

Perhaps I should be happy. These are minor incidents, after all. My dignity is bruised on such occasions but no greater harm is done. My name is not David Oluwale. I am alive to write these words. Still. To be othered is never less than painful.

—

Some months after my trip to Hereford I made a Zoom call to Yinka Shonibare, the artist. It was early autumn, a cool Saturday, and

Shonibare appeared on my screen, from a book-lined room in his East London home. Three years previously, he had been invited by Hereford Cathedral to make an artwork in response to the Mappa Mundi. Shonibare often explores relationships of power and presence between Africa and the West, and in Hereford he created a series of six quilts that depicted some of the monstrous races from the map – including the Blemmyae and the Cynocephali – using the brightly coloured Dutch wax fabric that is his signature material.

Shonibare's artworks offer a sardonic approach to complex topics of history and identity. The wax fabric he favours was originally made in Holland for export to Indonesia, before being widely adopted in West Africa in the nineteenth century. What's often regarded as an archetypal example of African authenticity is anything but. It is an example of how identity is fluid and not fixed, changing meaning across time and place. He considered his Mappa Mundi textiles 'a kind of Trojan horse, a masquerade' – works that were slyly questioning of Western notions of race even while they were joyously patterned enough to enchant visitors to the cathedral. 'They thought I was just depicting aspects of the map, not realizing that actually it was critique,' he observed.

He had also recently been commissioned to create a memorial to David Oluwale, by the David Oluwale Memorial Association. Shonibare was born in London and raised in Nigeria. He visited Britain on holiday throughout his childhood before returning at seventeen in the 1970s. Although his circumstances were far more comfortable than Oluwale's – his family owned property in London and Shonibare later attended boarding school in Hampshire – he identified with the experience of the other man. It was impossible to live in Britain as a Black person, he reflected, without encountering the experiences of racialization and discrimination that affected

David Oluwale. 'Even if you're not thinking about those issues, those issues are constantly projected on to you. That could easily have been me. I could have been in that situation.'

On the evening of 25 April 2022, a blue plaque commemorating Oluwale was unveiled on Leeds Bridge, close to where he was last seen alive. Less than three hours later, the plaque was ripped off the bridge and stolen. Racist graffiti was daubed in its place. A laminated paper copy of the plaque was put up as a temporary replacement the following day, but this was also vandalized, before a third plaque was finally installed on 23 October. Police called the thefts a hate crime.

Shonibare's proposed memorial is intended to stand next to the Oluwale footbridge over the River Aire. I was seeing his design for the first time as we spoke and it struck me powerfully. The protocols of remembrance can sometimes be prosaic. A statue or a plaque will duly honour a person but it rarely invokes empathy. Shonibare was determined to avoid the response the plaque had provoked. 'I didn't want his memorial, his legacy, to be defined by the same violence he'd suffered in life.'

Instead, the artist looked to his own childhood in Nigeria, where he'd been captivated by the hibiscus flowers that grew so profusely there. He'd play with them and even suck the sweet nectar from them. In creating a memorial, said Shonibare, he wanted to restore Oluwale's dignity. The artwork was called *Hibiscus Rising*, a huge, 9.5-metre-high sculpture of a hibiscus flower fashioned out of fibreglass, aluminium, steel and copper, and finished in yellow, orange and purple-coloured Dutch wax pattern. In the artist renderings, the sculpture stretched to the sky on a slender stem, towering over the heads of passers-by. It looked beguiling and beautiful, and perhaps because I'd spent the previous months reflecting on the bigotry and violence Oluwale had faced in Leeds, I was profoundly moved. I thought of David Oluwale, Yankee, brave and reckless, stowing away on the *Temple Bar*. Working where he could, at a factory, a building site, an abattoir, to get a foothold in Britain. Yankee watching westerns. Yankee dancing at the Mecca till the lights came up. And then the years locked in institutions. His decline. Being hounded and harassed. The hostility and hatred. How do you remember a life in its fullness? Its joy and potential as well as its pain? 'I didn't want to put something in the public realm that continued to portray him as a victim,' Shonibare told me. 'I didn't want that to represent him as a Black man. So the sculpture is bold, it's very tall. Yeah. It's bold. It will stand, not in tragedy, but in colour. In defiance. And as you approach it you will see it for miles.'

2

Matthew Henson

Greenland, July 1891

A hundred dollars. That's how much Lieutenant Scaptec bet you that you wouldn't make it back in one piece. Scaptec. Broken blood vessels blossoming across his cheeks. His face laughing in your face while the other boys at the Navy Yard leered behind him. A white man risks his sanity and his life venturing into the Arctic, he said. What chance does a coloured man have in such an environment? It is a cold hell and nothing more. Come back unharmed and you've earned the money. But it won't be my fault if the cold snaps off your fingers and freezes your Negro blood.

It's true that many of those who've come to the High North have departed crawling, beseeching God. Their ships crushed by pack ice. Crews dragging lifeboats across the frozen sea in pursuit of open water. Men driven mad by the sunless winter. Till they lie down begging to be left behind.

You might vanish off the Earth like the Franklin expedition: one hundred and twenty-nine men never seen again. Or resort to eating the flesh of your dead crewmates as did the last survivors of the Greely expedition, knowing if they lived they would carry the shame of their actions for all their days.

Yet once you row off from the *Kite* and set foot on the eastern shore of McCormick Bay, you forget to be afraid. Latitude seventy-eight degrees. A thick green moss, ankle-deep and spongy, spreads across the ground, punctuated by vivid clusters of azaleas and rhododendrons, yellow poppies and lilac anemones. Butterflies play in the air. Further back from the bay, the terrain looks less inviting. Bare and stony ground turns to red-brown sandstone cliffs topped with polar ice. The cliffs are a reminder of what lies inland. The goal of your expedition is to travel to the northerly perimeter of Greenland, a destination that no explorer has ever reached before. To do so means trekking for some hundreds of miles towards the unknown.

The interior of Greenland is an elevated plateau of snow and ice, piled up layer upon layer over centuries, until its accumulated mass lies eight thousand feet above sea level. A vast frozen shield high enough to bury even the tallest peaks on the island. You will camp in the bay over the winter and begin your campaign next year at the beginning of spring. Icebergs shaped by the wind and sun into abstract sculptural forms glimmer in the clean afternoon light. Seals bob in the water. In your diary that night you write, 'Imagine gorgeous bleakness, beautiful blankness. Such a light as never was on land or sea.'

You and Frederick Cook, the expedition doctor, carry Lieutenant Peary ashore on a plank. He broke his leg during the voyage and has been in a foul mood every day since. The lieutenant lies by the bay shouting orders and taking readings with his sextant, while Mrs Peary, who is joining the expedition for its twelve months in Greenland, sits beside him jotting his findings in a notebook.

The most urgent task is shelter. For two weeks you and the rest of the crew are busy building the big wooden cabin that will be your home for the next year. The Pearys name it Red Cliff House for the sandstone cliffs rising behind the bay, waiting for you to begin your march across the ice.

You lie in your bunk at night listening to the eerie groan of the wind and aching with the exertion of the last few weeks. Building the cabin and then rowing back and forth to the *Kite* to unload a year's worth of supplies. Corned beef, condensed milk, compressed pea soup, tea, coffee, biscuit, lumber, skis, snowshoes, guns, tins of alcohol fuel. Despite your exhaustion, it's a struggle to sleep in the deceptive polar light. A wan red sun sits over the bay without setting. You drift in and out of wakefulness. When you doze you see figures hovering at the edge of focus. Faces that you left behind long ago. Pa is there, glowering. So are your three sisters, who you haven't seen since you were children together in Charles County. In a dream you are walking with them across an empty field. Past trees with bare branches against a black sky. They are ahead of you. You can't see their faces or remember the sound of their voices. The desire to be with them is overwhelming. Yet you can't catch up. They move ahead into the woods, leaving you behind.

You wake. For a second it feels impossible to get up. A huge weight seems to be pressing on your chest, holding you down.

In the afternoon you are preparing a lunch of baked beans and corned beef when the lieutenant, who is sitting at the front of the house with his leg up, calls you outside. You follow his pointing finger to see a blue fox trotting along the bay by the edge of the water. You whistle at the animal and it stops, looks directly at you with dark, shining eyes, and then carries on walking. The lieutenant lifts the rifle lying beside him, takes aims and shoots the fox in the flank. Close up, the creature is a poor trophy, thin and ragged fur with badly worn teeth. You wish the lieutenant had left it to live. The blankness in its eyes brings back something of your dream from last night. A recollection of faces blurred and out of reach. The yawning sense of loneliness that left you gasping for breath.

September 1891

Preparations continue for the coming winter. The crew are hunting as much as they can before the long darkness falls. Hare, fox and reindeer hang in abundance in the larder, along with a large quantity of seal meat. Ikwah, a young Inughuit man who has come to pitch his sealskin tent beside Red Cliff House, along with his wife Manee and their two small children, has been acting as a guide to the expedition. In the boat with him, you shot a walrus. It weighed 1,569 pounds and measured nine feet. For Ikwah every piece of the animal is valuable. The Inughuit use walrus tusks for tools, walrus fat for lamp oil. Walrus skin lines the inner wall of the stone igloos they build during the winter.

The sun is visible for only a few hours now, in the late afternoon. It sinks lower and faster each day. The windows of Red Cliff House have been boarded up for insulation – soon it'll be too dark to see out of them anyway – and hung with heavy, brightly coloured Red Indian blankets. The effect is very welcoming. The embracive warmth and the flickering shadows bring to mind a Manhattan gentlemen's club. Or at least how you imagine one would look. The lieutenant and Mrs Peary have a separate room to themselves with an American flag on the wall, a Persian rug on the floor and his sextant and other instruments lined up on top of a trunk. For so remote a camp, there is a well-stocked library, consisting of Shakespeare, Dickens, Kipling and many works on polar exploration. When the wind is at its loudest, you think of Caliban's words: 'Be not afeard; the isle is full of noises / Sounds and sweet airs, that give delight, and hurt not.'

The men grumble about the constraining effect of Mrs Peary's presence on the expedition. She is prim and high-handed and requires them to wash before dinner and hold off from swearing in her company. Privately, she is less reserved. When the rest of the men are out, and it's just you preparing dinner while the Pearys take their leisure, she is terrifically dismissive of them. 'I hate these people more and more every day. Every action of theirs speaks of lowness.' Dr Cook is 'exceedingly coarse with not an idea of gentlemanly behaviour. A dirty specimen of manhood.' Verhoeff, a mineralogist from Kentucky, is 'an uncanny and very homely dwarf who is not quite right in the "upper storey"'. Langdon Gibson, a young blue-blood, has, she concedes, 'been brought in contact with a better class of people'. But he is 'a lazy, shiftless, thoroughly deceitful fellow, besides being a coward'. Astrup, a Norwegian champion skier, is 'foreign'.

It doesn't occur to her to hold back while you're in the room. She only appears to notice you when she's giving you chores, which she does with relish. When the other men are surveying the landscape, you are kept back to beat out the fur rugs for fleas, sweep the floors and empty the slop pails. Perhaps she doesn't credit you with having an opinion on matters in the cabin. In this behaviour, she's not much different from the rest of the expedition party. From their perspective you are only ever Lieutenant Peary's valet. Not Matthew or Mr Henson. Only Matt. His 'body servant'. His boy.

You are enough of a scholar of white folks to expect little more from them. Every Negro is schooled thus. When you were growing up, your pa was known as the most unyielding man in the whole of Charles County. He was no bigger than you are now, which is to say mid-height. But taut, sinewy. Frequently furious. This was Pa: when the cart he was driving got stuck in mud up to its axle, and the ox pulling it refused to move, he thrashed the animal half to death and then pulled the cart out himself. Mindful of his reputation, the three Homer brothers came by once with their hats in their hands, the younger ones pushing Joshua, the oldest, to the front, to ask, could Pa please stop his cattle grazing on their land. Pa broke Joshua's jaw with one punch and then threw all three of them off his property.

After a day working his farm, he was still energetic enough to beat you up and down the stairs and out into the yard.

Pa was at his most severe when he was warning you and the girls not to leave the house after dark. Go out late and you'd get caught by a Night Doctor, he said. A Night Doctor was a white man in a gown who caught black people careless enough to be out of the house after dark and attacked them with a knife or a syringe. Out of amusement or spite, no one could definitely say. But Pa swore they had struck in his town when he was a child. A person just vanishing one night without a trace. He knew it was them because a lynch mob left what remained of a body behind, whereas a Night Doctor moved in silence.

You never saw a Night Doctor but you witnessed plenty of other white men willing to exercise their power over black folks. When Mr Samuel, the owner of Pa's land, came by, you watched your father go into a gruesome act of abasement. Laughing too loud and practically rolling his eyes. It reminded you of a dog that's been whipped, lying down with its belly to the ground before you, whining and whimpering. Everyone was disgusted by Pa's grovelling; Mr Samuel, Pa himself, you. But he had no choice. Coming north, travelling as far in one direction as it's possible to get from America, you'd hoped you might see a different side to folks here.

And sometimes you do get a glimpse of what could otherwise be. Just a few weeks after landing, the men threw you a birthday dinner. As a way to maintain morale, one of the rules decided among you all is that each expedition member's birthday should be celebrated with a special meal of their choosing. In honour of your twenty-fifth, you were able to select whatever you wanted from the supplies. The dining table was only a wooden board, left over from building the cabin, with supply boxes for seats. But Mrs Peary draped it with a white muslin cloth and when it was laid out the meal was magnificent: mock turtle soup; a stew of little auk with green peas; broiled breast of eider duck, Boston baked beans, tinned corn and tomatoes. For dessert, apricot pie, sliced peaches, plum duff with brandy sauce. A Sauternes was passed around with the plum duff. Lieutenant Peary made a speech praising you for your 'intelligence and faithfulness'. A glow of pleasure spread through your body as you sat listening to him. It was the first time anyone had ever celebrated your birthday. You recorded it carefully in your diary that night.

The warm feeling was short-lived. The men make it their business to see you know your place. Usually Verhoeff is the instigator. He has paid $2,000 of his own money to join the expedition. He is much prone to spitting on the wooden cabin floor and talking of his relatives back in Kentucky, one of whom is a policeman and another who keeps a poorhouse. Verhoeff only speaks to you indirectly – as in, 'Tell the nigger to harness the dogs,' or, grinning, as you enter the cabin one afternoon, 'I don't know what stinks worse, the Esquimos in their filthy furs or this coloured boy.' You tell him you have a proper name which you'd like to be addressed by and he says, 'The nigger's getting airs about him.'

No one in the cabin comes to your defence. Either they consider nothing offensive about his words or else they agree with them. Mrs Peary is the only one to acknowledge the animosity between you. 'If the two of you can't resolve your differences, you should go out-doors and fight it out,' she says. You'd like a go at punching that sallow face of his but Verhoeff says he won't fight a man who isn't his equal. When you come in from the cold and find him holding forth in the cabin, you get a bitter taste in your mouth and you're tempted to spit on the floor as freely as he does. But in these last days of sunlight you have too much work to do to rise to his taunts. You are hunting, cooking, overhauling provisions, soldering tins of alcohol, shaping and building the sledges that the expedition will use on the ice cap in spring.

'All day,' you write in your diary, 'cries of Matt, do this, and Matt, do that and Matt, the lieutenant wants you. It is the same old story. A man's work and a dog's life, and what does it amount to? What good is to be done? Tired, sick, sore and discouraged.'

October 1891

The sun set today at 2.30 p.m., its last flares lighting up the hills across McCormick Bay and painting the icebergs in the water a gorgeous amber. You stood up to watch the view from in front of the cabin where you were shaping a sled. The sudden, encompassing brightness made your head swim and, for a second, you could have been back in Nanjemoy. Close your eyes and you could see an earth snake winding lazily across the back yard, its skin a dull, reddish-brown, the same colour as a scythe that lies rusting in the grass. The Potomac, near enough that you and the girls could go and stand by the river's edge while great unruly rafts of logs felled by lumberjacks floated past downstream. That was before you'd watched Pa fall to his knees one Sunday on the way back from church. Fall to his knees and slam his face sideways on the damp autumn earth. The blood running from his nose. His eyes already blank. A 'rupture', the doctor said. Your mother having long passed by then, it was left to Nellie, Pa's second wife, to raise you. A woman running a farm by herself with three children of her own and four stepchildren. You don't remember her smiling or sparing you any attention except when, her lips forming into a narrow line, she slapped you on the face or legs, or tore a switch and whipped you across the back.

When you could take no more from her, you got up one night, lined your shoes with newspaper and made off into the dark. After thirteen years on the farm, being in motion was liberating. So you kept walking, sleeping where you could, working when the chance arose. Forty miles until road surrendered to sea. At the docks in Baltimore you begged your way as cabin boy on to the *Katie Hines*, a three-masted cargo ship carrying wheat to Hong Kong.

Quite promptly you acquired an enemy, a white deckhand named Frenchy, whose repeated insults finally culminated in him knocking you to the floor in the galley, leaving you with a bloody mouth and an aching head. Captain Childs, the ship's master, came to your rescue. Childs was sixty years old and had spent most of his life at sea with no family or firm ties to land. He was the sovereign authority of his vessel. But the sea hadn't roughened him so much as made him more sensitive – to fluctuations in atmospheric pressure, and to people. He cared enough to take notice of a thirteen-year-old boy, hurting and frightened. Childs gave you Dickens and Shakespeare to read and taught you maths and astronomy. Each day, two to four, in the dark-wood warmth of his cabin, reading aloud, and when you couldn't make out a passage, Childs himself taking over for the satisfaction of hearing the words brought to life: 'It was the best of times, it was the worst of times, it was the age of wisdom, it was the age of foolishness, it was the epoch of belief, it was the epoch of incredulity, it was the season of Light, it was the season of Darkness . . .'

By the time you reached the equator you'd learned how to use a sextant and take a noon observation of the sun. Your friendship, because it was nothing less than that, lasted five years, during which you travelled as far as the oceans could take you: China, France, Murmansk, Casablanca. With Childs you found the love that had been absent when it came to your own father. Aged eighteen, you were returning from China when Childs caught a fever. He insisted there was nothing to worry about, sweating and shaking in his cabin. Within five days he was dead, his sheet-wrapped body sent to the ocean floor.

The pain of his loss was like being struck blind. For a long time, all you did was drift. You found your way to a foul job on a whaler in Newfoundland where the captain was a drunk. The memory of butchering a whale for the first time stays with you to this day. Slashing through thick layers of flesh and fat while steaming blood poured down the deck. Then there were spells as a stevedore, a messenger boy, a chauffeur, a nightwatchman.

Now you are on the move no longer. The eerie beauty of the Arctic has brought you to a halt. Pack ice massing silently in the bay. Frozen water vapour making wreaths of mist. You find you can think about the *Katie Hines* without yearning. The snowscape bathed in the dazzling light of the full moon. Here the Earth reveals itself as a living creature. The place has even given you friends.

One night a month ago, you saw moving lights on the other side of the bay, faint and flickering and coming closer. Having had no human contact outside the camp since the *Kite* left in July, the sight seemed so strange that you thought it might be an Arctic will-o'-the-wisp. It turned out instead to be Ikwah and Manee, who'd been camping across the shore. In their wake, other Inughuit have come. There are now seventeen at the camp, men, women and children, with more due to arrive as the bay freezes over, and the place is busy with the sound of talking and crying babies and barking dogs well into the night.

To your diary: 'In colour, the Inughuit are brown, their hair is heavy, straight, coarse, and black. In appearance they are short, fat, and well-developed; and they bear a strong resemblance to the

Mongolian race. The tribe of these people, the North Greenland Esquimos, numbers two hundred and eighteen. Rarely does a family remain in one place longer than one season, which is nine months, for after a season of hunting in one place, game becomes very scarce.'

Until the expedition led by Captain John Ross of the Royal Navy made contact with them in 1818, the Inughuit of north-western Greenland had lived in isolation for generations, cut off from the Inuit groups to the south of Greenland by vast stretches of icy wilderness. They called themselves 'the great and real human beings', believing they were alone on the planet. No trees grow on their lands so the Inughuit lack wood for tools or shelter. They do, however, have access to metal from the 'Iron Mountain', a secret, sacred deposit of iron from which they fashion basic tools, thought by Ross to be a meteorite that long ago crashed in the ice.

Whalers and other explorers have followed Ross, so that the Inughuit no longer find the sight of travellers remarkable. Until now, though, all of their visitors have been white. When they discovered a dark-skinned man, the Inughuit camped at Red Cliff House were fascinated anew. The competition that broke out among the young men to school you in the ways of the Inughuit was won by Ootah, a cousin of Ikwah. He is a skilled and serious-minded hunter whose parents' treasured possessions include a sextant box and a string of beads given to them by members of the *Polaris* expedition which came from America in 1871.

Lieutenant Peary regards the Inughuit in strictly functional terms. In exchange for what he calls 'trifling presents' – knives for the men, needles for the women and maybe a mirror for the children – the community will work for the expedition party until the spring. They hunt the seal, walrus and reindeer that provide meat for food, fat for fuel and skins for clothing. The women stitch the fur parkas and pants (polar bear for deep winter, Arctic fox for warmer months), stockings and kamiks – sealskin boots – that are far better suited than heavy woollens for this climate. The men have a good many sledge dogs and, from canny questioning, the lieutenant has information on all the best animals and what their owners will be prepared to trade for them.

'Of what use are Esquimos to the world?' he asks. 'They are too far removed to be of any value for commercial enterprise; and furthermore, they lack ambition. They have no literature; nor properly speaking, any art. They value life as does a fox, or a bear, purely by instinct.' However much the expedition is beholden to the Inughuit for their skills, it is they ultimately who should be grateful to him, says the lieutenant. 'To understand what my gifts have meant to them, imagine a philanthropic millionaire descending upon an American country town and offering every man there a brownstone mansion and an unlimited bank account.' The lieutenant stands a foot taller than the Inughuit. They are, he says, like 'little fur-clad aborigines'. You have to be firm but also kind to them, as you would to a child. 'I have made it a point to rule them by love and gratitude rather than by fear and threats.'

When you listen to him, your mind turns to the scene last month when Lieutenant Peary, in a burst of generosity, ordered a barrel of biscuits to be taken out of the stores. He had it placed before the Inughuit who had gathered around him. Then he kicked it over. Men, women and children hurled themselves on the biscuits like dogs. The lieutenant stood among them smiling coldly, his pale eyes gleaming.

You spend long days and weeks with the Inughuit. Ootah shows you how to drive a sledge being pulled by eight powerful dogs, one hand on the handle, the other holding the 28-foot sealskin whip that you snap over the ear of the lead dog to urge him on. Out on a hunt, Ootah sees the ice give way beneath you as you're crossing a frozen lake. He drags you from the frigid blackness on to solid ground, beats the water out of your fur pants and shrugs off your thanks for saving your life. It is no less than a brother would do, he says.

You are invited to a dinner one night in the stone igloo that Ikwah and Manee have built for the winter. Many of their family members are present, including Kyo, Ikwah's brother, and various cousins and elders. The place is pungent with their accumulated body odours – the Inughuit preferring to rub themselves clean with a bird skin once or twice a month rather than waste water with bathing. A walrus-blubber stove provides heat and a gauzy orange light. You find a space on the fur-covered ledge that runs round the inside of the domed room and share the feast of giviaq, little auks pickled in oil and stuffed in a seal's stomach bladder, that Manee has prepared in your honour. You follow Ikwah's lead in the frenzied eating, pulling a bird out of the bladder, plucking its feathers and tugging off its skin with a twist of the wrist, before finally getting to the meat. When the meal is over, Ahnalka, an elder who until now has been sitting quietly, stands up, making a deep humming in his chest, commanding the attention of the gathering.

While Ikwah beats out an echoing rhythm on an ayayut, a hand drum made from stretched walrus skin, Ahnalka begins to chant long and low, his voice initially tremulous but rising in force, singing of loss and love and yearning while the watching crowd sways and hums. His song reverberates around the domed interior and when he finishes, shoulders slumping in exhaustion, an emotional charge still fills the room. Without thinking, you stand up and gesture to Ikwah that he should start drumming again. You sing the first song that comes to your mind, 'In the Garden', a hymn that

Captain Childs liked to hum at the ship's wheel. Thinking of Childs brings tears to your eyes and you are embarrassed to be crying before these strangers. But you carry on singing anyway and the words bring you their own comfort. 'And He walks with me / And He talks with me / And He tells me I am His own.' By the time you're finished, you are as exhausted as Ahnalka was, and you sit down, at once empty and filled up.

Ootah and the other Inughuit take to calling you Mahri-Pahluk, 'Matthew the Kind One'. Through the months of dark winter you prefer to spend your time with them rather than at Red Cliff House. Often you feel as much Esquimo as American. Speaking their language, adopting their dress, eating the same food, sleeping in the same dens, sharing their pleasures and their griefs. You know every man, woman and child in their community. They are your friends and regard you as theirs.

May 1892

In spring you climb to the ice cap to carry out the purpose of the expedition – crossing the interior of Greenland in search of the northern limits of the land mass. You, the lieutenant, Dr Cook, Astrup and Gibson start from Red Cliff House with five Inughuit guides, including Ikwah, and twenty dogs.

It is hard-going from the beginning. The lieutenant envisaged an 'Imperial Highway' of ice and snow running flat and smooth from the edge of the cliffs to the north. The reality is a chaotic landscape of crevasses, gullies and pinnacles, over which you have to haul and push the sledges by hand. Treacherous gorges covered by drifts of snow threaten to open beneath your feet. Leaden grey clouds gather overhead, signalling an approaching storm. Five days into the journey, the

Inughuit refuse to go any further. Ikwah says the inland ice is the domain of the demon Kokoyah who does not welcome strangers into his home. His jaws are crevasses waiting to eat you up. There is no convincing them to stay.

The group moves on without them. Just you men and the dogs walking into one of the most damnable territories on Earth. The pace slows to only a few miles a day. Without their masters, the dogs grow restless and fight constantly among themselves. Four die and one escapes. In the evening all of you lay your sleeping bags out in the open. Dinner is a meal of pea soup and pemmican – ground beef mixed with suet, sugar and currants – the mainstay of expedition rations. You go to sleep in the lee of the sledges, taking shelter from the shrieking wind. Invariably, in the morning, the dogs are in a sorry tangle of knotted leads. Half of them have chewed free of their harnesses and are running at will around the sledges trying to gnaw at the provisions, and it's a painful task involving much snarling and biting of hands to get them back under control.

You wake up another week into the journey with a searing pain in your left eye, as if overnight someone has stabbed you in the pupil. Dr Cook applies a drop of opium solution to it to relieve the pain but he says the eyeball is frozen and the only remedy is to return to the warmth of Red Cliff House. The notion of turning back while the rest of the group fights on feels like a humiliation. You tell the lieutenant you won't let him down and you want to continue. But he has already made other plans anyway. To speed up progress, Lieutenant Peary is only taking one man with him for the rest of the journey, the champion skier Astrup, while you, Cook and Gibson will head back to base.

You leave in opposite directions the following morning, Peary and Astrup taking most of the dogs and a thousand pounds of supplies, while the rest of you travel with two light sledges and a fortnight's worth of food.

You are back at Red Cliff House by the end of May. June goes by without any sign of Lieutenant Peary or Astrup. By the end of July they are still not returned and the unspoken fear at the cabin is that they are lost or dead. On July 24th the *Kite* arrives from New York to take the expedition team home. The ship will leave by the end of August to avoid being frozen in for the winter, whether the two of them have made it or not.

All the men are keeping up a brave face for Mrs Peary, who spends many hours gazing out of the cabin window. Only the Inughuit are baleful. Kyo, Ikwah's brother, haunts the cabin muttering about Kokoyah taking his revenge on transgressors. Where his brother is kind and generous, Kyo clings to resentment, believing himself always cheated, always a victim. He is twice a widower and is thought to have killed both his wives. He has fits of terrible rage and twice during these spells he has cut his current wife across the face with a knife. Among his people Kyo is also feared as a shaman of considerable power. Yesterday morning, he came to Red Cliff House. During the night, he said, he had entered a trance in which the great expanse of the inland ice was laid out before him. Far to the north he saw a solitary white man walking slowly and painfully southward. Here Kyo raised his head, pushed back his long, greasy hair and gave a sustained pause, glaring around the room, while Ikwah, who was translating, sat mortified beside him. The man was not Peeuree, but a messenger from the other realm come to say that Peeuree is dead.

What will it mean for the expedition if the lieutenant is really gone? For all his arrogance, his loss would be devastating. Not least because you have him to thank for coming to this extraordinary place.

You were working at Steinmetz and Sons, a haberdasher's on G Street in Washington DC, when Lieutenant Peary came into the store. This was in 1887, during the lost times after the *Katie Hines*. He was a civil engineer in the navy. He had been put in charge of a survey mission to Nicaragua and required a sun hat, seven and three-eighths in size. The lieutenant also mentioned he was looking for a valet to keep his clothes and quarters clean on the expedition. Mr Steinmetz recommended you to him as an 'honest, intelligent boy with regular habits'. You agreed to go. The prospect of being someone's servant didn't appeal, but travelling to Central America certainly beat the tedium of the hat store.

Eighteen months in the jungle, hacking through rainforest, wading through swamp. All the time at Lieutenant Peary's side, bearing witness to his insatiable ambition, his boundless insecurities. The lieutenant had lost his father at the age of two and he was brought up alone in Pennsylvania by an anxious, overprotective mother who made him wear a sun bonnet with ribbons when he went out to play. He had a lisp and at school the other boys would put tacks on his chair before he sat down. As a man, his abiding urge is to dominate the people and landscapes around him. You once found a note he had written to himself on his desk: 'Tall, erect, broad-shouldered, full-chested, tough, wiry-limbed, powerful, tireless swimmer, a first class rider, a skilful boxer and fencer.' The physical description was accurate. But he could also have written: craves attention, imperious in attitude, liable to tantrums, desperate for advancement, fears obscurity. 'I would like to acquire a name which would make my mother proud and which would make me feel that I was the peer of anyone I might meet,' he told you one night, after another exhausting day in the caterwauling jungle. 'I cannot bear to associate with people who, age and advantages being equal, are my superiors.

I must be the peer or master of those about me to be comfortable.'
Growing up, he had read the accounts of polar exploration by Kane,
Hayes, Hall and all the rest. Without ever venturing any further
north than Providence, he had convinced himself that was where his
destiny lay.

After Nicaragua, the lieutenant was stationed at the Navy Yard
in Philadelphia. He found a job for you there as a messenger at $15 a
week. But all the time he was plotting to make his name. Having
raised $10,000 in donations, he chartered the *Kite* and assembled a
team to search out the northernmost point of Greenland. Despite
the scepticism of Lieutenant Scaptec and the other men at the yard,
and even though the pay is just $50 for the whole year, you joined the
party as his assistant. Assuming he and Astrup make it back, this
expedition is only the lieutenant's first intended step to making history as the discoverer of the North Pole: 'I must have fame and
cannot reconcile myself to years of commonplace drudgery. I see an
opportunity to gain it now and sip the delicious draught while yet I
have youth. I want my fame now.' If he dies in Greenland, blindly
searching for the edge of the land, his name will stand for nothing;
all his yearning will have been in vain.

26 August 1892

Lieutenant Peary and Astrup came back last night. They trekked
five hundred miles north, enduring fierce storms and a treacherous
landscape fissured with hidden crevasses. Finally they arrived at a
3,800-foot cliff face beyond which they couldn't travel. They had
reached the northern boundary of Greenland.

With their return, the mood at the cabin has lifted. The company
drink the last of the wine and whiskey and dine on venison before

embarking on the *Kite*. All is cheerful except for the fact that Verhoeff has gone missing. He was last seen ten days ago, leaving by himself to collect mineral samples further around the bay, with supplies for four days. You joined the search party and, after six days scouring the landscape, Ootah found his footprints at the edge of a glacier riven with crevasses, twenty-five miles from Red Cliff House. It is most likely, he says, that Verhoeff lost his footing on the icy surface and slid into a crevasse. You had no love for him but it's a terrible thing to die this way, alone and afraid. Kokoyah has claimed his sacrifice after all.

2

United States of America, January 1893

Each lecture opens on a stage decked out with tents and harpoons and bearskins, a miniature recreation of an Inughuit village. Lieutenant Peary walks onstage to a photographic slideshow of icebergs and muskox, and group portraits of the expedition team looking intrepid. He instructs the audience on building an igloo and how to hunt polar bear and survive the long winter. And as the crowd nods along he says, who among you would be brave enough to face the bitter cold and savage creatures of the Great North? This is your cue. You bound on to the stage dressed in furs, cracking a whip above the heads of six Arctic dogs. These are the animals that Lieutenant Peary took all the way to the edge of Greenland. They spring around the stage, yelping and swishing their tails at the sight of him. Then, at a word from the lieutenant, they fall silent and lie at his feet. At the climax of the lecture, as he describes the last perilous trek north with Astrup, the dogs raise their heads and fill the theatre with their howling.

Night after night, the audience is on its feet in awestruck applause. Sweltering in your furs at the side of the stage, it's hard to share the elation. The pace of this tour is gruelling. Two shows every day for three months, starting in Pennsylvania then on to Brooklyn, St Louis, Columbus, Toledo and city after city. If there's snow on the ground when you arrive, the lieutenant has you hitch the dogs up to the sledge and drive them up and down Main Street beforehand to get folks excited. The lieutenant has returned home a hero. They say the expedition is the greatest feat yet in Arctic exploration, second only to reaching the Pole itself. The purpose of this tour is to raise the money for an expedition which will accomplish that last illustrious goal. He is irrepressible. He will keep returning to the Arctic until he achieves success, he says. Meanwhile for you there is little glory in third-class train travel and searching out a hotel prepared to take Negroes at every new town. And there is a letter from Eva. 'When will you be back?' she asks. 'When will I see you?'

Philadelphia, May 1893

Eva belongs to another species altogether. The Flints, her family, are originally from Washington DC and are connected by complicated ties of marriage, blood and business to the Wormleys, the Shadds, the Syphaxes, which is to say, the best black families of that city. They are members of the Crescent Club and the Ugly Fishing Club and take their summers at Highland Beach on Chesapeake Bay. Sometimes you wonder if the only reason her parents let you court their daughter is because your complexion – as copper as a penny – makes you at least physically presentable in their eyes. When they ask where you are from and who are your people, you skim over the past and emphasize your future prospects. Now that the expedition is over, you're back to your old job as a messenger at the Navy Yard. It's a respectable position that comes with a government pension. And there are few black men your age to have had their name in the *New York Times* as you did after the Greenland expedition.

Eva herself is untroubled either by your obscure family roots or by your great triumph in the Arctic. You watch her out of the corner of your eye in the Flint parlour while her mother asks, 'Are you related to the Georgetown Hensons?' She gazes back at you, entertained by your discomfort, an arched eyebrow over a bone-china cup decorated with flowers and butterflies in yellow, green and blue. Run into her in the park on a Sunday with the other young ladies of her set and she has the same privately amused manner. A murmured, 'Good day, Mr Henson,' and then she walks on, arm-in-arm with her friends. The coolness with which she acknowledges and then looks past you, giving and withholding in one motion: this is the moment you know you want to marry her.

Her family is divided on the matter. Eva's mother finds you polite and well groomed, albeit lacking in the social connections she would prefer. Her father thinks she should marry a businessman like himself. 'They can't make you out,' says Eva. What kind of Negro takes leave from a good job to go to the North Pole for $50, comes back, and then proposes to do it again the following year?

Eva herself has not said yes or no. She seems happy working in a dressmaker's, going to church with her family, walking in the park with her friends, playing tennis at the club. It's hard to tell behind her ironic demeanour if she feels seriously about you. She is twenty-two, just four years younger than you, but seated together in her mother's parlour, the gulf between you feels immense. Eva has never known loss or feared for her life. She has grown up in this solid house with its books and paintings and two parents that dote on her. There is no presumption on her part that the future will unfold any differently. Yet surely you're not alone in being restless. In wanting more.

All over the country, black people are looking beyond the horizon. In Mississippi and North Carolina folks in their thousands are catching 'Kansas fever' and heading north. White Southerners say all that waits for them up there is loneliness and despair. They write songs claiming to speak in the authentic voice of the Negro: 'I'm Going Back to Kentucky Where I Was Born'; 'When I Hear a Gun, I'm Going to Run Back Home to Tennessee'. Even those black people who are staying in the South are rising up in their own way. In Atlanta, three thousand black washerwomen have gone on strike for higher pay. In Lamar County, Texas, armed black men on horseback are patrolling their own streets, refusing to be terrorized by the white-sheeted Klan. Your promise to her: the life you make together will be different to anything her parents have known.

Chicago, June 1893

On the World's Fair

The World's Fair in Chicago was opened by President Grover Cleveland at noon on May 1st in front of a 100,000-strong crowd. The president, who was rumoured to be suffering from mouth cancer, managed a tight smile at the roar that greeted his presence. His gaze took in the White City, from the vast Agricultural Hall to the life-size replicas of the *Niña*, the *Pinta* and the *Santa Maria* – the three ships with which Columbus discovered America – floating on the lake. Cleveland lifted his hand and the audience fell silent. The fair was proof of the unparalleled skill and ingenuity of a young nation, said the president, listing some of the wonders on display across the 690-acre site: the telephone, the typewriter, threshing machines, the moving walkway, Thomas Edison's kinetoscope, William Morrison's electric car, the 264-foot-high rotating wheel built by George Washington Gale Ferris. 'We have made here objects of use and beauty, but we have also made men who rule themselves.' Men who were fearless. Men whose spirit of invention and enterprise was bringing into being the mightiest nation the world had ever seen. President Cleveland pressed a special golden button on the podium. Two hundred thousand light bulbs flickered into life and an elevated electric railway began to whisk passengers around the fairground. 'At the push of a button,' declared the *Salt Lake Herald*, 'the electric age is ushered into being in America.'

Not long after President Cleveland's opening speech, Frederick Jackson Turner, a young historian, delivered a much-discussed paper at the fair to the Chicago branch of the American Historical Association. Turner summoned an ominous vision. Now that the country was becoming a manufacturing civilization, it risked losing the very spirit that had made it exceptional. A generation of men whose fathers and forebears were explorers and conquerors, exercising natural dominion over the land and the darker peoples, were becoming soft. 'The frontier is gone and with its going has closed the first period of American history.'

Others echoed Jackson's anxieties. The world of 1893, said historian Henry Adams, scion of the Adams political family and a direct descendant of two US presidents, was 'getting awful rickety'. His brother, Brooks Adams, another historian, went further. The remarkable display of native genius at events like the World's Fair was reason for gloom not celebration. It was a sign the nation had reached its apogee. Only collapse could follow. 'The energy of the race has been exhausted. We bear every mark of premature decay. The worm is at the heart, eating, eating.' The recently published *American Nervousness*, by neurologist George Beard, on sale at bookstores at the fair, seemed to offer evidence for Adams's pessimism. Across the country, wrote Beard, young men were being afflicted with 'neurasthenia', a nervous condition with a multitude of symptoms: ennui, listlessness, temporary paralysis, pressure in the head, impotence, premature ejaculation, constipation or diarrhoea, insomnia or excessive sleep. The cause, said Beard, was 'overcivilization'. Cut off from the frontier and left to atrophy in the city, young men were falling victim to the spinning force of urban change. Neurasthenia was 'the cry of the human system struggling with its environment'. Its sufferers were being consumed by 'the whirl of the railway, the pelting of telegrams, the strife of business'.

The question that followed from such concerns, unspoken but hovering in the air with the scent of cigars and sausages and fried onions, was how would America renew its vitality? If the frontier was closed and the city capable of breeding nothing but enfeebled young men, who would write the next chapter in the nation's history?

Maybe it was the fear that America had run its course, foreshadowing the demise of the white race, that had led to the creation of the human zoos. The fairground was divided into two sections. The White City: grand neoclassical buildings dedicated to science, technology and the arts. And the Midway Plaisance: a mile-long strip of gleefully vulgar attractions, such as burlesque dancers, Wild West shows, beer halls – and living, 'anthropological' exhibits. The Midway was designed by the fair's creators as a 'Street of All Nations', where the crafts and cultures of a multitude of countries would be presented side by side in neighbouring village compounds. The order of the villages was supposed to replicate the hierarchy of world cultures. To walk east away from the splendour of the White City, representing American exceptionalism, was to take a reverse journey through the development of civilization. It was an opportunity, as the *Chicago Tribune* put it, 'to descend the spiral of evolution, tracing humanity in its highest phases down almost to its animalistic origins'.

A visitor began with the cultures most similar to America's in status, including a German village, a Japanese bazaar and an Irish village featuring a replica of Blarney Castle. Then came the 'half-civilized' nations of North Africa and the Middle East, offering camel rides on Cairo Street and exotic dancers performing the scandalous *danse de ventre*. At the end of the Midway, visitors finally arrived at the 'least evolved' peoples. This was the location of the Dahomey village, a collection of wooden huts where a large group of half-clothed men and bare-breasted women performed songs, dances and, according to a sign, other 'native pursuits'. The villagers, wrote the *Tribune*, were 'blacker than buried midnight and as degraded as the animals which prowl the jungles of their dark land'.

The neighbouring compound was the 'Esquimo' village, populated by inhabitants from Labrador, on the eastern coast of Canada. They had arrived in Chicago during the winter of 1892 and been housed in their two-acre encampment on the fairground months before its official opening by President Cleveland. For a while they'd been happy. They went kayaking on the lagoon and, when the water froze, they harnessed their dogs and took visitors on sledge rides over the ice. But by the summer, the situation had deteriorated. Their huts lacked any sanitation and many were sick with pneumonia. They were barred from leaving the village and, despite the warm weather, the managers insisted they remain dressed in their sealskin furs as visitors would expect. When one young man came out of his hut in blue jeans, he was locked up until he agreed to change his clothes.

———

In July, you visit the World's Fair. You have been married for the past month, following the grudging acceptance of Eva's family, and in a fortnight you will leave with Lieutenant Peary's next Arctic expedition. Perhaps because departure is on your mind, you explore the White City with an unsettled feeling that's a poor match for Eva's sense of excitement.

As you make your way down the Midway Plaisance, your unease blooms into disgust. At the Dahomey village, the crowd seems oblivious to the pantomime of savagery on display. You overhear one woman ask her husband whether the Dahomeans are real cannibals. Beside you, Eva screws up her face and turns away. Coming from a good family, her sense of propriety is offended as much by the bared breasts of the African women as it is by the demeaning fact of black people being put on show.

The Inuit compound is almost worse. The people there speak a different language from the friends you made in northern Greenland. But all the same you think of Ootah and Ikwah and how they would hate to be here. They are hunters and fishermen, used to travelling across the expanse of their always-changing landscape. The tedium of being penned up in a compound to be jeered at by the public would drive them to despair.

The indignity of these 'villages' is unbearable. Among the noisy mass of visitors, you feel abruptly alone. It strikes you that you have spent almost a third of your life away from America, travelling first with Captain Childs and now Lieutenant Peary. To leave, and to come back, is to recognize the strangeness of the place supposed to be your home. Yes, your marriage to Eva is a wonderful and unanticipated occurrence. You are looking forward to building a life with her. Even so, it is hard not to think of yourself as an exile, out of step with the manners and conventions of your wife and the rest of the country.

In your mind, you picture icebergs in a bay and a riot of spring flowers unfurling across the grass. The fuggy heat and human smells of an igloo in winter. Black skies scattered with stars hard and brilliant as diamonds.

3

Greenland, August 1893

From its start the expedition has been running awry. Intoxicated by his previous success, the lieutenant has shipped north an excess of men and animals, most of whom quickly prove redundant. It's one thing to return with the same sledge dogs that were such reliable companions on the last trip. Quite another to bring three times the number of men, none having any qualifications for polar work beyond an Ivy League education and a callow sense of self-regard. Many rounds of the Yale 'Whiffenpoof Song' were heard as the *Falcon* steamed away from New York. Also on board were a small herd of sad-eyed South American burros that the lieutenant was experimenting with as pack animals, and a flock of messenger pigeons he hoped to use to communicate between expedition teams on the ice. These experiments were short-lived. The pigeons adapted poorly to the cold, huddled in their cages sullenly refusing to fly. One of the burros died on the ship and was fed to the dogs. When the *Falcon* made land, the rest of the burros had to be locked in a paddock for their safety because the dogs had gained a taste for their meat. A fortnight later, a huge iceberg broke off from a glacier near the bay. It triggered a tidal wave that surged a hundred yards up on to the shore, dashing to pieces precious barrels of fuel oil and dragging most of the burros, as well as a litter of puppies, to their deaths in the water. The last two surviving burros were shot for the dogs.

Matters only got worse from there. Peary's intention was to return to Red Cliff House but you landed to discover the cabin had been smashed to pieces by Kyo, the shaman. Since the *Kite* left last year, his behaviour had become increasingly violent. He had stabbed his wife, Klayuh, in the leg and threatened to kill his daughter. Klayuh had fled with the girl. Kyo had pursued them, but not before ransacking the cabin for its remaining supplies and then smashing up the building itself. Ikwah, who related this story to you morose and embarrassed, fears what his brother will do if he catches up with Klayuh. So far, the rest of the Inughuit have conspired to keep him off her track.

With the old cabin destroyed, you've set up camp in a neighbouring inlet, Bowdoin Bay, and built a new base, Anniversary Lodge, modelled on the same design as your former home, but large enough to hold fifteen men. In place of the lost fuel, you're forced to burn seal oil and vile-smelling walrus blubber.

Although you live in close quarters with these men and do much of the important work of hunting, cooking and building sledges, they pay you little attention. They belong to the same fraternities and rowing clubs in Massachusetts and Maine and Connecticut and share the same friends up and down the East Coast. In their eyes, the Arctic is the ground on which to prove themselves real men. They pose for photographs beside the walruses they've shot, gazing sternly into the middle distance and keeping score of how many days they've spent away from the lodge, how far they've travelled, who has notched up the most kills.

Shortly after arriving, you take part in a hunt, travelling with Samuel Entrikin, a teacher from West Chester, and two other men in a steam launch, while Uutaaq and his friend Kessuh follow behind in kayaks. Seven miles from shore the engine of the steam launch breaks down and the boat begins to drift further out to sea. Uutaaq and Kessuh manage to tie the launch to their boats. You, Entrikin and the other men clamber in beside them and start to row back across the ice-strewn waters, towing the heavy launch. The boats have already drifted out of sight of the shore and with the ice floe impeding your progress it is arduous-going. Exhausted and hungry, you row day and night for seventy hours through the icy waters before making it back to the cabin. Afterwards you notice how Entrikin boasts of the incident, embellishing his role with each telling, although it was Uutaaq and Kessuh who had saved your lives.

March 1894

The expedition has made it through the winter months and, with the days brightening, the principal march can finally begin. Lieutenant Peary aims to lead a team back on the 600-mile route to Navy Cliff, the northernmost point on Greenland, which he reached on the previous expedition, mounting a full survey of the terrain as they travel. If conditions are good, he might continue on and try for the Pole.

Given your experience on the earlier tour, you expect to be part of the team. Instead the lieutenant orders you to stay behind with Hugh Lee, a newspaperman from Connecticut, who is the youngest member of the crew.

You watch with a sting of envy as they prepare to take their leave accompanied by five Inughuit guides and much howling from their ninety dogs. There's another round of the Yale song as they stand by their sledges and then the lieutenant reaches for an epic register before they sweep out of the camp: 'Never before has such a sight been seen on this great, desolate ice. Never will the scene be repeated.' Six days later, the Inughuit are back, having refused, as before, to go deep inland. Entrikin and Clark follow a fortnight afterwards, suffering a gastric infection.

Then Davidson hobbles back with a frozen foot, bringing stories of fearsome conditions out on the ice cap. Fifty-mile-an-hour winds tore one of the two big tents to shreds, forcing the men to huddle together under one covering as the storm raged for days.

Sleds fell apart. Food stocks ran low. Lice infested their furs. More cases of frostbite. It was the lieutenant's intention to struggle on with the remaining men but finally, after one hundred and twenty-eight miles of impossible conditions, he calls a retreat. Six weeks after its departure, the expedition team is back at Anniversary Lodge, cowed and haggard.

Once they have recovered, the men busy themselves with hunting trips and modest explorations of the immediate terrain. But they do so aimlessly. There is no disguising the situation. The expedition has ended in premature failure. A mood of shame and resentment settles on the cabin. Burning with the humiliation of surrender, the lieutenant blames the men: 'They have discovered that Arctic work is not entirely the picnic they had imagined.' They in turn grumble at his haughtiness. Entrikin complains that Lieutenant Peary is 'not as unselfish as the commander of a scientific expedition ought to be'. He wants the glory of the enterprise for himself.

With four months still to go before the return of the *Falcon* and nothing to look forward to but a journey home in ignominy, discipline begins to break down. Having failed to master the frontier, talk at the lodge turns to conquering the Inughuit women. Carr says he will make it his mission to sleep with at least two of them before going home. Vincent hints he's already had an Esquimo girl, although he is widely known as a liar and his word rarely believed. Swain and Davidson take a pair of young women down to the bay one evening to play 'cooney' with them. The game involves pushing their faces close to the girls and inhaling their smell. Afterwards they give them cider and try to convince them to lie down right there on the shore but the girls run off in dismay. Baldwin, the expedition meteorologist, appeals to Lieutenant Peary to stop the lodge being 'converted to a whorehouse'. To Baldwin's consternation, the lieutenant does not act. In fact, he condones the men's behaviour. According to him, 'feminine companionship' is a necessity for 'both physical and mental health and the retention of the top notch of manhood'.

Ultimately relations between white men and local women will benefit all of civilization. 'If colonization is to be a success in the polar regions let white men take with them native wives. Then from this union may spring a race combining the hardiness of the mothers with the intelligence of the fathers. Such a race would surely reach the Pole if their fathers did not succeed in doing it.' The lieutenant believes the make-up of the ideal expedition party is like the body of a 'tough, hardy man'. It has one intelligent white man at the head; the arms comprise two more white men, selected for 'their courage, determination, physical strength, and devotion to the leader', and for the body and legs there are the natives.

The lieutenant has turned a corner of Anniversary Lodge into a makeshift photography studio. This is a project he began while waiting out the winter, and now he returns to it with renewed vigour. With you as his assistant, he makes scientific studies of Inughuit men and women, posing them before the camera, front and profile, clothed and undressed. In the case of Aleqasina, a sixteen-year-old girl and a favourite of his, the lieutenant abandons his veneer of objectivity. He takes her out to the bay and photographs her naked on the rocks like a pin-up girl, breasts bared to the camera, her smile uncertain. Lieutenant Peary has had his eye on Aleqasina since the last expedition, when she was fourteen. Behind Mrs Peary's back he called her the 'belle of the tribe' and 'a girl just beginning to develop into a woman'. You believe he intended to make her his mistress even then. Mrs Peary has not joined her husband on this second trip and there is nothing now to stop him.

The fact that Aleqasina is herself married makes no difference. Peary regards both her and her husband, Piugaattoq, as his property. Over these past months, you've seen how he drew them into his service. The lieutenant made sure to give Piugaattoq prized gifts like a rifle even though he was a younger, less experienced hunter than many other men. He sent Piugaattoq on extended hunting trips that kept him away from the bay for weeks at a time, and during these absences Aleqasina was often at the lodge in the lieutenant's private quarters, where all the expedition crew, including you, colluded in the fiction that she was his 'laundress'. Piugaattoq has never objected. Inughuit men sometimes engage in wife-exchanges with other men and it could be he sees this situation in the same light. What is he to do if he is unhappy anyway? What could he, or Aleqasina, a shy, quiet girl, say to a man with so much power? You want to tell the lieutenant to keep away from the girl yourself but he is a king out here and you are just as much his subject as any of the Inughuit.

Sometimes it seems the Inughuit women can't take any more of being treated like chattel. As Swain, Davidson and the other men continue to hound them, a nervous condition, known to the Inughuit as pibloktoq, starts to spread among the women. Its symptoms are startling. You have seen Atunginah suddenly freeze while cutting up a piece of seal meat and start to shout obscenities, uttering a strange, unsettling laugh. Another time, Tongwe tore off her clothing, paced up and down screaming and gesticulating, and then ran out naked across the ice. She was half a mile distant before some of the men caught up with her. They wrapped her in a muskox robe and brought her back still shouting and thrashing. An attack of pibloktoq can last an hour or more and some sufferers become so wild that they would continue running about in the cold until they froze to death if not restrained.

Dedrick, the expedition doctor, calls pibloktoq a form of female hysteria little different to that suffered by American women. He prescribes quinine or brandy, or a one-tenth grain of morphine by hypodermic. Often, says Dedrick, an attack is caused by 'pure cussedness'. A woman wanting her way and making trouble when she doesn't get it. In such cases, he says, a more punitive response is called for. Some of the women are injected with a potion of mustard water. Last week he ordered Alnayah, who he takes to be an 'attention seeker', to be wrapped in sacking and lashed to a post. This caused much amusement among the Anniversary Lodge group, who gathered around her making lewd jokes as she writhed and yelled. You have nothing but sympathy for the women. Who wouldn't scream at living with these men?

August 1894

A year since you arrived in Greenland. The *Falcon* is anchored off the bay, but last night Lieutenant Peary gave the men an ultimatum. There was still work to do here, he said, and he'd be staying at the lodge for another year. If any man wanted to remain with him to try and carry out the expedition's original plan, they should say so now. Perhaps he didn't realize how unhappy the men had become under his leadership. He looked crestfallen when they stayed silent, nobody looking up to meet his eye. Eventually Lee, the youngest member of the team, said he'd stay. No one else followed. In that moment, you had the choice of leaving too and being free of the lieutenant and his ceaseless desire for domination. But you know it is not yet time to leave this place, even if that means staying under his control for another season.

So this morning you sit reading through a year's worth of letters from Eva that have arrived with the *Falcon*. Letters that begin in hope and excitement, asking what sights you're seeing, if you're staying warm, how you're enjoying the raw seal meat you told her the Inughuit liked so much. Letters saying, *I miss you, I miss you.* And which diminish in intensity over the year until they offer only perfunctory details of the dances she has attended and who will be at which resort this summer. You fear the effect on your relationship of the letter you're writing now, which is coming back to her in place of you. She may rightly ask if this is a real marriage. If there can be loving involved in remaining so far apart. You plead your obligation to remain here, beside the lieutenant, although it's still not too late to join the men packing their furs and walrus-tusk carvings in anticipation of the stories they'll tell when they get home. The connection you feel to this land runs deeper than you can put into words, deeper than you can admit even in a letter.

The Arctic is a desert. Bone dry, a cold Sahara. But beneath the surface, surely the earth is rich and thick. Surely the ground is alive. Do worms and star-nosed moles burrow through the soil? Listen close. Can you hear the shallow roots of grasses whispering in the dark?

Greenland, April 1895

Out on the ice cap the mind is liable to lose itself. Try steering a sledge in a straight line across an endless white space with nothing to fix the eye. Sky fuses with snow. An endless low light throughout day and night. It is impossible to tell if you are moving forward or floating on a still point. You have seen a man step abruptly off his sledge, befuddled by his surroundings, only to be dragged along on his face by his dogs who have continued running at a furious pace in the meantime.

Back at the lodge, the windows are closed, and the doors nailed shut. Letters have been written and given to Ikwah to deliver to the *Falcon* in the event the whiteness closes behind you forever. You follow Lieutenant Peary. Lee follows you, long shadows stretching across the ice. Six hundred miles to Independence Bay.

Out here, the temperature can drop as low as minus forty-five degrees Fahrenheit. Yet when the wind falls, the weather seems almost mild, and the exertion of snowshoeing and driving dogs leaves you sweating so much inside your furs that you strip down to your deerskin undershirts. The ice cap sits over seven thousand feet above sea level, the height of a small mountain. At this elevation, you can walk comfortably at a pace of two miles an hour and keep going for up to twenty-five miles in a day. But a run of a few yards to overtake the sledge, after stopping to pick up a mitten or tie a kamik string, will take your breath away completely. Often your nose bleeds, freezing into your moustache on exposure with the air.

From the day you left camp, the expedition team has been short of food. Last year, an advance party buried fourteen hundred pounds of pemmican in the snow along your route. But the flags marking the site have since been blown away and, despite a whole day of searching and digging, the cache remains impossible to find. The loss of such a large quantity of supplies is a harsh blow. Neither walrus meat for the dogs, nor frozen venison for you men, can fill its place. The closest you come to cooked food is warming the frozen venison in your tea. It is hard to care for this as a meal. Already you can see the effects on the dogs, who are running slower and breathing faster than normal. Man and beast alike daily growing weaker. You are racing against starvation.

Four hundred miles. To save rations, you go among the dogs with your hatchet, looking for the weakest of the pack. This is the occasion for a certain bleak humour.

Lieutenant Peary: 'It must now be a case of dog eat dog, until we find game.'

Lee: 'The dogs are going to the dogs.'

You bring the hatchet down on the back of the dog's neck. The rest of the pack barely wait for the animal to fall to the ground. They tear it open, rip out its insides, lap sticky blood from the snow.

Five hundred miles. Days of travelling for twenty-four hours at a time without a break.

Fixing the broken runner of a sledge, on your knees in frigid winds. Walking in a trance. The ice cap hidden in the clouds and fog, everything invisible in the grey shroud. There are few experiences more physically draining than the monotony of dragging hour after hour at a sledge. Twenty-two miles of this punishing work. Face chilled and covered with thick scabs. Your eyes are bloodshot from sun-glare and you walk lame from a frozen toe. It gives you a deal of pain, but you walk just the same and let it hurt.

The last of the walrus meat was finished today, a chunk about the size of a man's head. You sliced some of it up for you, Lee and the lieutenant and fed the rest to the dogs. The meat had disintegrated into a mix of flesh, fur, grit and rancid blubber. You were grateful for it anyway.

There are now just eleven dogs out of an original thirty-six, all of them completely exhausted, and three so nearly dead that they are fit only as food for the others. You are forced to get into the ropes and drag the sledges yourselves.

Six hundred miles. Thirty-six days after departing you reach Navy Cliff. Three exhausted men and nine starved dogs wandering through a gelid wilderness. Thousands of feet below, the peaks and valleys of a new land lie wreathed in mist. The glistening snow and the cold white sun.

At this latitude, you are alone on the planet. If the Arctic is a frontier, then you stand at its edge with only the frozen sea between you and the Pole. Yet there's no sense of triumph. Only a bone-deep exhaustion and an awareness that unless you find food soon this will be the very end of your journey. You make camp on the crest of the ice cap, all three of you completely spent. It is several hours before you open your eyes again. Heavy grey clouds obscure the sun. You agree on a plan.

You and the lieutenant are to go down to the land and search for muskox while Lee remains in camp with the dogs and tries to recover from a frozen toe. You make a tinful of tea and eat some biscuit. By the time you've finished breakfast and are ready to start, the clouds have descended upon the ice cap and the summit of the land, hiding it from view.

All day in a drizzling snowstorm you scramble down cliffs and climb over jagged rocks, in search of a way to reach the mainland. Your legs and backs ache savagely. The rocks tear your kamiks and stab your feet.

You see fresh hare tracks and the pawprints of a wolf. There are muskox droppings, but only very old ones, as if it has been an age since they came through here.

You make camp in the open air, stretching out to sleep regardless of the cold wet ground beneath you and letting snowflakes settle on you as you doze. When you wake, it is still snowing and you can only climb empty-handed back up the ice cap, breaking the news of failure to Lee. It is a very silent party gathered round the cooker in the evening, and it is a long time before you manage to sleep.

Another whole day of searching and scrambling, both of you light-headed for lack of food, before you finally come across a muskox herd. It takes your last remaining strength to lift your rifle and shoot a calf at the edge of the group. You butcher the animal there on the rocky ground, slashing off chunks of its meat and stuffing them into your mouth raw and warm. Feeding like a dog. Your face and hands are covered with blood but you can't stop.

June 1895

Ahnalka, the elder, finds you passed out on the floor of Anniversary Lodge after making the 600-mile return journey. He tells you he will bring you to his own home to recover. Lee and the lieutenant are similarly done in. He leaves them behind in the cabin, knowing that other Inughuit will look after them, and lays you down in his sledge. Days go by as you are borne across the snow, too weak to move. Days marked only by the changing colour of the sky, which is sometimes white, sometimes pink, sometimes orange. Close your eyes and you're back on the *Katie Hines*, nodding asleep in the warmth of Captain Childs's cabin. Finally you reach the Inughuit settlement where Ahnalka has his summer tent. Unknown figures crowd around and carry you into the tent and lay you down on a pile of furs. When you wake up, Ahnalka is squatting beside you, calling up to the spirits and beating on his drum. His wife crouches next to you and puts a bowl of dark, thick seal blood to your lips. The taste is strong and tart, but it has a narcotic richness that sends your eyes slipping back in their sockets and your body sinking into the fur. At night, Ahnalka and his wife lie naked under the furs with you, one on either side, warming you with the heat of their bodies.

On the Iron Mountain

At Anniversary Lodge, Robert Peary reckoned with a second year of failure. Two years away from home and nothing to show for it. This expedition, with Lee and Henson, had merely reached the same point as his 1892 journey, without making any significant new discoveries along the way. 'Has the game been worth the candle?' he wrote to his wife Josephine. 'As I look out on the scenery that a few years ago would have filled me with enthusiasm, as I think of my high hopes then, and contrast them with my present lack of energy, of interest, of elation; as I think of the last years and what I have been through; as I think of all the little petty details with which I have been and am still occupying myself, it all seems so small, so little worth the while that I could cry out in anguish of spirit.'

It was at this low point that Peary thought of the Iron Mountain. The Inughuit's secret source of metal, from which they made the harpoon heads and knife blades that were indispensable to their survival. The 'heaven stone' had been sacred to the Inughuit for generations, considered by them a gift from the skies, its location too valuable to be revealed to outsiders. If he could find the Iron Mountain, prove correct Ross's theory that it was really a meteorite, and bring it back home with him, then he might yet manufacture a triumphant return.

Peary bribed Tellikotinah, a young hunter, with the promise of a rifle if he would lead him to the secret site. Tellikotinah agreed and took him to an isolated peninsula two days away by sled. Iron Mountain proved to be three enormous fragments of bluish-brown ferrous rock, a meteorite which must have broken up into pieces on impact hundreds of years ago. The two smaller parts, known as the Woman and the Dog, lay close together. The largest, eleven feet across and called Ittaq, the Tent, was six miles away, lodged in permafrost.

'The brown mass,' Peary wrote in his journal, 'rudely awakened from its winter's sleep, found for the first time in its cycles of existence the eyes of a white man gazing upon it.' And what use was the rock to the Esquimos now there were white men to trade with? On its surface he scratched a rough 'P'.

As it turned out, the Tent was reluctant to surrender to him. Peary organized its extraction when the expedition relief ship, the *Hope*, arrived. In the waning days of summer it took most of the ship's crew, working day and night, to dig the rock free of the permafrost and drag it the eighty yards to the ship. If, in the darkness, a sledge or shovel struck its side, wrote Peary, 'a spouting jet of scintillating sparks lit the gloom, and a deep note, the half-pained, half-enraged bellow of a lost soul answered the blow'. Sailors never have to look far for an ill omen and they took the arduous progress and the high winds and fog that surrounded them as sure signs that the 'brown monster' was cursed. They watched the ice floes accumulating between the ship and open water and muttered that if the weight of the Tent did not sink the *Hope*, then the ice would surely lock them in for the winter. When the meteor was eventually fixed on deck, Peary draped an American flag over it and posed for a photograph, one hand on its flank, like he was a hunter, and the rock the still-warm body of his prey.

As well as the Tent, the *Hope* departed Greenland with some other unanticipated guests. Shortly before Peary left for the Arctic, he was contacted by Franz Boas, an anthropologist at the American Museum of Natural History. Boas had helped organize the Esquimo hut at the Chicago World's Fair and he wrote to the lieutenant asking that he bring back with him a 'middle-aged Esquimo' since 'this would enable us to obtain leisurely certain information which will be of greatest scientific importance'. The lieutenant obliged. Two years later, he returned with not one but six Inughuit.

New York, October 1895

Your Inughuit passengers consist of Nuktaq, an accomplished hunter in his forties; his wife Atangana, a shaman, and their twelve-year-old daughter Aviaq; a younger man in his thirties called Uisaakavsak who is also a skilled huntsman; and Minik, a seven-year-old boy, with his widowed father Qisuk, both of them still mourning the death last year of Minik's mother. The four adults have worked with your party for the past two years as guides and hunters and, in Atangana's case, a seamstress. The lieutenant has told them their visit south will last one year, after which they'll return home rich with guns and goods. Even though it means their community will be without two of its best hunters as winter approaches, they said yes. How could they refuse – now the Iron Mountain is gone, they are entirely dependent on him for trade.

You stay close with them through the voyage, answering Minik's many questions about New York and parrying Uisaakavsak's queries on how to go about acquiring a wife in the city. You are beside them as the *Hope* docks at Brooklyn Navy Yard where a crowd of ten thousand is waiting to see the Tent and the exotic visitors.

'Their first object was to get a view of the wonderful piece of iron, which is supposed to have dropped from the heavens,' says the *Boston Post*. 'After that they gave all their attention to the six red-faced natives of the Arctic who made a laughable sight as they ran up and down the deck in their native costumes.' The *New York Times* reports: 'The children attracted considerable attention, and were plentifully supplied with candy and peanuts, which they seemed to enjoy immensely. One of the officers of the vessel said, "The children are sick from the quantity of sweet things given them. We feed them with raw meat, and the candy has had a bad effect on them."'

You are their guide and their only family in this city, as they gawk at skyscrapers and trolley buses and flinch at the blare of car horns. Everyone wants to shake their hand or pat them on the back. A passer-by pins an American flag on Uisaakavsak's cap. Qisuk, a keenly inquisitive presence among the group, is gifted an overcoat several sizes too big but which he wears with a swagger, matched with a noisome pair of argyle golf stockings. Minik and Aviaq, the children, are petted and fussed over wherever they go. Minik now wears a knickerbocker suit, blue flannel waistcoat, and a baker's-boy cap cocked at an angle. You take him for a ride through Central Park and he marvels at the 'big dogs', by which he means horses. The sight of a bicycle makes him howl with glee. He has already picked up some English and can say, 'My name is Minik and I am glad to be in America.'

Philadelphia, November 1895

Eva is at home with her parents when you arrive. For a while, it's as if nothing's changed, and you are once again the tentative suitor sitting on the edge of a brocade armchair, fumbling for words. Two years have passed. Two years since you were married and were last together. She sits opposite you, smiling vaguely at the gift of a carved walrus tusk in her hands. She seems even more arch and remote than you remember. You feel like a child bearing toys in her presence. You think about her most recent letters, which you read on the *Hope*. Their dry formality: 'I should be glad to see you.' And even this was effusive in comparison to your present encounter – a meeting, an interview, hardly a homecoming. 'For a long time I wondered if you'd come back at all,' she says. 'And now here you are.' Another faint smile. She puts down the tusk and knits her fingers. You know she's waiting for you to explain why you stayed away for a second year. Why you preferred a cold wilderness to her. And for you to answer the question, who are you, this stranger in the room, with so little to say after such a long time?

With Ikwah and Ootah, you learned to sit by a hole in the ice for hours on end, waiting, harpoon in hand, for a seal to poke its head out of the water. The silence in that waiting is an active one. You're listening to the creaking of the ice, the water flowing beneath it, the wind as it moans or sighs or sometimes sings. The serenity of feeling absolutely connected to the life and landscape around you is the very opposite of how it feels to sit now amid these polished walnut side tables and crochet-knit quilts. An oil painting of a prairie scene fixed above the mantel. The rich, floral scent of Eva's mother's perfume that still lingers in the room.

You know that the idea of the frontier is as seductive for you as it is for Lieutenant Peary. And you know too its meaning could never be the same for a white man as it is for you. In the unwritten terrain of the Arctic, you are always discovering yourself anew rather than contorting yourself to the expectations of others. A black man in America can be arrested for walking down the street or standing still. Opening his mouth or keeping it shut.

Eva's expectations aren't unreasonable. But they are absolute. Her silence says, since you're back, I expect you to stay for good. If you can't, then leave now and don't return.

New York, December 1895

The change in the Inughuit group in the weeks since they first arrived is troubling. The museum was expecting one Inughuit, not six men, women and children; no one is sure how to take care of them. Lieutenant Peary passed them to Boas, the anthropologist, who in turn has given them over to William Wallace, a building superintendent at the museum. You find the group together in the windowless basement where Wallace has made up beds for them. In the midst of an unseasonal heatwave, the place is stifling and ripe with the smell of damp. Qisuk, normally the liveliest of the six, barely looks up when you enter. No one speaks. Without immunity to American infections, all of them are miserable with colds and homesick for the open horizons of the north. The silence is broken only by the occasional shouts of museum visitors crouching at the grating above the basement and calling down to get their attention: 'Kushu! Minny! Ah-Wee-Ah!'

The papers are still following the story with some interest. 'One of the most amusing forms of entertainment consists in the manner in which the Esquimos attempt to conjure away illness,' says the *New York Times*. 'This in their opinion can only be accomplished by rubbing the sides of the body and singing a weird sort of lullaby that with all its peculiarities is not absolutely discordant. It is sung in a plaintive strain, the inflections of the voice being accompanied by a rhythmical shaking of the head. The grimaces which are thrown in to make the conjuration complete are indescribable.' You recognize 'the entertainment' for what it is. Atangana, the shaman, is trying to call down healing spirits to cure their illness. But her invocations go unanswered by the gods.

May 1896

One by one they die. Atangana succumbed to tuberculosis in March, as did Nuktaq, her husband, this month. Ten days later, their daughter Aviaq followed. Uisaakavsak, refusing to stay in America any longer, has managed to get a place on a ship bound for Greenland.

Qisuk's health has been fragile for months. He was sent to Bellevue Hospital over the winter and Minik has stayed with him, sleeping in the next-door bed and pining over his father. By the time you arrive to see him, he has already died. You find Minik sitting alone and try to embrace him but he will not move. His face is as blank and still as the meteorite that Peary ripped from the frozen earth.

You attend Qisuk's funeral in the museum grounds with Minik, standing beside the boy as he weeps. You have hardly seen him since that day. Minik has been adopted by William Wallace and stays with him in Cobleskill. Lieutenant Peary did not come to the funeral or send any word of condolence.

August 1896

For a black man who has spent so many of his recent years far from civilization, finding a respectable job is no easy task. Eva's family won't countenance the idea of their daughter's husband working at a steel factory or a meat-packing plant. The best you can do is become a Pullman porter, even if it takes you away from Eva again. In the past, the company only hired former enslaved men from the South. George Pullman, the founder, believed they knew best how to behave around white people: keep smiling when a white man tells you to kneel down and shine his shoes, or unpack his cases in the compartment while he sits watching you from the toilet with the door open, taking a shit. You ride through Washington and New England, Chicago and Newark, and also down to Florida. The company expects you to stay on duty for forty-eight or even sixty hours at a time, snatching sleep at night on a hard wooden stool at the end of the coach, always alert for the passenger who wants a midnight whiskey or more firewood for their stove. Porters are known to have fainted on the job or tumbled out of a moving coach through lack of sleep.

Nonetheless, travelling through the country in the wood-panelled interior of a Pullman car, rich carpets underfoot and a chandelier shimmering overhead, you are deliciously insulated from the world outside. As America whispers past, framed by velvet curtains, its farms and towns and great cities look only benign.

Yet every porter from the north dreads the prospect of going south. Charles, who's worked for Pullman for twenty years, says he still gets a deep, roiling kind of feeling each time he comes out the tunnel that runs under the Potomac River from Washington DC to Virginia. The change is tangible. It's in the thicker air and the scent of orange blossom. And the attitude of the passengers. In Chicago or DC they might call out, 'George', which is the name all Pullman porters are known by. Go south and it is 'boy' or 'nigger', and you must come running.

The train pulls into Fort Myers, Florida. You're descending the steps backwards, arms full with suitcases, when something hard hits you between the shoulder blades. An orange rolls to the floor. At the far end of the platform, three young white men in dungarees are loading crates of the fruit into a goods car. Another orange strikes you on the side of the head, splitting open and smearing your face with pulp. You hurry along the platform, head bowed, still clutching the cases. Fruit hails down around you, smacking you on the head and shoulders. 'Get back on that train where you belong, nigger,' the men shout. 'Don't look back, nigger. Just get out of town.'

The more time you spend on the Pullman lines, the more you come to understand that the trains are describing, point to point, a map of violence across America. In Birmingham, Alabama, sailors stab a porter in the face with a glass bottle after he refuses to dance for them. Early one morning a porter named J. H. Wilkins is found to be missing from a train coming into the town of Locust Grove, Georgia. His body is discovered a couple of hours back along the track in a grove of trees separated from the train line by a ploughed field. Wilkins's skull is fractured in two places, indicating he may have been hit over the head and thrown from the train. He has been tied by the neck to a sapling tree by the white coat of his porter's uniform. The police investigation that follows is lacklustre and in the absence of information the porters offer their own speculations. The train's conductor was known to feel that Wilkins had made himself 'more familiar than he should be' after he was seen picking up a white woman's handbag and returning it to her in her compartment. It's likely that Wilkins was forced out of the window by the white train crew and then lynched during the night. No one is arrested for his murder. A coroner's report rules he died of 'causes unknown'.

North as well as south, the violence is inescapable. You read in the *Philadelphia Mercury* about 'a prominent physician of this city' who wears shoes made from the skin of Negroes. The doctor insists that 'the tanned hide of an African makes the most enduring and the most pliable leather known to man. He obtains the skins from the bodies of Negroes which have been dissected in one of the big medical colleges. The best leather is obtained from the thighs.' The story is hardly isolated. A 'young society lady' in Philadelphia is similarly known for her beautiful dark slippers of 'remarkable lustrousness' which have been stitched together from 'a Negro cadaver'. The rosettes on the slippers are 'deftly fashioned from the Negro's kinky hair'. The *St Louis Post-Dispatch* carries a report on a physician's wife who is having 'a dead Negro's skin tanned for a Christmas gift for her husband. A part of the Negro's hide is to be made into a razor strop.'

You are waiting at a window as the train draws into Fort Myers one afternoon. A white man stands on the platform, holding a stick. As he sees you he raises the stick, which now reveals itself as a rifle. You dive for the ground as the weapon goes off, shattering the window and showering you with glass. It is not then, as you're trembling on the floor, but later, in the renewed calm as you ride through the Florida night, that you realize you cannot go on. Just to live in this country is to feel like you're dying. Sitting on the wooden stool at the end of the coach, you write a letter to Lieutenant Peary, asking to join his next expedition.

After you tell Eva you're returning north, what's left of her affection evaporates. You're not the man she imagined, she says. You wallow in your fantasies, chasing dreams instead of working your way up to a place among the better class of black people. Rather than talk to each other, you both vent your anger via Lieutenant Peary.

Dear Sir
    I hear you are going to Greenland again. Will you please inform me when you expect to go and how long you are going to stay and oblige yours truly,
    Mrs Eva Henson.
    PS As Matt says he is going with you again.

The upcoming expedition is the lieutenant's first explicit attempt to reach the North Pole. This time there will be no Ivy League dilettantes, only you and Dedrick, the doctor accompanying the lieutenant. You write to him to say you're happy to stay away 'for five or ten years . . . Anything to get away from this town.' Even before the expedition departs, Eva has petitioned for divorce.

4

Greenland, December 1900

The Earth speaks. The Inughuit say that every feature of the land has a voice and when you learn to listen to it you can never be lost or alone. As you walk across the ice you make a map in your mind, noting each rock formation you pass and the pattern of the striations carved by the wind into the hard crust of the snow. The map feels so rich in detail it's hard to understand how you used to see the terrain as empty and featureless. By comparison it's America that now seems flat and remote. Two years since you came back to the north. Two years that have snaked and meandered like a wayward river. There's no way to account for time as you'd do at home. Not when a single night lasts for five months. Or when you can look up from contemplating the melting of an icicle in the spring warmth to find a half day has passed. Amid the eerie groan of shifting ice and the ripple of the aurora borealis across the night sky, you come to share the Inughuit perception that the barrier between the physical world and the spirit realm is porous and indeterminate, neither domain more real than the other. Out on the ice you can glimpse whole mountain ranges in the distance and pass the sight off as an atmospheric hallucination, although who's to say it's not a glimpse into a world beyond.

Sometimes a spectral presence is closer to hand. A giant bear that leaves no pawprints as it pads through the mist. The sound of a harp being played backwards emanating from a cloudless sky. A demon in the form of a man standing at the window of the cabin, his countenance grave. It seems to you there are two ways to handle the unknowable Arctic. You either fight or surrender. This is what separates you and the lieutenant. He seeks to dominate the land whereas you want to be absorbed by it. So far it has not gone well for him.

You, Dedrick and Lieutenant Peary arrived in '98 on the *Windward*, aiming to base yourselves at Fort Conger, an abandoned US military outpost on Ellesmere Island in the Arctic Archipelago, no more than five hundred miles from the Pole. As usual, the lieutenant was confident of success. From Fort Conger, he said, you would 'shoot forward to the Pole like a ball from a cannon'. Unfortunately, thick ice floes forced the *Windward* to make land 250 miles further south. It was December but the lieutenant couldn't bear to wait till the spring to begin the campaign. He set out at once for Fort Conger.

For eighteen days you groped through winter darkness over a riot of broken and heaved-up ice. The temperature was lower than you'd ever known it, dropping by night to minus sixty-nine Fahrenheit. It was so cold that snow fell inside the tent. You held Primus stoves under your furs to melt the ice that had formed on your bodies. When you finally reached Fort Conger, the lieutenant complained of a 'wooden' feeling in his feet. You sat him down, slid the blade of your knife under the top of his kamiks and cut away his boots. Both legs were a bloodless white up to the knee. As you peeled back his rabbit-skin undershoes, three of the toes on each foot came away, snapping free at the joint. For a month, the lieutenant lay confined to bed, the bandages on his mutilated feet stained yellow with pus. When it was finally safe to move him, you and Dedrick tied him to a sledge and returned south to the *Windward*, which was iced into the winter bay. Lieutenant Peary was laid out on a table while Dedrick began a clean amputation of his toes. There wasn't enough ether available for the operation and you had to hold him down when he came to, groaning and kicking, while the doctor was still at work with the scalpel. The lieutenant was left with just the little toe on each foot. When he had recovered enough to walk again, he did so with a splayed, shuffling gait, as if wearing a pair of flippers.

He was able to rally himself by spring to direct you in an attempt on the Pole. But you faced fierce winds and ice fields so rough and broken up that they were impassable. After advancing no further than twenty-two miles in a week you were forced to turn back. A second effort the following year fared little better. Since then

Lieutenant Peary has hardly been himself. Where previously he strove to give the impression of an iron man, he is now wrecked in physique, wrecked in hope. There is a glaze to his eyes, and the skin hangs on his body in baggy folds, its colour a gruesome grey-green tinged with yellow. His health is not helped by his refusal to join you and the Inughuit in eating raw seal and muskox. The diet helps stave off anaemia and scurvy but he says he would 'rather die' than eat uncooked meat.

The small group of Inughuit at Fort Conger occupy a hut next to your cabin, where they live together, working for the expedition in return for metal tools and guns. But the land this far north is unfamiliar to them and the seasonal hunting less predictable. After two years, even good friends like Ootah are restive. Cut off from their families and obliged to undertake arduous, abortive marches through blizzards and rubble fields of ice, they have become increasingly despondent. The lieutenant sent Soundah's husband Pooblah out on a hunting trip recently, and she was unable to shake off the fear that he'd die on the ice. There was no consoling her. She was listless and downcast, sleeping through the day. And when she did get up, she sat shivering, saying she couldn't eat and complaining of a permanent headache.

The mood of the expedition is not improved by the fact that Fort Conger was the base of the disastrous expedition led by Lieutenant Adolphus Greely in 1881. Greely and his twenty-five men were marooned at the base for three years after successive relief ships failed to make it through the ice in 1882 and 1883. By the time a rescue vessel eventually arrived the following year, eighteen of the crew had died of starvation and some of the survivors had resorted to cannibalism, slicing flesh from the frozen corpses of their crewmates laid outside in the cold.

When you first arrived at the cabin, it felt as if the former occupants had just left. The place was littered with empty boxes, cast-off clothing, and tins of tea and coffee, their contents spilled across the floor. There were still dishes remaining on the table, along with dirty cutlery, overturned cups, and biscuits scattered in every direction. For months afterwards, you found it impossible to enter the cabin without thinking of how those men had become another species of ghost haunting the Arctic, and wondering what your own fate would be by comparison.

Earlier this year, a summer relief ship, the *Erik*, arrived from New York. It had been sent north by Lieutenant Peary's sponsors, who feared that, having been out of contact for the past two years, the expedition crew might have fallen prey to the lethal wilderness. Perhaps it was in their minds to reach you before you succumbed to the same desperate means as Greely's men. In any circumstances, it was cheering to see faces from home, although sadly for the lieutenant the *Erik* came with a letter from Mrs Peary saying his beloved mother had passed away last November. She had died believing her absent son must have perished in the north. Another letter was even more painful. Mrs Peary had given birth to a daughter, Francine, shortly after the *Windward* sailed. Seven months later the girl had died suddenly of cholera. The *Erik*'s captain gave a memorial dinner. The lieutenant sat silent and withdrawn through the meal, barely lifting his eyes.

At times in the past, you have loathed the lieutenant, even feared him. But when you spend months and years in close company with a man, nothing stays hidden, no sorrow or shame. Seeing him suffer through what he called the 'interminable black days', you have come to understand him in a different way. No longer the would-be master. Only a man carrying his allotted pain. In the simple recognition of your shared humanity, it is hard not to love him just a little bit.

Ellesmere Island, September 1901

To surrender to the land is to wander its surface, only acting as a sympathetic witness to its aliveness. To hear in the shrieking wind and the groaning of the pack ice a praise song for the ordinary day. When spring arrives, lilac bluebells unfurl themselves in the benign air. You look forward to their shy beauty and the way their presence turns sparse scrub ground into putative meadow. If he's lucky, a man will have a woman to walk beside him on the Earth. A woman who's as much of a marvel to him as the unbroken sky.

There are exactly two occasions in your life when time has stopped still. The first was on the *Katie Hines*. Three days into your first voyage, when the land had slipped away for good and there was nothing tying you to the thought of Pa or Nellie or Charles County, except for the ship's wake dissolving in the water. The sight of the horizon ahead awed you and, to this day, the realization of promise and possibility that came with it can make you stop in wonder.

The other occasion is the first time you are alone with Elatu. The morning is cold and your vision is blinkered within a hood. You feel her presence beside you. Elatu is a cousin of Ootah and she has the self-assurance of one born to this precarious place. She treks in silence, gaze hidden behind long hair. Her breath mists the air. Normally there are people around you, calling and chattering, and you share no more than the occasional moment. Out here today there is nothing to interrupt your solitude.

Later, lying side by side in your tent in the darkness, you might be castaways on a tropical island, adrift from the world, alone but together. No one has ever held your gaze like she does. No one has ever seen you as plainly or fully or openly as her. When she touches your face, the warmth of her fingers runs beneath the skin and

through your body. Unlike the lieutenant, you have no urge to turn a
woman into your property. Better, surely, to find a place beside her.
And beside her your thoughts turn to Qisuk and the other Inughuit
who came south with the Iron Mountain. Your failure to warn them
beforehand about the abstract cruelty of America or to protect them
once they arrived in New York weighs heavy on you. And where is
Minik, the boy? Is he in trouble? Is he even alive? The idea that he
might be suffering is agony.

Elatu's voice is soft in the darkness. She tells you about her
father's death on a hunt while she was a child and how her mother,
overwhelmed by grief, died a few years later. The only consolation
for losing them was that she was brought up amid the love of her
aunts and uncles and cousins. To die far away and alone like Qisuk
and the others is a tragedy for an Inughuit, she says. But maybe
Minik is all right. Maybe he is even now returning home to be with
his people. And maybe, she whispers, you and I can make our own
baby and raise it here, in warmth and love. There is not much more
talking between you that night. Only a decision that you make
together that feels easy and inevitable and true. There is no wedding
ritual among the Inughuit. All that's required is for two people to
choose to be together. So by the time you're back at camp you've
already become husband and wife.

January 1902

Lieutenant Peary is considering one last run at the Pole and there is
work to do in camp. But it has been an unseasonably warm few days
and you have travelled further along the coast with Elatu, the two of
you treasuring the glimmer of the red sun passing across the horizon. The lieutenant will be angry that you are not in his constant

attendance but it is worth it to escape with her even for a short while. During much of the trip, though, Elatu has been sick with an inflamed stomach. She lies in the igloo groaning while you sit beside her with tea. When she fell asleep last night, you saw a meteor score a line across the sky and wondered again at what lies beyond this world and whether the living as well as the dead can ever reach those other realms. In the morning Elatu is fully recovered. She is light-hearted all the way back to Fort Conger.

1 February

Elatu is sick and vomiting. She has eaten nothing that she can keep down these past four days. Dedrick comes to examine her but he leaves saying he is not much concerned and that whatever is afflicting her will pass. Atunginah, the oldest woman at the camp, is an angekok, a healer, and takes charge of Elatu's care. She clears everyone out of the Inughuit communal hut and then sits over Elatu with two younger women, chanting and singing, their voices rising to fill the air. Dedrick, hearing the sound, comes rushing back and shoos them away, saying he won't have the camp ruled by superstition.

2 February

Elatu is back on her feet and eating, free of pain. Maybe Atunginah worked her cure after all.

2 March

Ootah has returned from a journey north to visit another Inughuit community. He was gone for ten days with a small group that included Elatu. Now he is back alone, carrying Elatu on his sledge. She is groaning with discomfort. Dedrick tells Ootah to lay her down in his hut where she can stay under proper medical care.

8 March

Dedrick reports that Elatu was delirious all night, talking and struggling and soiling her bedding. She is pale and thin. His diagnosis now is liver trouble. He has her on doses of potassium bicarbonate, iodide potassium, mercury chloride and opium. He says she'll be up in no time.

28 March

You keep her with you in your quarters. She is weak but eating well and seems to no longer be in pain. Mostly you sit beside her, taking no notice of whether it's morning or night. After a few days she's strong enough to go outside. The lilac bluebells are flourishing. You pick a few and hand the posy to her and she smiles wanly. You sit outside the cabin in the evening's mild warmth, saying little, letting the hours stretch by. You think of how there will be much more of this in the years to come. You imagine this same quiet intimacy when you are both old, unable to picture where'll you live or if you'll have children, or anything much but the fact of your love, of which you have enough to last a lifetime. Then Elatu says she's feeling tired again and goes inside to lie down.

Robert Peary

Arrived back from a supply mission to find Matt sitting forlorn and cold. He is in bad shape mentally and physically. His woman Elatu had died on the 13th, after two weeks' illness. Gave him a good drink then made coffee and cooked some fish for him. I know what it is to lose some of those who are most dear, and I feel for him. Gave him my deerskin shirt to put on and got him to sleep.

20 April

It seems to you that you can still hear Elatu's breathing. You know it's only the sighing of the wind but the sound torments you all the same, as do the shadows in the hut that appear to promise the shape of another body. Three nights ago, Lieutenant Peary and Ootah came with Ionah, another cousin of hers, to conduct the funeral. They wrapped her body in a muskox skin and carried her to the lieutenant's hut. To your shame you stayed in bed, unable to get up, while the lieutenant took your place in all the rites. For three nights, they watched over the body without lying down or leaving the hut except to answer nature's demands. Following Inughuit custom, her body was dragged away from the camp, laid on the ground in the burial place with the head pointing south, and covered with more animal skins which were weighted down with stones. Your body has been weighted down with stones too. Lieutenant Peary is not a religious man and, having no Bible verses to hand, he recited as much of Mark Antony's funeral oration from *Julius Caesar* as he could remember.

You feel Elatu's loss like a physical presence, not an absence. It is a shrieking wind. A winter without sun. Lieutenant Peary has been your only companion since her death. After the funeral rites were done, he came to sit beside you in silence and in the dark, neither of you reaching to light a lamp in the cabin. When he did speak it was to talk about his daughter, lost at seven months, who he had never known beyond a photograph that came with Mrs Peary's letter. But who he grieved for with all his heart. At some point you fell asleep and, when you woke, he was still there beside you. At that moment, he was as close to being your brother as any man you've ever known.

5

New York, July 1908

It's seventeen years since you first visited the Arctic and, succeed or fail, this will be your last expedition. After Elatu died the idea of returning north again felt too painful to contemplate. Yet here you are, six years later, on your way back again aged forty-two, beat up and scarred, outside and in. At the International Geographic Congress in New York last year, Lieutenant, now Commander, Peary announced a final bid for the Pole. No one in the audience of distinguished explorers exactly laughed out loud but the sniggers were audible. With two decades of failure to his name, some consider him an embarrassment, others a crackpot. Bookmakers offer extravagant odds against the success of the coming expedition. Would-be adventurers propose their own rival schemes in the press. Flying machines, submarine boats, a giant cannon, motor cars 'guaranteed to run over any kind of ice'.

The expedition ship is a battering ram of a vessel with a thirty-inch hull and two 1,000-horsepower engines designed to punch through ice floes up to a hundred feet thick and penetrate as far north as possible before disembarking the team. It is named the *Roosevelt*, after the president, who Commander Peary idolizes. On the day of your departure, Roosevelt comes to see you off and the two men stand like twins in white summer suits, straw hats and walrus moustaches. Like Commander Peary, Roosevelt was a weakling child who has reinvented himself as a big-game hunter and a dominator of men. Standing at the bow of the ship he addresses the crew.

'Over-sentimentality, over-softness, in fact washiness and mushiness are the great dangers of this age and of this people.' The Pole is the last true frontier. It is the duty of this expedition to claim it for America and for the good of civilization itself. All the way up the East River, ships dip their flags and factories blow their whistles for you. Even the convicts on Blackwell's Island line up outside to cheer you on.

Etah, August 1908

The *Roosevelt* stops in Greenland to collect the Inughuit who've agreed to go north with the expedition. Forty-nine men, women and children, along with two hundred and forty-six dogs, scrapping and barking, cram on to the ship. The dogs foul every surface on the deck, the stench of their excrement combining with the odour from the fifty dead walrus hanging in the rigging and the thirty thousand pounds of whale meat you've taken on board to feed them. To your final passing, you will never forget the noise and commotion and choking smell that mark the final stage of this voyage.

1 March 1909

The day of departure for the Pole begins without fanfare. One after another, teams of two men, an American and an Inughuit, each man with his own sledge, head out across the ice. Bartlett, the *Roosevelt*'s captain, leads, followed by you and Ootah; then MacMillan, a college professor; Marvin, the commander's assistant; and Borup, a Yale letterman in wrestling. Commander Peary brings up the rear. The advance team breaks trail and builds igloos for the followers. Every five marches the leaders will drop back and be leapfrogged by the second-place men. In front of you, Bartlett's team is swallowed up almost immediately by whirling snow. You follow his trail into the blizzard.

2 March

The going is often vertical. A region of pressure ridges frustrates your progress. Even with Bartlett ahead clearing the way, you need to chop a further path through the ice with a pickaxe. The shattered blocks of compressed ice can be as high as a house and wide as a quarter mile. Clambering over them means crouching behind the 500-pound loaded sledges, shoving and pushing them to the top and lowering them down the other side, hoping the strain doesn't tear your arms free of their sockets. Underfoot, the broken and raftered ice is so jagged it cuts through your sealskin kamiks and hareskin stockings, to pierce the soles of your feet.

10 March

You march as though advancing into a dream. A dull, lead-coloured haze spreads across the sky, obscuring the sun. Between the diffuse, shadowless light and the white surface of the ice and snow it is impossible to see ahead for any distance. Sky and ice seem equally wan and unreal. When you look back, you can make out neither men nor dogs, only a low-lying bank of fog glistening like silver, which is the steam of their breath suspended in the air.

You come across the tracks of two foxes, some two hundred miles north of their natural habitat. The same of course could be said for this caravan of sledges, trekking across terrain where no man has been before.

You are two thirds of the way through the day's march when you see an ominous band of dark cloud ahead extending across your course. Clouds are always a sign of open water, forming as the water vapour condenses in the colder air above. Sometimes they are as thick and black as the smoke of a prairie fire. They are a reminder that much of the Arctic is not a land mass at all but a frozen sea, constantly fracturing and re-forming, with the Pole lying somewhere at its shifting centre.

16 March

For the past six days, the whole team has been stuck by the side of a lake of inky black water, a quarter of a mile wide, throwing off dense clouds of vapour which gather in a canopy overhead. Each day the river widens. The men have named it the Styx.

Tensions are growing in the camp. The commander paces up and down, fretting at the days lost. The Inughuit men are increasingly anxious. They cluster in groups of twos and threes, talking in low voices. Ootah says they fear the channel is a sign by Kokoyah to go no further. Yesterday, Pooadloonah and Panikpah, the two oldest and most experienced men, went to the commander, complaining they were sick. He sacked them on the spot and told them by all means to go back to the land just as fast as they could while the rest of us carried on. You were sorry to see them leave, although the commander insisted they were too cowardly to continue as part of the team.

By night, the ice sheets beneath your camp stir with the movement of the tide. The continual groaning and creaking, as the pieces of ice crunch together, keeps you awake, hour after hour. In the morning you find a passage across the river on some fragments that have frozen together to form a tentative bridge. The young ice is so thin you have to shuffle across one by one at intervals of fifty feet. Once you start across the bridge you can't stop or lift your feet. You inch forward, trying to glide smoothly, keeping an even pressure, achingly conscious of the undulations spreading out over the film of ice with each movement.

24 March

Eighty-five and a half degrees parallel. Now it's a race to the Pole. Every few days the commander sends another member of the expedition back to base so that the team can travel lighter and faster as you close in on your goal. This has been his dream for the last two decades but, truthfully, in all that time you've never shared his obsession. To your mind the Pole isn't a specific place waiting to be conquered. It's a landscape, a people, a realm natural and supernatural, a state of possibility. Throughout those two decades you've remained officially the commander's servant, never an explorer in your own right, even while all the would-be adventurers on previous expeditions have come and gone. Yet here you are, days from the Earth's last horizon, continuing to do what an explorer must always do – go further.

28 March

The expedition teams are camped overnight at eighty-seven degrees parallel beside another wide channel of water. You are asleep in your igloo when you're woken by shouting and the dogs howling. Everyone is yelling and running about. The ice has split open through the middle of the camp, marooning Bartlett and his dogs on an island of their own, and turning the rest of the ground into a lattice of fissures. The only light comes from the silvery glow of a half-moon and, as you try to find a way to solid footing amid the melee, the ice suddenly tilts beneath you and you're sent sliding feet first into the freezing water, into blackness and cold, your heavy furs dragging you deeper. Then you feel yourself being grabbed by the nape of the neck and Ootah hauls you to safety and leaves you sprawled on the ice, spluttering for breath and too stunned to register the burning sensation in your face and your hands, as your body comes back to life.

30 March

You travel ten hours at a time, the dogs often on the trot, and the course, by dead reckoning, straight north. Zigzagging through pressure ridges sometimes fifty feet high, so that finding a way through the gaps between them brings with it abrupt clarity about the scale of the planet and your tiny place scrambling across its surface. The sun sits low above the horizon mirrored by a pallid full moon, a disc of silver and a disc of gold.

31 March

Today Commander Peary told Bartlett to return to base. With his departure there's now only you, the commander, Ootah and three other Inughuit left: Egingwah, Seegloo and Ooqueah. You are one hundred and thirty-two miles, or about seven days, from the Pole.

This evening, sitting together drinking tea, the commander was frank about why he'd chosen you at the last. He meant to be complimentary but the conversation has only left you unsettled.

'You've been with me all these years, Matt,' he said. 'And you're the best man here for this kind of work, with the exception of the Esquimos. You're a part of this travelling machine that I've built. If I'd selected another man he'd ultimately be a passenger, while you're more useful to me than any other member of my expedition.' If he'd stopped there, you'd have been proud to complete the journey with him. But the commander continued talking. 'The second reason, I'm afraid to say, Matt, is that you just wouldn't be as competent as the rest of the men in getting yourself back to the land. If I sent you back now, you'd never reach the land. You're faithful, and when you're with me there's no one more effective in covering distance with a sledge. But you don't have the daring and initiative of a white man – of Bartlett, or Marvin, MacMillan, or Borup. I owe it to you not to subject you to dangers and responsibilities which you're temperamentally unfit to face.'

The commander spoke casually, as if the evident truth of his words was beyond dispute. The idea that you'd be angry did not seem to occur to him. And why should it? In all the time you've known him, you have never set yourself against him. In return for your loyalty, you imagined he respected you as his equal in competence. In the Arctic, if not America, you thought of him as the friend of sixteen years, the brother who sat with you after Elatu's death. His assistant, yes. But a man nonetheless.

5 April

Eighty-nine degrees twenty-five. The Pole is no more than a day away. 'Mine at last,' says the commander. 'I can't bring myself to realize it.' Before he turned in last night, Commander Peary gave his instructions. For this final stage of the march, you've broken trail every day while he's remained at the back, carried in a sledge by Egingwah – his mutilated feet make it impossible for him to walk any great distance. Tomorrow, he said, you should stop short before reaching ninety degrees latitude, make camp, and wait for him to catch up and lead the team over the final miles to the Pole. After he was asleep, Egingwah came to talk to you. He said the commander had quietly planned with him and Ooqueah to leave you in the camp tomorrow and claim the Pole by himself. It was mean, said Egingwah, because we were all so near, and you had worked so hard to make the trip a success. Your first impulse was to protest that the commander wouldn't be so cruel. He would not betray you at the last. But you knew that wasn't true.

6 April

You wake up as tired as when you went to sleep, weighed down by the accumulated weariness of days and nights of forced marches, the constant peril and anxiety. It is the early hours of the morning and the rest of the men are still asleep. In the pre-dawn stillness, the only sound is the tramp of your boots and the runners of the sledge, scraping across the granular surface of the ice as you leave camp.

You stop at around the fifteen-mile mark. By your reckoning you're just short of the Pole. The commander's instructions are to wait here for his arrival. You make tea, eat some pemmican, and rest the dogs. And then you stand up and keep walking, heading straight north.

According to some, the Earth is hollow and from the Pole you can find the way down to an interior of oceans, mountains and vast continents peopled by undiscovered races. Others say the Pole is a mirage, floating unfixed in a frozen sea, an abstract point on the map marking nothing more real than an idea. Yet to stand at the notional point that signals the top of the world is a far from insubstantial act. It's true that when you finally stop at the location of the Pole, there is nothing to see but a cracked plain of ice and snow beneath a grey sky. But to claim this land is to make your own myth of place and presence. It is to insist on being seen on your own terms, even if there's no one else present to mark your achievement.

Hold here. Feel the strangeness of standing at this point, real and imaginary, where east and west are one and every direction leads south. If you could stay on this spot across the six months of the Arctic winter night, you would see every star of the northern hemisphere circling the sky at the same distance from the horizon, with Polaris in the zenith.

Later, in the afternoon, the rest of the team arrive at the camp you have made, with the commander carried on Egingwah's sledge. You've busied yourself in the meantime by building an igloo and brewing more tea. And you've taken the cartridges out of the rifle and buried them in the snow because you can't predict the commander's reaction when you tell him you have overrun your mark and believe you are the first man to stand on top of the world.

'I do not suppose that we can swear we are exactly at the Pole,' the commander says stiffly. He sweeps out of the camp with Egingwah without another word. When you rejoin him he is lying on his stomach, taking observations with a sextant and a pan of mercury. His gaze fixed on his findings, he says he is satisfied that this is the correct location, ninety degrees latitude. You wonder, what did he make of the footsteps already in the snow when he arrived?

—

Of course, Commander Peary claims the Pole as his anyway. A small ceremony takes place. The commander raises an American flag with a collection of square holes cut into its fabric that Mrs Peary gave him for his first expedition and which he has carried, wrapped around his body, on every subsequent journey, leaving a square of its silk in a cairn to mark his furthest north position each time. Alongside it, Peary hoists the flags of the Navy League, the Red Cross, his alma mater Bowdoin College, and the Daughters of the American Revolution, the society of American women who can trace their pure white heritage back to the founding of the nation. The six of you stand in a line under the flags and pose for a photograph. Feeling that the time has come, you unglove your hand and step forward to congratulate him on the success of your shared eighteen years of effort, but he turns away without returning your gesture.

From this point on, the commander barely talks to you. Throughout the return journey he rises in the morning and departs without rapping on the ice for you like he used to. On the rare times he does speak, it is in the most matter-of-fact way, simply, 'There is enough wood left, and I would like to have you make a couple of sledges and mend the broken ones.' Not a word about the magnitude of your success or your part in its accomplishment.

You think this over and it grieves you sorely. You reflect on the years you've worked together for the great aim and the different acts of kindness you've done each other. You wonder if he remembers with any gratitude those awful days in 1900 when he lost his toes and became an invalid in the care of you and Dedrick. How you kept the men and dogs in order as you travelled. How you foraged with the dogs, like a dog yourself, hunting for food to keep him alive, chasing hares and any living thing that could be eaten, until you finally got him back to the ship, mutilated but safe.

You have travelled with Commander Peary for almost two decades. You hope to have been a good assistant and friend over those years. You had hoped that the scale of victory at the Pole might be great enough to encompass both of you. How could its attainment ever be his alone, given that you have been standing alongside him the whole time?

When the *Roosevelt* docks at Sandy Hook, the commander doesn't wish you well as you disembark. He affects to be absorbed in giving orders to the crew. The last you see of him is a figure crossing the deck with a shuffling gait and ducking down the stairs to his cabin, closing the door behind him without looking back. It's only when you're alone on the wharf with your kitbag that you realize you've no money for a cab fare. Some of the newspaper reporters at the harbour see you looking about dazedly and give you a ride into the city. As you get out, one of them puts $5 in your hand and says, 'Good luck, buddy.'

6

New York, October 1909

It's the type of occasion that Eva's parents would have swooned over. Tuxedo Hall. Chandeliers, a string quartet, and two hundred members of New York's black elite. A glass of champagne as you enter and a steak dinner at eight. As the guest of honour, your role is to do little except sit beside the energetic toastmaster, Charles Anderson, as he bobs up and down to introduce each dignitary speaking tonight. James A. Cobb, Assistant District Attorney in Washington. Frederick B. Watkins of the Liberty National Bank. Gilchrist Stewart, who led the legal fight for black soldiers in the Brownsville riot. Anderson himself is Collector of Internal Revenue, a position he was personally appointed to by President Roosevelt. With each speaker that stands to toast you, your heart sinks further. Their words don't summon pride so much as an accumulating sense of unease. They are talking about another man. A hard-working, diligent black man who has striven above all to be a credit to his race. He bears your name but you do not recognize him.

After dessert – blueberry pie and ice cream – Anderson presents you with a gold watch and chain. You face the audience. When you went to Greenland for the first time, they swore you'd never come back, you say. They told you that you couldn't stand the cold, that no black man could. You said you were willing to die, if necessary, to show them. You survived all right. And here you are. Cheers and laughter fill the hall. You wave to the guests and sit down.

Their applause continues to sound but the heavy feeling within you will not lift. Anderson pats the air for silence. This evening, he says, pulling a telegram from the breast pocket of his dinner jacket, we have received a message from Booker T. Washington. More cheers from the audience. Washington is the most powerful black person in America: educator, author, orator, and adviser to President Roosevelt. 'My congratulations to the guest of the evening, our distinguished and deserving fellow citizen who has by his achievement lifted the race to a higher level,' says Washington. Listening to the telegram, you understand that this evening is no different to those long afternoons in Eva's parlour, nodding mutely while her parents declaimed on how progress for the black race would come step by step, as men and women proved their worth to the nation through unresentful hard work. This was the creed that Washington had espoused for respectable blacks. 'Cast down your bucket where you are,' he urged his black audience in the speech fourteen years ago that catapulted him to national fame. Do not go north or embrace anger. *Earn* the respect of white America through your industry and faithfulness. In his telegram, Washington weds you explicitly to this philosophy. By your 'fidelity and devotion' you have proved yourself 'the trusty companion', 'the splendid follower' of a great explorer, and shown that 'courage and ability' can be found 'under a black skin as well as under a white'. The words leave you queasy. The string quartet has struck up again and you close your eyes, wanting the music to carry you out of the hall, beyond the reach of these people.

———

Soon after your return from the Arctic, William Brady, the Broadway agent, offers you a nationwide lecture tour. Before leaving on the *Roosevelt*, you and the other members of the expedition signed a contract giving the commander all rights of publicity. You write to him anyway, asking his approval for a speaking tour of your own. His reply is blunt. He will not allow you to cash in on *his* success by undertaking the tour or showing any of the dozens of photographs you took on the journey.

The commander's response is maddening. Apart from the banquet organized by Charles Anderson, you have been almost entirely overlooked since coming back. All public acclaim for the expedition has gone to the commander. The Royal Geographical Society of Britain has awarded him its gold medal. He has received awards from scientific bodies across Europe, and Edinburgh University has given him an honorary doctorate. By contrast, the commander still describes you in interviews as his body servant, a man 'as loyal and responsive to my will as the fingers of my right hand'. While he is now lauded, you are jobless and broke.

A reporter from the *New York Times* is writing a story on the commander and he approaches you for a quote. For all the years you've known him, you say, Commander Peary has been a selfish man committed to his own glory and that of nobody else. Soon after the article runs, you receive a final payment sent to all members of the expedition, of $750, plus a bonus amount of $1,000. The money is not intended as a peace offering, says the commander. The message comes through one of his supporters. 'I would not have Henson get the idea I am endeavouring to do anything for him for a thousand dollars. He has deliberately and premeditatedly deceived me and I am done with him absolutely.' Mrs Peary adds her own thoughts, letting it be known that in her opinion you are 'a vainglorious braggart'.

Yours is not the only dispute dogging Peary's triumph. It turns out that the commander's telegraph home, declaring victory at the Pole, was superseded a week previously by an announcement from Frederick Cook, the surgeon from your first expedition in 1891. Dr Cook had subsequently staged his own journey north and claims he reached the Pole on 21 April 1908, a whole year before your final trip. Hearing this news upon your return to New York, and knowing Dr Cook from that earlier expedition, you were immediately sceptical. Cook was never much good for a day's work, and the idea of him battling through hundreds of miles of hazardous terrain to reach the Pole was so ludicrous that you burst out laughing. But enough people have taken his claim seriously to divide the country. The *Herald* is serializing his story at the price of $25,000 and you can already buy fur-clad Dr Cook toy figurines in the stores. The commander has the *New York Times* on his side, hailing him as a hero and Cook 'a deliberate swindler'.

Even after the bonus, you decide to accept Brady's offer. The commander may not like it but you are determined to make your voice heard as a principal figure in such a great adventure. The tour begins triumphantly in October. On the opening date, in Middletown, Connecticut, a marching band greets you at the train station and leads a crowd down Main Street to the theatre where the governor is waiting to welcome you. The next night, at the New York Hippodrome, you draw an audience of eighteen hundred. At Wonderland Park near Boston, you dress up in furs and talk through your slideshow of photographs with one knee propped on a sledge. The response is enthusiastic. The *New York Times* describes how you were 'bombarded with questions' and 'heartily applauded many times for quick wit and frank answers'.

But the dispute between Commander Peary and Dr Cook is growing increasingly heated and soon the mood of your audiences becomes more rancorous. Cook supporters turn up to barrack you. Each night brings shouts and jeers and coarse laughter. The morning after a chaotic lecture in Providence, the *Christian Observer* writes, 'So rapidly were questions showered upon him that he did not get to even begin his lecture, and after several vain attempts to do so, lasting some forty-five minutes, the lights were turned out.'

The commander is avoiding public appearances while the controversy rages and, in his absence, the spotlight falls all the more harshly on you. Above all, the critics demand to know, why did Commander

Peary take only a black man to the Pole, instead of a white member of the expedition? 'The moral support of a white man would have done much toward establishing an unqualified claim to success,' reflects an English reporter, Henry Lewis. Did the commander choose his 'swarthy companion' in order to avoid sharing the honours with another white man? Were you, as Congressman Robert Macon describes it, 'Peary's useful Negro tool'? Could you read a sextant? Could you even *read*? Whatever the reason was for your selection, the *San Francisco Bulletin* says, it is unconscionable for you to try passing yourself off as an equal to a man of such accomplishment. 'Once his way of reasoning is accepted, we shall have to look upon Peary as the white and Matt Henson as the coloured polar champion. And then the whole affair will be cheapened, and future generations will not care a gum-drop who discovered the Pole.'

February 1910

Five months in and your audiences have dwindled to a trickle. Receipts for an evening lecture in Baltimore were $23. A matinee in Philadelphia the following week brought in $13 and 80 cents. In total, the tour has earned just $2,800. By comparison, one of Brady's sell-out shows can make $100,000 in a single night.

Black people, who you'd hoped would be supportive, are staying away. Perhaps they don't want to pay $2 to see a white crowd bait a black man onstage. Or maybe you're the problem. 'Mr Henson,' says the *Chicago Defender*, a black newspaper, 'is not an orator or scholar. Neither is his delivery good.' In the nervous tension of appearing before a hostile crowd each night, you've lost forty pounds. You tell Brady you can't go on.

Brady makes some sympathetic noises about how disgraceful it is that 'your own people' haven't turned out for the show. You suspect he'd already made up his mind to axe the tour before you came to him. This evening in Chicago will be your last performance. You're not sure if the decision is a relief or a humiliation. Either way, it's done.

In the dressing room, an unbearable tiredness wells up inside you. The face that looks back at you in the mirror is a defeated one. See the downturned mouth. The hollow cheeks. The bloodshot eyes squinting against the light.

Someone has left a copy of the *World* on the table. Pick it up, turn to the front page and there is the sensation of falling, like you have been hurled bodily into a well, its smooth sides offering no purchase as you plunge to the bottom. The paper's headline reads: 'Give Me My Father's Body'. Underneath, there's a photograph of Minik, who you haven't seen since you stood beside him at the funeral of his father over a decade ago. Except, as you read in the story, the funeral was a sham.

Before the service, Qisuk's body was swapped with an old log a similar size to a human corpse, which was wrapped in a cloth. The mock burial was held at dusk to avoid attracting attention. The log was placed in the ground and a mound of stones piled on top of the earth in the Inughuit fashion. Minik stood sobbing by the grave, suspecting nothing. Qisuk's real corpse was taken back to Bellevue Hospital, where it was dissected by medical students. His skull was opened up and studied by a scientist who published a paper in *American Anthropologist* titled, 'An Esquimo Brain', complete with photographs of the cerebrum, seen from above and below. Qisuk's corpse was then sent to a macerating plant, where it was stripped of its flesh. His skeleton was returned to the Museum of Natural History and mounted for display, where it has stayed ever since. Upon discovering the truth, Minik has been begging the museum to let him have his father's remains, but with no success. Now, despairing and angry, he is going home to the Arctic. 'I know I'll never get my father's bones. I am glad enough to get away before they grab my brains and stuff them into a jar.' The story sets the nerves jangling through your body. The horror of it.

An interview with Minik accompanies the report, recalling his last sorrowful days at Bellevue, beside his father.

He was dearer to me than anything else in the world – especially when we were brought to New York, strangers in a strange land. You can imagine how closely that brought us together; how our disease and suffering and lack of understanding of all the strange things around us made us sit tremblingly waiting our turn to go – more and more lonesome and alone, hopelessly far from home, we grew to depend on one another, and to love each other as no father and son under ordinary conditions could possibly love.

Aside from hopeless loneliness do you know what it is to be sad – to feel a terrible longing to go home, and to know that you are absolutely without hope? Ah, you cannot know. And then to add to this the horror of knowing that death was waiting near for us, and that one must go first and leave the other all alone – awfully alone; no one who even understands your language – no one except grief! Aside from these tortures my poor father's neck was swollen from tuberculosis, and his chest ached so badly that he could not rest. And yet, in spite of all this, his whole thought was constantly of me. He watched over me night and day, denying himself sleep and even food, and when anything was brought for me to eat he insisted on giving

148

it to me himself and if I seemed to like it, big tears would come in his eyes and he would half laugh and half cry and pat me on the cheeks. He knew that he must leave me, and his grief was terrible. 'Father's spirit will stay with Minik always,' he said. The next day father died. I think his poor heart broke and that is what killed him. I thought my heart was broken too. That sad, long, lonesome day.

The tears come easily as you read. What a place this country is, you think. So devoid of love or honour that it will steal a man from his son, strip him to the bones and stand him bare for the world to see. As for the boy, now a man himself, you wish you could go to him and hold him by the hand. You want to tell him that not every step he takes will be accompanied by betrayal or abandonment. Although, God knows, you're familiar enough with both to also argue the contrary.

A rap at the door from the stage manager. It's time. You're so preoccupied that it takes a while after you arrive onstage to see that the theatre is almost entirely empty. Rows of vacant red velvet seats and just a few folks scattered in ones and twos, as if embarrassed to be seen together.

You're dressed in your furs, isolated from even this meagre crowd by the bulk of the suit and the perversity of delivering a talk on the coldest place on Earth from inside clothing so warm you might faint. As usual you open with a slideshow of icebergs and dog teams, of Arctic flowers and a midnight sun. Brady has written the script for you and it describes the two decades of struggle for the Pole in an unbroken arc of adventure capped by the moment when you, the commander and the Inughuit men stand in triumph beneath the stars and stripes. Your role in the story is that of faithful servant, 'a lowly member of your race', who feels a stab of 'savage joy and exultation' at being 'chosen by fate to represent it, at this, almost the last of the world's great work'.

You know the lines by heart, yet you can't stick to them this evening. Your eyes keep drifting across the listless room. A man slumped in his seat with his hat low across his face who appears to be asleep. A woman sipping on a bottle of cola while her two sons make their way through a bag of peanuts, scattering the shells on the floor. You cannot form a connection between the dutiful figure of the script and you, sweltering onstage. They are two separate people, each in their own way lost.

The memory comes of forcing yourself through a blizzard. Snow crystals stirred up by the wind, whipping into your face. The broken ice beneath your feet and a pressure ridge as high as a house blocking your way. It strikes you that since this is your last performance there is nothing keeping you to the script. You're free to say what you like. Instead of speaking to the picture of Red Cliff House being projected on the screen behind you, you shut your eyes. You describe the view in your head. It is March and you are following the coast at the start of that last trek to the Pole. The route ahead passes through a region of sombre magnificence. Huge cliffs overlook the path; dark headlands project out into the ice-covered ocean. The Arctic night still holds sway, but its power is waning. The day is translucent and at noon, far to the south, a thin band of light shows, promising the return of the sun. Every day now will increase in brightness. It's as though you're walking from the past into the future.

When you open your eyes, there are more vacant seats. The sleeping man seems to have roused himself and left. The two boys with their mother are now taking turns to see who can spit peanuts furthest forward into the unoccupied rows in front. You carry on talking all the same. You tell the emptying theatre about Minik and

Qisuk as they were before coming to New York, the boy trailing after his father on a seal hunt. Minik excited because the last time they went out Qisuk killed a polar bear which, among the Inughuit, is the rarest and richest prize for a hunter. You recall Ahnalka, the elder, who sang in the igloo, and even the face of the malign Kyo, who was said to have killed two of his wives. The words tumble out of you with a sense of release you haven't felt in years. You speak the names of all the dead you've carried these times past. You welcome them on to the stage beside you in an act of final farewell. To Ma and to Pa. To Captain Childs. Qisuk. Nuktaq. Atangana. Aviaq. In time their presence will fade. Just as the whole idea of walking to the top of the world will come to seem fantastic. In times ahead, as you're riding the subway or walking down the canyon of a New York street, the memory of trekking for months in the company of cold and fear and hunger will return to you and you'll stop and shake your head at the absurdity of the endeavour. Yet the truth of the place far beyond this dismal theatre, this cruel country, will never really leave you. As you speak, you are beside Elatu. The night is full and vast and silent. She brushes her fingers down your face, over your eyelids and your nose, lets them linger at your mouth, leaving behind a faint taste of salt. You hear her whispering voice, soft as mist. Her gaze encompasses you like the night.

Like Paradise

An hour before moonrise on the night of 11 October 1492, Christopher Columbus first glimpsed the New World. From the deck of the *Santa Maria*, he saw, across the water, a light 'like a little wax candle rising and falling'. The following morning, sixty-one days after leaving Spain, Columbus made landfall on the island he named San Salvador. 'There are wonderful pine woods, and very extensive ranges of meadow land,' he wrote in a letter, describing his discovery. 'There is honey, and there are many kinds of birds, and a great variety of fruits. The seaports there are incredibly fine, as also the magnificent rivers, most of which bear gold.' Columbus's account of a remote Eden set the template for travellers to the Caribbean for generations to come. Gonzalo Fernández de Oviedo, author of the *Historia general y natural de las Indias*, a first-hand account of the New World widely read in the sixteenth century, was moved to rapture by the land he encountered. 'Such variety of animals . . . Such an untellable multitude of trees . . . useful plants and herbs . . . such variety of roses and flowers and sweet-smelling fragrance.'

Offering a similar perspective to those earlier travellers, the English landscape artist George Robertson journeyed to Jamaica in 1774 and depicted idyllic scenes of swaying palm trees and mist-wreathed mountains. Robertson had been brought to Jamaica by the plantation owner William Beckford, to record what Beckford called the 'variety and brilliancy of verdure' of his estates. The softly romantic paintings were consistent with the pro-slavery views of a landowner whose family owned over nine hundred enslaved Africans on the island. The reality of plantation life was a starkly different matter.

The diaries of Thomas Thistlewood, an English plantation overseer and contemporary of Beckford, offer a grotesque insight into the true nature of the slave colonies. Thistlewood, a bland, bookish figure when among his peers, maintained a regime of astonishing sadism on the plantation. The enslaved were flogged, branded, scourged and dismembered as a matter of routine. To punish a recaptured runaway, Thistlewood 'gagged him; locked his hands together; rubbed him with molasses & exposed him naked to the flies all day, and to the mosquitoes all night, without fire'. Another runaway received a punishment of Thistlewood's own devising: 'Gave him a moderate whipping, pickled him well, made Hector shit in his mouth, immediately put a gag whilst his mouth was full & made him wear it 4 or 5 hours.'

Violence was also enacted on the landscape of the West Indies, and on its indigenous peoples. Europeans coming to the Caribbean brought with them a portmanteau biota of plants and animals wholly novel to the islands, including yam, mango, coconut, coffee, banana, breadfruit and sugar cane. They also introduced diseases such as smallpox, measles, typhus, chickenpox and bubonic plague, many of which proved fatal to the local populations. Within fifty years of Columbus's arrival, the Taino people of Hispaniola, who may have numbered up to eight million, were virtually extinct. This genocide remained absent from the idealized picture of the Caribbean promoted across Europe for many centuries. When Charles Rampini, of Edinburgh, travelled to Jamaica in 1873, he described an encounter with some surviving members of the Taino people in baffled terms as if their continued existence on their own lands was an exotic mystery. The Taino were 'a curious colony of blacks whose origin has puzzled most travellers . . . They have no religion, no tradition; they are extremely shy, and shun the society of, or even intercourse with, white men . . . They form a curious and by no means uninteresting problem to the ethnologist.'

European presence radically remade the population and ecology of the West Indies. The St Lucia-born poet Derek Walcott has described the West 'look[ing] at a landscape furious with vegetation in the wrong light and with the wrong eye'. To speak of Caribbean identity is to talk of exile and loss, dislocation and alienation. 'We were all strangers here,' observed Walcott. 'The migratory West Indian feels rootless on his own earth, chafing at its beaches.'

—

On an early morning in 2020, I was walking along a beach shrouded in mist on the north coast of Jamaica. The few other figures I passed – a woman and her boisterous terrier, a couple locked in what seemed an anguished conversation – appeared and vanished like ghosts. Further down the beach I came upon a string of abandoned buildings, former hotels or guest houses, one after another, that had collapsed into ruin, perhaps after falling victim to the indifference of tourists or some sudden economic crisis. Many of the structures were overgrown with vegetation, their ceilings caved in and their remaining walls latticed with mildew and climbing plants. A large palm tree reached up, three storeys high, through the very centre of one building. A girl ran barefoot up and down the concrete steps of another. She wore a yellow dress and stood out against the tumbled-down walls brilliant as a tropic flower. Later, when I recalled the encounter to a friend, he reflected, 'In Jamaica, people very rarely wear dark colours. There's always a brightness that projects them forward.'

I turned his words over in my mind. A brightness that projects them forward. What, then, would it have felt like for West Indians coming to Britain in the drab 1950s? They arrived in an exhausted nation, drained by the struggle of war and the demands of rationing and rebuilding. Fog and dust choked the streets. The modish colours of the season were donkey brown and 'greige', grey and beige. With their bright clothes and their dark skin, Caribbeans were regarded as a strange, alien presence. 'Thirty Thousand Colour Problems' went the headline in *Picture Post*, above a photo of a disembarkation hall at Liverpool docks crowded with the latest 'boatload' of new arrivals. The fashion journal *Tailor and Cutter* sought to diagnose what was behind the 'sartorial sickness' of the flashy zoot suits favoured by many West Indian men: 'It is a reflection of the Negro's connections with the tropics — where his instincts were attuned to extremes of growth and colour and heat and excitement and are now reflected in his adoption of these sartorial exaggerations.'

This cold reception raises the memory of Sam Selvon's description, in *The Lonely Londoners*, of forlorn Caribbean immigrants struggling through the busy streets and vast indifference of their new home, 'the black faces bobbing up and down in the millions of white, strained faces, everybody hustling along the Strand, the spades jostling in the crowd, bewildered, hopeless'. In each direction they looked, West Indians saw further evidence of the disdain with which they were regarded. You might buy a new coat and discover the colour of the fabric was 'Nigger Brown'. Or you could read John Wyndham's *Day of the Triffids* and find an analogy for immigration in the invasive species that came from 'jungle country' to contaminate Britain. 'Bloody unnatural brutes,' curses a character in the novel. 'I always did hate them bastards.'

The 'colour problem' of Caribbean presence in Britain revolved around a fundamental conundrum: could Black people shed their loud clothes and manners and learn to fit in with the British way of life? Or did the very fact of their Blackness mean they were doomed to remain perpetual outsiders in the host country? 'In our culture, the coloured man is the archetypal stranger,' wrote sociologist Michael Banton in the *Listener* in 1958. A year later, in his book *White and Coloured*, Banton expanded on the point. 'Strangers are people who are unaware of norms of conduct. The coloured man is considered the most distant of strangers.'

Stranger. An outsider or foreigner. An intruder. One not admitted to communion or fellowship. Stranger: related to alien, non-resident, outcast, pariah, drifter. A stranger is in the group yet never fully of the group. A stranger remains associated with their origins irrespective of how far they have travelled from them. A stranger is not an individual in their own right but the representative of a particular type.

To be a stranger is to be at odds with the everyday. It is to walk through the world in a situation both of proximity and remove. 'I remain as much a stranger today as I was the first day I arrived,' wrote James Baldwin in 1953, having gone to stay in the same Swiss mountain village of Loèche-les-Bains for three years running. 'And the children shout Neger! Neger! as I walk along the streets.'

Soon after returning to London from Jamaica, I received an invitation to participate in a talk at a stately home in Yorkshire. I looked up the house online. It was an extraordinarily regal property, set in an estate of one thousand acres, with paintings by Titian, Tintoretto, Bellini and Turner adorning the walls. The invitation explained that the event was part of an effort to 'widen the conversation' around the history of the house, which was built on the fortune made by its owner through the slave trade. I couldn't make the date. But I was intrigued by what it meant to 'widen the conversation'. The wording on the property's website was carefully phrased. Its goal seemed to be to absolve its founder's wrongs, as much as to acknowledge them. The words swallowed themselves:

> However abhorrent the nature of his business, he was a very astute businessman, who became one of the richest men in England . . . The money came from owning plantations, slaves, ships and warehouses, a fact that was pervasive throughout British society at the time . . . For better or for worse there is nothing that any of us can do about history and the past.

—

In September 1767, Olaudah Equiano arrived in London. He was by then a free man. But his journey to individual liberty was painful and hard-fought. Equiano was no more than eight years old when he was kidnapped by slave traders from his home in the Igbo region of Nigeria. From there he was marched down to the coast, a forced trek which took several months, and sold to a British ship bound for Barbados. 'The stench of the hold while we were on the coast was so intolerably loathsome, that it was dangerous to remain there for any time,' he wrote later, describing the dreadful conditions in which he was transported across the Atlantic. 'The closeness of the place, and the heat of the climate, added to the number in the ship, which was so crowded that each had scarcely room to turn himself, almost suffocated us . . . This wretched situation was again aggravated by the galling of the chains, now become insupportable; and the filth of the necessary tubs, into which the children often fell, and were almost suffocated. The shrieks of the women, and the groans of the dying, rendered the whole a scene of horror almost inconceivable.'

From Barbados, Equiano was sold to Lieutenant Michael Pascal, an officer aboard the Royal Navy man-of-war, the *Roebuck*, who named him Gustavus Vassa, after Gustav I, a sixteenth-century king of Sweden. The Seven Years War against France had just begun. Equiano joined the 'good number of boys', or officers' servants, at the lowest rung of the ship's hierarchy. During sea battles he was a powder monkey, running gunpowder from the ship's stores down in the hold to the cannon above deck. Carrying combustible material in the middle of a sea battle was a hazardous occupation. 'I was a witness of the dreadful fate of many of my companions, who, in the twinkling of an eye, were dashed in pieces, and launched into eternity.' The boys worked, ate and slept side by side. Often they were corralled into boxing matches on the quarterdeck for the enjoyment of the officers, with a prize of 5 shillings for the winner of each bout.

Equiano learned to read and write. He grew practised at cutting hair and made some pennies shaving officers with a cut-throat razor. Lieutenant Pascal liked him and saw he was promoted to the rank of able seaman, the highest grade beneath an officer in the navy. In return, Equiano saw Pascal as the surrogate father in his new seaborne family. 'I began to consider myself as happily situated; for my master treated me always extremely well; and my attachment and gratitude to him were very great.' During the months-long intervals when the *Roebuck* was berthed in London, Pascal sent Equiano to stay with his cousins, the sisters Mary and Elizabeth Martha Guerin, who enrolled him in school, and arranged for him to be baptized.

After the defeat of the French at the end of 1762, the fleet was ordered to return to England, and Equiano began to hope that the end of the war would also mean the end of his enslavement. 'I thought now of nothing but being freed, and working for myself, and thereby getting money to enable me to get a good education . . . For though my master had not promised it to me . . . from all this tenderness, I had never once supposed, in all my dreams of freedom, that he would think of detaining me any longer than I wished.' His hopes were misplaced. Pascal learned of what he took as Equiano's impudence and, on the night their ship dropped anchor in the Thames, put a sword to Equiano's neck, threatened to cut his throat and vowed to sell him to the first buyer that would take him. Before the night was over, Equiano had been rowed to a ship bound on the next tide for Montserrat and sold to its captain. From the deck, he watched the boat carrying Pascal and the men he'd thought of as family recede into the darkening river. 'I followed them with aching eyes as long as I could, and when they were out of sight I threw myself on the deck, while my heart was ready to burst with sorrow and anguish.'

Two months later Equiano was back in the Caribbean, the site of his original arrival in the New World. Return meant reacquaintance with the many cruelties of the slave colonies, though his new master, Robert King, a Quaker merchant from Philadelphia, was at least 'charitable and humane'. Instead of being put to work on a plantation, Equiano was allowed to serve as right-hand man to Captain Thomas Farmer, one of King's most trusted employees, who ran a merchant ship between the West Indies and North America. By proving himself useful in myriad ways – as clerk, seaman, valet, hairdresser – Equiano secured a deal from King: if he could earn enough money by trading small goods of his own on Farmer's ship, then he could buy his freedom at a price of £40, the original sum that King had paid for him from Pascal. Starting with 'a very small capital . . . one single half bit, which is equal to three pence in England', Equiano became an assiduous entrepreneur. He bought citrus fruit in Montserrat, sold glass tumblers from Sint Eustatius, and travelled between islands with barrels of pork, hogsheads of sugar, and, on one occasion, a flock of live turkeys. In just three years, he became 'master of about forty-seven pounds' and was able to secure his freedom and depart for his chosen destination of England. 'With a light heart I bade adieu to the sound of the cruel whip, and all other dreadful instruments of torture ... adieu to oppressions ... and adieu to the angry, howling, dashing surfs.'

All of this was only prelude to the main act of Equiano's life. He was twenty-two when he arrived in London, bearing with him thirty-seven guineas, his manumission papers, and a heart 'full of hope'. For some months Equiano worked as a hairdresser in Coventry Court, Haymarket. In his spare time he took evening classes in mathematics and learned the French horn. But he was restless. Short of money and being too much of 'a roving disposition', he found it impossible to settle. In May 1768, Equiano decided to 'try the sea again'. For much of the next decade, he was on the move, trading goods back and forth between Asia Minor, southern Europe, North America and the Caribbean, even taking part in a disastrous Royal Navy expedition to the North Pole. In this time he also formed the Sons of Africa, along with other formerly enslaved men including the writer Ottobah Cugoano, a corresponding society that campaigned to end slavery. And in 1789, at the age of forty-four, he published his autobiography, *The Interesting Narrative of the Life of Olaudah Equiano, or Gustavus Vassa, the African*, which traced his journey through enslavement and liberation.

In the introduction, Equiano played coy, begging the pardon of his readers for a work 'so wholly devoid of literary merit' as produced by 'an unlettered African'. In fact the book, the first widely published personal account of the horrors of slavery, was a sensation. Supported by the Prince of Wales, the Bishop of London and leading politicians, artists and writers, it turned Equiano into a literary celebrity and ran to nine editions during his lifetime. Sales of the book enabled him to live the life of a gentleman. By the time of his death in 1797, he was the wealthiest man of African origin in Britain.

Writing of his travels as a free man, Equiano sometimes took the nonchalant tone of a young aristocrat on the Grand Tour. In Nice, he was 'struck with the elegant buildings' and enjoyed 'plenty of extraordinary good wines and rich fruits'. Approaching Naples by sea – 'a charming city, and remarkably clean' – he watched the awful majesty of Mount Vesuvius in eruption, the ash piling high and silent on the deck of his ship. At Smyrna, in Turkey, 'a seraskier or officer took a liking to me here, and wanted me to stay, and offered me two wives.' But the pleasure he took in travel was only ever partial. In each place Equiano visited, he was reminded of his marginal and precarious position. The beauty and grandeur of Europe's ancient cities were blighted by the sight of enslaved men 'whose condition [. . .] is truly piteous and wretched'. Passing through the slave colonies of the New World, he faced the constant duplicity of merchants who knew no court would side with a black man over a white one, and who were free to cheat him in business whenever they could – or worse. In Georgia, two white men tried to kidnap him into slavery, claiming he was their runaway property. Another merchant in the same city swore to take him 'dead or alive' over a dispute. Equiano was forced into hiding for five days in fear of being flogged. 'Hitherto I had thought only slavery dreadful,' he wrote of those years. 'But the state of a free Negro appeared to me now equally so at least, and in some respects even worse, for they live in constant alarm for their liberty, which is but nominal, for they are universally insulted and plundered without the possibility of redress.'

Neither enslaved nor fully free, travelling through a white society that he regarded with a black gaze, Equiano was both a wanderer and a stranger. The ground unfixed beneath his feet and no place to call home. It was a condition forcibly imposed upon him, but also one that he seemed to pursue, making considerable efforts to remain in motion – propelled by a belief in his right to claim the earth and the sea that surrounded him on his own terms.

On this point, one episode from his memoir strikes me with particular force. Having already secured his manumission, in 1766, Equiano undertook one last voyage to Georgia on behalf of Robert King. Anxious to leave the Caribbean, he accepted the job reluctantly. All the more so because the cargo, along with various goods and supplies, included two dozen enslaved men.

Equiano regretted his decision as soon as the voyage began. The sloop, *Nancy*, was led by an arrogant young captain, William Phillips, making his first journey on the ship. Knowing the route to Georgia well, Equiano found Phillips's decision to steer a different course through more hazardous waters 'very extraordinary'. He suffered a recurring nightmare in which the *Nancy* was smashed to pieces on rocks. Before they were even out of Caribbean waters, the dream had come true. At half past one in the morning on the fourth day at sea, the lookout at the helm called to Equiano, who was also on watch, to see the dolphins he had spotted. Equiano's suspicions were roused as he peered down at the grey shapes in the water: 'I said it was not a fish but a rock.' He rushed to warn the captain but Phillips refused to stir from his bunk. Running up and down the ship with increasing alarm, Equiano eventually managed to rouse Phillips. By the time the captain came on deck, it was too late. 'The breakers are around us,' reported Equiano. 'And, with one single heave of the swells, the sloop was pierced and transfixed among the rocks!'

Phillips called for the crew to abandon ship and to nail down the hatches on the enslaved men in the hold, leaving them to their fate.

At this Equiano 'could no longer restrain' his emotion. Effectively seizing command from Phillips – 'I told him he deserved drowning for not knowing how to navigate the vessel' – he ordered the crew to stay on board, patch up the hull as best they could and leave the hold unfastened. Daylight brought a calmer scene. The waves quieted and in the distance, about six miles away, it was possible to see a small island that could be reached by lifeboat. But the island was ringed by a reef reaching nearly to the surface of the water, forming a jagged, virtually impassable perimeter. Unless they found a way across it, the crew would be marooned on a sinking ship.

Here the difference between Equiano and the wastrel Phillips could not have been clearer. The captain and his closest men remained on board the swamped vessel, making no attempt to address their perilous situation. 'Not one of the white men did any thing to preserve their lives; and indeed they soon got so drunk that they were not able, but lay about the deck like swine.' It was left to Equiano and four other men of colour to row back and forth all day in the lifeboat, taking the same care with each person, from the enslaved men they helped out of the hold to the drunkards who they had to lift bodily over the side of the ship. Each time they neared the island, Equiano and his allies had to drag the boat over the reef, at the cost of much 'labour and fatigue . . . our legs cut and torn very much with the rock . . . the skin entirely stript off my hands'.

Safe on land, Equiano oversaw the building of shelters while Phillips only disgraced himself further. From the distance there seemed to be a group of men approaching across the beach. Phillips was alarmed and made to flee back to sea. 'Our captain swore they were cannibals. This created a great panic among us.' Equiano insisted they go and meet the islanders. Only when they got closer did it become clear that the suspected cannibals were just a flock of flamingos that took lazily to flight on their approach.

Once this phantom threat was seen off, the castaways concentrated on collecting fresh water and food. The warm coastal waters were rich with turtles and fish. White crewmen and black captives ate and slept together in contentment. All were grateful to Equiano for saving their lives. He was treated like 'a kind of chieftain amongst them'.

The satisfaction Equiano felt at their approval can only have been bittersweet. The next day, they would need to find a way back to Montserrat. That meant returning to the same place that presumed Phillips a better man than him based on the colour of his skin alone. And consigning the enslaved men he'd saved from death on the *Nancy* back into a life of bondage. For a single, precious day, Equiano had stepped outside of that harsh world, to glimpse a life beyond race. A land predicated on kinship not bigotry. On shared status not domination. And maybe it was with this sense of fragile mutuality in mind that, later in the day, as his shipmates dozed, Equiano walked to an isolated spot set back from the beach. He carried with him some fruit – oranges, limes, lemons – he'd brought from Montserrat, intending to sell in Georgia. On his own, in the quiet that fell quickly once he was away from the other men, he dug a hole in the earth and began to bury the fruit. 'Finding it to be a good soil . . . I planted several of them as a token to any one that might be cast away hereafter.' Symbolically, his actions marked a closing of the circle first opened by Columbus and the European travellers who remade the flora and fauna of the Caribbean in their image. In planting his fruit, Equiano made the island his, designating its 'good soil' as a place of refuge and sustenance for those cast as strangers in the world beyond. A temporary republic that might, by another name, be known as home.

3

Frantz Fanon

I

Blida, Algeria, 1953

The psychiatric hospital is a village of its own on the edge of the city of Blida, in northern Algeria. Within its high stone walls there are eighty-nine hectares of tropical gardens and landscaped walks shaded with olive trees. Blida-Joinville Hospital was built before the war to house seven hundred patients in spacious, modern, white-washed pavilions with shuttered windows and terracotta roof tiles. Today it holds some two thousand people and conditions are over-crowded and often tense.

You arrived from Lyon three months ago after completing your doctorate. At twenty-eight, you are the youngest of the hospital's five chief physicians, with two hundred and twenty-five Muslim men under your care. Although you speak no Arabic or Berber, you hope to form a good connection with your patients. During five years of study in France you were never made to feel at home, but you still believe you can be part of the civilizing mission in the col-onies. You are a French citizen and you will bring the light of learning here to the sick and the lost.

You came by bus from Algiers, rattling past groves of gnarled olive trees twisting out of ochre soil. The sun beat against the window the whole way and by the time you made it to the hospital your head ached and your linen suit was orange with dust. But you were excited all the same. The thought in your head: maybe this is where you prove yourself. Maybe this is where you're supposed to be. Even the churlish welcome from the bursar, sweltering behind the reception desk in a black wool suit, didn't put you off. He leafed suspiciously through your papers, squinting up at your face, apparently unable to accept that someone who looked like you could really be the new head physician. It took a phone call to the local prefecture for him to let you through, mumbling something about how your face was so dark in the passport he couldn't make it out properly.

You have a house in the hospital grounds. It's only a small place but there are palm trees at the front and the blue-and-white patterned floor tiles are cool underfoot in the afternoon heat. And there is much work to be done. Most nights you sleep no more than four hours, preferring to cross the grounds in the dark and be seated at your desk by dawn, reading up on the new psychiatry journals that have arrived from France, and updating your patient notes while a thick quiet blankets the ward. At eight, Jacques Azoulay arrives, and you sit together over coffee as the day begins. Azoulay is your intern, but he's only four years younger than you, and the proximity in your ages has brought you together as friends. That, and the fact that you're both outsiders in the colonial system of the hospital; you a Martiniquan and he an Algerian Jew.

Azoulay arrived at Blida a month after you did. He's energetic, inquisitive, and as eager to make a difference here as you. He's the only person who you feel free to confess to that you are appalled by the state of the wards, having known nothing about the hospital before coming here. There is a shortage of beds, a shortage of machines and a shortage of drugs. The day rooms and refectories have been converted into dormitories to cope with overcrowding, so after breakfast the men have nowhere to go except the courtyard, with no shelter from the bare sun. Some of them have been here for a decade or more with no improvement in their condition. Unless you find a way to reach them, they will still be here in ten more years. Others aren't even mentally ill. They are the senile grandparents or the autistic children of families that have abandoned them to the institution. The place is choking with people forgotten by the world outside.

It used to be the case that agitated patients were tied down to their beds or lashed to trees. The most overwrought were stripped naked in isolation cells and fastened to the floor with iron rings. Those days are thankfully gone but an uneasy atmosphere still reigns. The men shuffle around in drab uniforms. They are dirty and unshaven. Fights are common. When the hospital barber comes, he insists they be strapped into straitjackets before he will begin work.

The medical staff at Blida are split into two camps. Azoulay, along with some of the other interns and Muslim nurses, takes a progressive view on how to run the wards. So does Raymond Lacaton, one of the five senior doctors. Lacaton is courteous and compassionate. He comes from an old French settler family but he speaks fluent Arabic and is a dedicated student of Muslim culture. By contrast, the remaining chief physicians, led by Dr Huyghe, who has been at the hospital since it opened, are all Frenchmen who act more like colonial administrators than doctors. They seem more concerned with ensuring the patients make their beds properly in the morning and are locked up at night than in actually addressing their needs.

Their attitude is typical of how the French in this town see Arabs. On Sundays, in the elegant Place Toute, French families dressed in white linen drink sweet anisette while a military band plays beneath the wrought-iron pagoda. They might be in Arles or Cannes rather than North Africa. They would never stray from the *place*, into the narrow lanes of the Muslim quarter, crowded with people, fragrant with the scent of paprika and powdered coriander, babies' cries echoing off the walls of rough-cast buildings. This is a town of two halves.

The French minority have held power here since the country became a colony in 1830 and they continue to look down on Arabs and Muslims as if they, not the French, are the interlopers. In the slang of the settlers, Muslims are ratons: 'coons'. Their value compared to Europeans, says the mayor of Algiers, is 'as feathers against gold'. Accordingly, the hospital doctors treat patients with disregard. In their eyes, Arab patients are by their very nature unbalanced. Madness is part of their character.

The roots of that belief run deep. Nineteenth-century travellers to North Africa saw the land and its people as exotic and frightening. You yourself read Guy de Maupassant's account of his travels in Algeria and Tunisia in school, though the histrionic tenor of his narrative is only obvious to you now, as you come to know this country first-hand. In Maupassant's description, Algerian men dressed in tattered robes and dozed in the daytime by the side of the road, their slothful behaviour indicative of the Arab tendency to indolence. Through filigreed gates, a woman in a shaded courtyard cast him 'a sad and gloomy look' with her kohl-lined eyes. In Tunis, Maupassant visited an asylum that was more zoo than hospital. Inmates pressed pallid faces between the bars of their cells. 'One of them, extending his hand and shaking it outside his cage, shouted an insult. The others, jumping up suddenly like animals, raised their voices' until the cries were deafening. Upstairs, an old man shouted and capered, 'dancing like a bear'. A 'continuous laughter with a menacing air' filled the courtyard, leading the author to flee the asylum in fear of the 'contagious and terrifying emanation, the breath of unreason' that threatened to overwhelm his own sanity.

Blida opened its gates in 1938, the largest psychiatric institution in North Africa, an outpost of Western rationality in the midst of Muslim decadence. When you arrived, you had a brief and unsettling interview with Dr Huyghe. 'Muslims live in the present and the past but are indifferent to the future,' he said, taking a long draw on his pipe. 'Their mentality, which has developed on a level very different from that of our own, is characterized by enormous changeability and contradiction.' For much of its past, the hospital was run according to Huyghe's belief in Muslim degeneracy. Patients were subjected to a vast regime of experimental treatments. Digging into the archive of patient files, you and Azoulay have discovered the full extent of this programme – 4,510 insulin shocks, 2,483 cardiazol shocks, 383 lumbar punctures, 5,805 laboratory examinations in 1940 alone. Two lobotomies carried out every month for much of the following decade.

The whole scheme, disturbing as it was, took place in public, without shame. Azoulay found a note by Huyghe in the files: 'When it comes to the Muslim we must first remember that it is a diseased personality that we are operating on.' The records even detail the visit of a reporter from the *Alger Républicain* in 1948. Left to wander the hospital, the journalist described the alarm he felt 'when one has seen a revolting face through the bars of a courtyard, heard a soulless scream mount through the clear heavens on a beautiful morning, and remembered the poignant Baudelairean prayer, "Lord have pity on the madmen and madwomen." '

As a doctor it is your responsibility to bring the true meaning of civilization to the hospital. The human imperative must be at the heart of everything that takes place. That means a total break with the old methods of shackles and shock treatments. You tell your staff all the time, a hospital is a mirror of the world outside. Treat the patients as people not prisoners and they will thrive. As soon as you could, you introduced a new programme for the men in your care. In place of the monotony of mealtimes and medicine and perfunctory exercise in the courtyard, you instituted a weekly basket-weaving workshop. You organized movie screenings in the chapel: *Rio Grande*,

King Solomon's Mines, Cocteau's *Daughter of the Sands*. And you founded a weekly newspaper, *Our Journal*, made up of contributions by patients and staff. 'On a ship it is commonplace to say that one is between sky and water; that one is cut off from the world; that one is alone,' you wrote in your first editorial. 'This journal, precisely, is to fight against the possibility of letting oneself go, against that solitude.'

At first these interventions were well received, and you were pleased at the changes you were bringing so quickly to the ward. You had the nurses submit reports about patients' responses to your new initiatives, when you weren't able to supervise them in person. On games night: 'We all met together and played hide and seek, cards and dominoes. The atmosphere was good.' But as the weeks passed, enthusiasm among the men tapered off. They became increasingly indifferent to the activities. The film screenings and basket-making workshops were cancelled for lack of participants. Attendance at games night faltered. 'At the start there were ten patients, but later, only six patients remained. M, N, B and L refused to take part in the discussion; the reason being they were "too tired".' After three months of this, you are back to where you started, the men lethargic and the atmosphere on the ward disconsolate.

———

Dear Joby

I am glad to be settled in the hospital, though I am only now realizing the scale of the task I have accepted. Most of the staff here seem content to let the situation continue as it stands, but I can't bear to see these men sunk into such a low state of dignity. My fellow chief doctors in particular view my idealism as folly. I must

concentrate my energies where they will be welcomed, or at least
not blocked.

I hope you and the others are well. Send my love to Maman.
Your brother
Frantz

—

You have been walking since dawn, following a rocky path that leads above the town, a sliver of moon in the pale sky, cicadas humming in the laurel bushes. Since coming to Blida you've been trying to understand the world of your patients: not just life in the Arab quarter but also how the Berber communities in the foothills of the Atlas Mountains live. Lacaton knows many of the villages well and he offered to take you and Azoulay up on a visit this morning. The three of you walk the trail in single file as the sun rises steadily higher, Lacaton at the front.

At noon you stop at the side of a slender river. You unpack a picnic – a baguette of merguez sausage and a bottle of beer each – and sit beneath a glade of trees. When you've eaten, you wade into the water up past your ankles, hobbling over the flat, slippery stones underfoot, pushing against the surprisingly strong current that threatens to send you tumbling, until you find your balance, your toes digging into sand, savouring the exhilarating contrast between the stinging cold at your feet and the hot sun on your face.

By the time you reach the village up on a ridge, the river is no more than a ribbon running silvery along the valley floor. Smoke drifts from the houses, dissolving into the dusk air and dimming the flank of the mountain rising up above.

A villager who Lacaton knows invites you into his home. You sit cross-legged on a rug in his house while children run in and out and his wife, her face hidden by a veil, sets large dishes of couscous and lamb before you, and then retreats from the room. More men arrive and sit around the food, talking energetically in Berber and Arabic. Lacaton dives into the conversation, while you struggle to follow except for the moments when talk veers into French. Still, in the warm room, amid the clamour of voices, cigarette smoke unfurling into the air, drinking one glass after another of sweet mint tea, you feel content. More than participating, your aim is to observe and absorb the perspective of these local people, to try to understand why your efforts with the Arab and Berber patients have proved such a failure. You, Azoulay and Lacaton have occupied long hours discussing how important it is to see the world from the point of view of your patients. Especially when it comes to questions of the mind.

As you understand it, the Berber people perceive only a thin line between the physical and supernatural worlds, between sanity and madness. In between those quotidian and mystic realms travel the djinns, the genies, agents of good as well as chaos and evil. With the help of Lacaton, you've joined pilgrimages to saints' tombs to expiate curses, meeting the men and women who blame their headaches or vomiting on spirit possession. Madness too is believed to be caused by possession by a djinn. The remedy is an exorcism conducted by a marabout, a spiritual guide. On one long night, the three of you watched one such guide, solemn and angular, sit over a woman whose family believed her to be possessed. The woman thrashed about on a mat, her back arching, shouting and screaming uncontrollably. The healer laid a thin hand on the woman's forehead, demanding the spirit to identify itself while she raved. 'Are you djinn or ghost, devil or red wind?' he called. Then he blew into her mouth, cursing at the spirit, commanding it to release its hold on the woman. And this continued for many hours, the marabout reading aloud passages of the Qur'an, until, sometime around dawn, the woman's body relaxed and she lay spent on the mat, apparently free of whatever condition had seized her.

One of the consequences of believing in spirit possession is that madness ceases to hold a stigma. An Arab mother attacked by her mentally ill daughter would not blame her but rather the djinn that has possessed her. Viewed this way, insanity is freed from shame or mystery. It becomes simply another element of kaleidoscopic everyday life. How different this is to the clinical approach taken at the hospital, which sees mental illness as a disease afflicting a victim to the very core of their being. Yet it still eludes you how to apply this knowledge to the ward. The gulf between you and the men remains.

—

Today you make a new attempt at group therapy. To create a sense of occasion you cover the table in the big refectory with a white cloth and place a vase of flowers at each end. Azoulay and Lacaton sit beside you, along with another young, progressively minded intern, Charles Géronimi. The men shuffle in, not looking up as they take their seats.

You try to rouse their spirits. This hospital can be a place of equality where the sick and the well work together to create a world even better than the one outside, you say. That is why the liberation of patients is not just a matter of individual treatment. The structures that surround you men – the hospital itself – must be reformed. Not just the old practices of restraining and locking up patients. But also the regimes of forced idleness and numbing routine. Your days here must evoke the texture of everyday life.

Slowly, hand in hand with the doctors and nurses, you can become your full selves again.

When you finish speaking, the men stare blankly back at you. One patient yawns noisily, scratches his stubbly chin, then slouches off to the courtyard. The only one of them who seems to be paying attention is a middle-aged man, a former customs official and notorious bore, who launches into a long monologue in French – chiefly, it seems, to make it known he's 'made of better stuff' than the others. The whole session was nothing more than an empty exercise, you complain to Lacaton afterwards. Absurd. Devoid of meaning. An embarrassment.

Your fellow doctors watch your efforts with amusement. Huyghe takes you aside one afternoon to offer his advice: 'When you've been in Algeria as long as I have, you'll understand how futile it is to expect anything from Muslims. They are simply too undeveloped in their thinking to ever change.' Behind your back, says Azoulay, the other physicians call you the 'Arab Doctor'.

You know they are mocking more than your sympathy for the men in the hospital. To your colleagues, there's no fundamental difference between you and your patients. If you're not European it's all the same to them whether you're Arab or West Indian. The first time you understood that this was how such people thought was when you arrived from Martinique to study in Lyon. It was an ugly realization. There were some twenty students from West Africa at the university, while you were the only one from the Caribbean. At home you'd been brought up believing in Martinique as a district of France, seeing yourself as a child of the home nation, rather than belonging to the colonies like a Malian or a Senegalese. It turned out your white classmates made no such distinction.

You were even taken for an African at a party near Place Guichard, the old town with its narrow, dark buildings, the student district. A girl called to you from the other side of a crowded room, 'Omar, Omar!' She rushed over to you and then, realizing her mistake, dropped your arm, saying, 'I'm sorry, I thought you were Omar Traoré.' She smiled and you smiled, and you both agreed it was an unfortunate error. Except that similar mistakes kept happening, often enough that you were forced to understand it as a deliberate refusal to recognize you as the Frenchman you'd been raised to believe that you were. Your friends at the university praised your 'good French', as if you hadn't been speaking it all your life. In the next breath they told you they didn't 'see' colour. Once, during a class, you made an observation about the connection between Caribbean and European poetry that won the praise of the professor. As you filed out of the lecture hall, one of those friends patted you on the back. 'Well done, Fanon, at heart you're basically a white man.'

—

You have been invited to witness another exorcism. Although Lacaton arranged the visit, he is away from the hospital at present, Azoulay too, so it's just you walking up into the foothills through the afternoon. It is dark by the time you arrive. A group of villagers are sitting in a circle around two women lying on the ground, their faces illuminated by a fire, rapt and grave. The village marabout kneels over their supine bodies, chanting and singing while they struggle and fit. Sometimes the onlooking villagers join, raising their voices to accompany the marabout. At other moments, the only sound is the crackle of the fire, the popping of logs. The ritual continues into the night until your hands and feet tingle with cold. Eventually you wander out to the edge of the village. In the perfect

177

blackness you can see nothing before, or below, you. Just the constellations above are visible, hard and bright, the stillness of the tableau interrupted only by the forlorn grace of a shooting star in descent.

By the time you return to the fire the two women are gone, but the villagers are still gathered around, singing now and ululating and dancing. Against the backdrop of the silent mountains, this coming together of music and bodies feels like its own kind of exorcism, a collective conjuring away of the forces, whether social or supernatural, that might haunt each villager, and an affirmation perhaps of the bonds that unite them. Later, when you read them back, you're struck by the delirious quality of the notes you made that night. 'There are no limits inside the circle. The hillock up which you have toiled as if to be nearer to the moon; the riverbank down which you slip as if to show the connection between the dance and ablutions, cleansing and purification – these are sacred places. There are no limits – for in reality your purpose in coming together is to allow the accumulated libido, the hampered aggressivity, to dissolve as in a volcanic eruption. The evil humours are undammed, and flow away with a din as of molten lava. When they set out, the men and women were impatient, stamping their feet in a state of nervous excitement; when they return, peace has been restored to the village; it is once more calm and unmoved.'

You are still thinking of the villagers days later. It occurs to you that perhaps the reason you haven't got through to your patients is because you've been trying to introduce activities based on a European, Christian worldview. What does a film like *Daughter of the Sands*, with its caricatured depiction of Arab nomads and princesses, mean to men who know the real desert? Come to that, why expect them to contribute to *Our Journal*, when, as it transpires, most of them can't read or write? You have insisted on the sovereignty of Western values. These colonial delusions are hard to shake off. It is so easy to become the colonizer yourself.

———

Dear Joby

At last, a breakthrough! I have been wrestling with how to reach my patients for months and it's only now I understand how badly we were on the wrong track. We naively thought it possible to transplant Western frameworks to a Muslim society — forgetting that any attempt of that kind must be preceded by gaining a real insight into the foundations of the indigenous society. I am now investing all my energies into moving the clinical staff away from the assumption of Western cultural supremacy and fostering a position of cultural relativism instead. I am chastened and will resolve to be wiser.

Faithfully

Frantz

———

Now, instead of the basket-weaving course, you introduce a Moorish cafe with low tables and floor mats where the men can drink mint tea and play dominoes as they do at home. The therapy sessions are run, more successfully, by Muslim and Berber nurses and a local musician comes to perform for the patients every week. Twice a month, a mufti visits the hospital to lead Friday prayers. You get the patients playing football and digging earth and planting crops in the hospital gardens. Coming mainly from rural origins, even the most catatonic among them have responded well to this activity. Across the ward they are rising from their sunken state. All around you, they are returning to life.

At a bar, you and Azoulay are sharing a bottle of good St-Émilion and talking about the past. You haven't been home in over a decade, you say, and you miss your brothers and sisters. But the idea of returning to the stifling atmosphere of Fort-de-France feels exhausting. You tell him about Martinique's social stratifications, its exactingly differentiated layers of class and skin colour. And how Maman forbade you and Joby from speaking petit nègre when you were children. If she caught you, she'd slap you round the head and say, 'Stop acting like a nigger.' Maman, who was the illegitimate daughter of a white man and a black woman. Even though her father never acknowledged her, she took all her pride from having roots that stretched back to Alsace, France. The family may be Caribbean by blood, she said, but it was French by birthright. Your very name is a testament to that belief. Frantz – a nod to the family's European heritage that also marks you as a loyal child of the colonies: in old German 'Frantz' means 'Frenchman'. How elated Maman was when you passed the examination for the Lycée Schoelcher, the island's most distinguished school, the glass dome of its library adorned with the names of Enlightenment philosophers: Voltaire, Rousseau, Diderot and Montesquieu. To walk into that grand building was like claiming your inheritance.

You shake your head with a rueful smile. You thought you were coming to Blida to spread the same civilizing values that you grew up with. But all you see now is how narrow your own perspective was. Azoulay nods silently and reaches for his glass of St-Émilion. You can't tell if he's amused or embarrassed on your behalf.

2

1954

The fighting begins soon after midnight on All Saints' Day, 1 November. At the start, it seems a minor affair. In Algiers, a warehouse full of oranges is set on fire. Bombs explode outside a gasworks causing little damage. In the city of Batna, a nightwatchman at a factory holds off an armed assault with an antique cavalry rifle. Responsibility for the attacks is claimed by a little-known group called the Front de Libération Nationale. They are demanding an end to French rule. 'Think of your humiliating position as colonized men,' say their leaflets. 'Under colonialism, justice, democracy and equality are nothing more than deceptions and tricks.' An army commander shrugs off the attacks as no more than a 'tribal uprising'. *Paris Match* carries a report on the 'terrorist wave' in Algeria, but the story is overshadowed by a photograph of a dazzling Gina Lollobrigida in a silk evening dress.

Some of the younger hospital staff are already talking excitedly about the coming war of liberation. When Huyghe catches you joining in with their conjecturing, his opinion of you sinks yet further. He is heard to say to another of the old-guard doctors, 'Who is this nigger who thinks he can teach us about psychiatry?'

These men, with all their certainty about the world, they know so little of what's happening. They think the fighting will blow over. But you have a presentiment of what's to come. Revolutionary ideas are spreading, whether they like it or not. You saw it yourself back in Lyon – a city in turmoil, the streets still pocked with bomb craters and collapsed buildings from the war, its people half-crazed with hunger and anxiety, and workers on strike everywhere: train engineers, metro conductors, chemical plant workers, the women in the garment factories, the men on the Citroën factory line. Through your young eyes, the drama of blockades and picket lines and factory sit-ins was exhilarating. You plunged into the melee, joining the student gatherings in smoky cafes, wild, driving jazz on the jukebox, turning up to demonstrations and marches that collapsed into running battles with the police. It felt like everything was speeding up and breaking down at once. Graffiti on a wall echoing the words of Marx: 'All that is solid melts into air, all that is holy is profaned.' Huyghe and his cronies might want to close their eyes, but the world is turning nonetheless.

Dear Maman

Have you heard about the fighting in Algiers? If you have, please don't worry for my sake. Blida is far away from the capital and untouched by trouble. Nothing has changed here. The Europeans are still taking their Sunday coffee in the Place Toute and looking down on the Arabs and Berbers whose land they occupy. But I must tell you that if the conflict spreads, there's no doubt whose side I'm on. I know you will read this with dismay and feel I am betraying my heritage. Please remember when I volunteered to fight for France, and you were proud of my beliefs then. I told you that I had no choice but to join up because the future of freedom was at stake. Surely the same principle applies here. I am for freedom, even if this time the war is against France.

Love

Frantz

1955

April. In response to increasing FLN attacks on police stations and army barracks, the colonial government declares a state of emergency. Paratrooper units are dispatched from France. Many of these are the same troops that returned in humiliation from the Indochina War last year, defeated by Viet-Minh guerrillas. They are determined to absolve their shame on the 'Viets' of the FLN. All the more so because Tunisia has given its support to the liberation movement and there is fear of a conflagration spreading across North Africa.

Under the state of emergency, the killing of a single French soldier is punishable with the destruction of an entire Algerian village. French troops go searching for FLN guerrillas in the village of Carrières Romaines. On discovering that the men have fled, they drag some fifty women, children and elderly people from their homes and kill them all. On its front page, *L'Express* publishes stills from the film footage of the massacre. The images show a policeman raise his rifle, take aim at a man and shoot him in the back. In the final frame, the policeman stands watching as his victim falls to the ground, his hat flying high into the air. Some French settlers are forming themselves into militia groups. They go out on armed 'Muslim hunts'. One man tells *Le Monde*, 'I shoot first and then afterwards I look to see if it was a good one or a bad one.'

'The days to come will be terrible days for this country,' you write to Joby. 'Every passing hour is an indication of the gravity and imminence of the catastrophe. European civilians and Muslim civilians are going to take up the gun. And the bloodbath no one wants to see will spread across Algeria.'

———

You are on the ward when Géronimi, the intern, hurries over to say that Mustapha Bencherchali is in the hospital, insisting on seeing you. Your first instinct is to have him turned away. You tell Géronimi you're too busy for a clown like Bencherchali. But then you pause and sigh and walk down the corridor to meet him.

He's waiting in your office wearing a pair of sunglasses, his hair slicked back and shirt open to the chest. Bencherchali's natural habitat is a bar, the air thick with cigarette smoke and loud music. Everyone in Blida recognizes his car cruising around town – a large, red American convertible, big and powerful like a speedboat. You greet him stiffly from behind your desk, trying to signal that unlike him – the son of a wealthy tobacco grower, slouched on a chair, legs apart, smoking a Marlboro – you have work to do. Bencherchali says he would like to begin seeing you for a course of psychotherapy and, again, you have the urge to say, stop wasting my time. You can't imagine someone less suited to intensive therapy than this playboy. 'Don't be put off by the clothes,' says Bencherchali, gazing down at his houndstooth jacket in response to the sneer on your face. 'Underneath I'm a serious person.' He looks up and fixes you in his gaze. 'What about you, doctor? Are you serious about our people?'

The question is pointed enough to make you start. For the first time you give him your proper attention. 'I have a lot of friends,' he continues in a quieter voice. 'Some of them are fighting for our nation. They are leading a unit in the mountains.'

As it turns out, all those times you saw him driving around in his red convertible, acting the bigshot, Mustapha Bencherchali was ferrying supplies to the fighters. He plays it so boisterously that the army never thinks to stop and search him at a roadblock. He comes and goes as he pleases.

The FLN want to know if you too can help them. They've heard about what you're doing at the hospital. Some of their combatants are suffering from shellshock. They want you to talk to the men, to help them get themselves together. Bencherchali would act as a go-between, under the guise of psychotherapy sessions, reporting back to the leadership. 'Will you be a friend to the cause?'

You tell him you'll do what you can, and he stands up and leaves the office, stopping to joke with Géronimi outside, his voice booming along the corridor as he heads to his car.

———

Conversations with Azoulay and Lacaton at daybreak. Lacaton is red-eyed with lack of sleep. He says, 'Every time I close my eyes I imagine women and children being torn from their homes and shot in the street.' Something must be done. The three of you agree that it's not possible to support the struggle of the colonized without also opposing the injustice of the colonizer. That means fighting back with whatever means you have.

As senior doctors, you and Lacaton open a day clinic for psychiatric patients. Officially the clinic has no connection to the war. In practice, most of the new patients being admitted are participants in the conflict, colonialists and freedom fighters alike. And its open-door policy means that wounded FLN guerrillas sent to you by Bencherchali can be smuggled on to the wards for treatment. Some are so worn down they're suicidal. Or they're wounded and need surgery. Mostly they are just young men sick of the death they've seen and the killing they've taken part in.

From the beginning, many of the clinic cases you encounter are hard to bear. DJ is a nineteen-year-old former student, a fighter in the FLN, who comes to see you each Tuesday. He suffers from insomnia and when he does manage to sleep he is haunted by nightmares of emaciated women in a blood-filled room. Twice in the last few months, before he started visiting you, he tried to commit suicide. On the morning he finally tells you enough to start making sense of the dreams, he sits, fidgeting uncomfortably in the chair, biting his fingernails and tugging at his hair. He regards you with bloodshot eyes. 'I have lost my path. My whole life is ebbing away.' It has taken many weeks of appointments to put together his story. At the start of this year, DJ left home to join the guerrillas. Some months later, he received devastating news from his family. His mother had been shot dead by a French soldier.

Shortly after, DJ took part in an FLN raid on the estate of a settler who had killed two Algerian farmers. His unit broke into the house at night but the man wasn't there. Only his wife was at home. She begged them not to kill her and they kept her in the room with them while they waited for her husband. 'When I looked at that woman I thought of my mother,' recalled DJ. 'I wondered why we didn't kill her; then all of a sudden she noticed I was looking at her. She flung herself upon me, screaming, "Please don't kill me . . . I have children." A moment later she was dead. I'd killed her with my knife.' DJ claims he 'didn't give a damn' about the woman's murder. But he can't eat a meal now without throwing up afterwards. And when he goes to sleep his room is invaded by spectres of the woman he killed. They are gaunt and pale and each of them has an open wound in the stomach where he stabbed her. The women stand over him, demanding he give them back their spilled blood. At that moment DJ sees that the floor of his room is drenched with blood – his blood – while the women's wounds begin to close and the colour comes back to their faces. He wakes up soaked in sweat, a scream half-formed in his throat.

What can be done with D J except to listen and to talk and for him to eventually admit that he does indeed 'give a damn' about this woman's life. Over the course of your sessions, his nightmares disappear and his suicidal thoughts recede. There is nothing to condone in his actions, but you admire his willingness, albeit belated and reluctant, to begin grappling with the morality of his conduct.

———

Even in these unsettled times, there is a rhythm to the hospital day. You make ward rounds, talking with the patients, taking notes, and in the evening, you lead a study group with the nurses and housemen. The hours flow by and in the midst of routine you can forget what's happening beyond the hospital walls. Early in the morning you walk by yourself in silence through the corridors, conscious of their antiseptic smell. A pink half-light seeps through the windows. You treasure these soft moments before the day begins in earnest. But, increasingly, you are stretched taut with the effort of maintaining a double life. Everyone is on edge. All it would take is a word from Huyghe about suspicious activity on your ward and you're finished.

The police make regular searches of the hospital looking for guerrillas. You complain to the Resident Minister about soldiers with loaded guns on the wards. But they come all the same. A settler militia has put up a barrier on the main road. Each time you drive to or from town in your Simca Aronde, you are obliged to stop and show your papers to some puffed-up farmer or dentist with a gun. At night, the sound of jet fighters taking off from the army airbase close by rends the air.

The police raids become more aggressive. Some of the male nurses are taken for questioning and only let go after being beaten. In June, Lacaton is arrested. It's not clear if he's been detained as the result of a tip-off to police about clandestine activity in the hospital or whether he's just been caught up in a sweep. If it's the former, you wonder how soon it will be before they come for you. Awful as it is to contemplate, you know that he, along with thousands of others being held across Algeria, is probably being subjected to torture. Policemen slap and punch and kick captives. They press cigarettes to their skin while demanding, 'Who is your commanding officer? Who is in your cell? Give us a name!' But there are also more elaborate methods they deploy. A prisoner might be made to sit on a bottle with a broken neck and pressed down upon it by the shoulders, the risk being, amid the intense pain, that the membrane of their intestine will tear, causing death. Or their head can be submerged in a tub of water until they are on the verge of drowning. Or a high-pressure water hose might be pushed into the mouth and another inserted up the anus. Or electrodes attached, one to the penis, the other to the inside of the cheek, each delivering 220 volts, will freeze the body in spasms of pain. The muscles lock. The jaws feel soldered shut. Geometric shapes, red against black, black against red, flash against the eyelids. The prisoner passes out but after they regain consciousness the shock treatment leaves no physical mark, as if it had never happened.

In the end, it's not important if an interrogation suspect has information or not. The goal is the subjugation of the individual and, by extension, their village or city, or the whole country. Some prisoners are driven into the woods following torture. They are told they're free to go and when they leave the van they're shot in the back for trying to escape. Others are flown by helicopter to a point above their village and then pushed out of the open doors to land among their people.

After days of questioning, Lacaton is released with no evidence connecting him to the FLN. The police drive him to a farm owned by a settler and fling him half-conscious into a pigsty, leaving him to crawl out of the slurry.

He returns to the hospital but the man is clearly suffering. He was always kind and well mannered but many times now he erupts into a fit of rage at a nurse over some minor incident, his face red, the spittle flying. One morning you find him crying in his office. Two months after coming back to work, he quits the hospital and leaves Blida altogether.

—

The horror grows. Hundreds of thousands of Algerians living near the Atlas Mountains, where the FLN are strong, are forcibly evicted from their homes. They are transported to resettlement camps ringed with barbed wire and their villages declared forbidden zones, the surrounding woodlands set ablaze. Anyone found there will be shot dead as a rebel. In response, the FLN call for Algerians to take up 'sticks, pitchforks, axes, sickles and knives' against the settlers: 'No pity, no quarter!'

The first major attack by the FLN against Europeans takes place in August, in the port town of Philippeville. A crowd of Algerians surges on to the streets, hurling grenades into cafes, dragging motorists from their cars and hacking them to death. The violence spreads to El-Halia, a nearby mining town. One morning, without warning, a mob forms. It goes from house to house, burning buildings, breaking down doors, and taking lives. In one family alone, an eleven-year-old girl has her throat slit open and her 73-year-old grandmother is stabbed to death. The father is killed while in bed, his limbs hacked off, and the mother is disembowelled, her five-day-old baby stabbed and inserted into her opened belly. Seventy-one people are killed. French reprisals are indiscriminate. For two hours, troops move through the town turning automatic fire on anyone they find. Prisoners are taken into the local football stadium where they are mowed down by a row of machine guns. The dead number in the thousands. There are so many corpses they have to be scooped up by bulldozer to be buried in a mass grave.

—

The fighting haunts your thoughts. When you wake up for another day on the ward, your head is already unquiet. You picture yourself back in Battalion 5 during the war. Slogging through gloomy pine forests in southern France, besieged by German mortar rounds and the regiment's artillery supplies running low. Dodging through the trees. Desperate to stay safe. You volunteer to lead a group carrying ammunition to the forward positions. The thought – 'keep down, stay alive' – is still running through your head when you are caught by a blast. There is a flash of light then everything turns starlit black. Then red. Then soft nothing. Afterwards, shapeless days of waking pain and morphine hallucinations, the latter preferable to the former, even though they are liable to slide into nightmares of writhing bodies and melding flesh, and the scent of liquorice which stays with you long after the grotesque visions themselves have faded.

—

Every time you take the car out, there seem to be new roadblocks in Blida. The sight of the settlers manning these barriers, self-appointed guardians of Western values, makes you furious. Yesterday afternoon, driving home, the placing of a new barricade up ahead left you so maddened that you pushed your foot down hard on the accelerator, and sped directly at the barrier, savouring the settlers' panicked response, the men unsure whether to raise their rifles at you or dive out of the way. At the last minute, you came to a noisy halt, rolled down the window, and nonchalantly handed your papers to them like nothing was amiss.

The bitter pleasure of the incident provides only a minor distraction from the unravelling of life taking place around you. A new patient comes to see you, complaining of what he calls 'fits of madness'. R is French, a police inspector, big-bellied, and short of breath by the time he's made it through the afternoon heat to reach your office. By nature, he is boorish and bullying. He's used to getting his own way in the police station and expects the same deference outside it. 'As soon as someone crosses me, I want to hit them, even for nothing at all,' he says, wiping the film of sweat from his forehead with a stained handkerchief. 'I say to myself, "If I had you for a few hours, my fine fellow, you wouldn't look so clever afterwards."'

He hates loud noise and, when his young children make a racket at home, he beats them heavily, even the twenty-month-old infant. Last week, as he was hitting the seven-year-old boy, his wife grabbed his arm and begged him to stop. Immediately he turned on her. R tied her to a chair and began to beat her 'black and blue', yelling, 'I'll teach you who's master of this house.' These fits of madness have intensified since 'the present troubles' began, says R, meaning the war. 'The fact is nowadays we have to work like troopers.' At his station, R is in charge of interrogations. The work is ugly, he says, but it's a necessary job. And his nostrils flare with pride as he describes what it takes to beat a confession out of a prisoner.

'By God, you don't know what it's like, doctor. Sometimes I'm at it for ten hours at a stretch,' he says, smothering his face again with the handkerchief. 'We take it in turns but each chap thinks he's going to get the information at any minute and get the honour and glory. It's a question of personal success. You see, you're competing with the others. You have to know when to lay it on or off. You have to have a flair for it.'

Unless you interrupt him, you suspect R might talk in this manner all morning, a connoisseur of the interrogation room, blithely detailing how best to 'soften up' a prisoner and why he insists on handling every beating personally, even if 'in the end your fists are ruined'. R is disturbed by the intensity of his mood swings, but he has no desire to quit being a policeman. After talking to you at the hospital he goes back to the station to resume beating the prisoners. He wants your help to carry on torturing suspects without suffering the symptoms of a guilty conscience. It's a relief when, after just one more week, R fails to turn up for his appointment, and does not return.

———

This morning you shouted at Géronimi in front of the other interns. It was during your ward round. You were at the bedside of that pompous former customs official, who was taking the opportunity to hold court at great length. Across the man's bed Géronimi rolled his eyes ostentatiously. An intern beside you stifled a laugh. You began instantly to yell at Géronimi, for being so juvenile, threatening to throw him out of the hospital and finish his career before it had even started. Later, he came to your office, begging forgiveness. Forget it, you said, brusquely, because by then you were more angry at yourself, for having allowed the pressure of the war outside, and your own covert part in it, to affect you so obviously. Is this how Lacaton felt before he decided he couldn't take any more?

You have a particularly difficult appointment waiting for you this afternoon. Two Algerian teenagers, thirteen and fourteen years old, who have confessed to killing a French boy of the same age, a former friend. At three, the boys arrive at the hospital with a policeman. 'Doctor,' he says, 'are they quite mad?' The more accurate question, you think, is what does sanity look like after two years of war?

The thirteen-year-old is first into your office. He perches on the edge of the seat, small and skinny inside an oversized shirt. The French boy was their friend from school, he says. His father was in a militia and he said Muslims should have their throats cut. But the boys still played together. Every Thursday they took their catapults and carried out target practice on the hill above town. One day they decided to kill him.

'Why?'

He looks up at you with a quick birdlike movement, narrow lips taut. 'Because the French want to kill all the Arabs. We can't kill big people. But we could kill ones like him, because he was the same age as us.'

'And yet you were friends?'

'Well then why do they want to kill us Muslims?'

First they considered throwing him in a ditch but that didn't seem like it would be effective. So the younger boy got a kitchen knife from home. He held their schoolfriend down and the fourteen-year-old stabbed him in the belly three times. The French boy started jerking like he was having a fit. The front of his shirt was red with blood. The Algerian boys left him in the scrubby grass on the hill. They went back into town. Back to their homes. 'It was sad,' says the boy flatly. But it had to be done.

The fourteen-year-old is next. The afternoon heat has left you parched and you wish you'd drunk some water before you had to hear more about the killing. This boy wears a smirk and the ghost of a moustache. He gazes about himself when he comes in, taking the measure of the scuffed walls, the desk stacked with patients' files, the doctor in his white coat sitting across from him.

You ask him why he stabbed his friend and he replies with a question. 'You know about the Rivet business? Well, two of my family were killed then.' Rivet is a village near Algiers. A settler militia came at night a few months ago and dragged away forty men. They killed them all. Afterwards no one was arrested. 'Has any European ever been jailed for killing an Algerian? No. And yet they kill us every day. And we're the only ones in prison. Can you explain that to me?'

'But is that a reason to kill your friend?'

'Well, I did kill him. So that's all there is to it.'

After the fourteen-year-old has gone, you fetch yourself some water. The carafe has been sitting out in the sun. The water is warm and silty with dust. In your case notes, you write, 'A whole generation of Algerians, steeped in wanton, generalized homicide with all the psycho-affective consequences that this entails, will be the human legacy of France in Algeria.'

3

1956

For months Blida has been wrapped in a stifling heat. The days are airless. The nights heavy and thick. Bencherchali arranges for a group of FLN fighters to come to the hospital after dark. Bringing them here is risky. But after Lacaton's arrest you're more determined than ever to fight back against the French. Besides, you're not alone in your efforts. Azoulay often helps to smuggle the fighters into the building and, once they're inside, you can also rely on the nurses, who are locally recruited Muslims, to be supportive. The same goes for the patients, who take offence when French soldiers enter the wards by day, and are content to turn a blind eye to the unexplained presence of an Arab combatant at night. Even so, it's better to keep the window shut in the small meeting room where you've assembled them, despite the oppressive temperature. The FLN leadership have sent instructions for you to coach the men to 'discipline their minds'. They're so nervous that they're giving themselves away before they can plant a bomb or stage an ambush. So, under cover of darkness, you instruct these six men on how to leave a bomb in a cafe or a shop without calling attention to themselves. Walk languidly. Don't run. Don't look back. 'Try not to sweat,' you say, and there is choking laughter in the sweltering room.

How has it come to this, you reflect later that night, as you walk back across the hospital grounds to your house. Even at the start of the war you could not have envisaged yourself here, training guerrillas. Look at these young men. They are boys really. Not much older than you and Joby were when you'd wander out beyond Fort-de-France, down a haphazard path through the rainforest to a waterfall, to leap from the top of the cataract into the water below, consumed by joy. Instead, for these boys, ordinary life means lessons in how to avoid capture and torture. What is taking place in this country is horrifying.

But however much you abhor the loss of life, you're also convinced of the rightness of the nationalist cause. The promise of the colonizer is that they will bring progress and order to the conquered. But the reality is just the nightmare of killing carried out in the name of civilization. For all their claims to a higher rationality, it's Europe that has brought the breath of unreason to this country. In Martinique, in France, in Algeria, the same circumstances replay themselves: the misfortune of the coloured man is to have been enslaved. The misfortune of the white man is to be the enslaver, robbed of his humanity by his own actions. What reigns now, you write in your journal, is a bloody, pitiless atmosphere, the generalization of inhuman practices. You have the sense that you are witnessing a veritable apocalypse.

You shut the journal, return it to the drawer of your desk, and begin a letter.

Dear Joby

Colonialism is not a thinking machine, nor a body endowed with reasoning faculties. It is violence in its natural state, and it will only yield when confronted with greater violence. When it's wielded in aid of resistance, violence is a cleansing force. It frees the native from his inferiority complex and from his despair and inaction; it makes him fearless and restores his self-respect. It is an act of rebirth that brings forth the creation of new men.

Even before you have finished the letter, you rip it up. You have the feeling it's no longer safe to express your thoughts openly.

Géronimi has cousins in the police force. He has heard that the hospital is an increasing target of scrutiny. Before long it will be impossible for FLN fighters to come and go as they have done. Better not to write anything incriminating. The security forces might already be opening the mail.

—

A major raid on the hospital is coming. It will take place any day now, says Géronimi. On his cousins' advice, he has already made plans to leave for Paris. When the raid happens, he says, you and Azoulay will be arrested and the hospital purged of any suspected FLN collaborators. Huyghe and his allies will doubtless be pleased to see the back of the Arab Doctor, you think. You imagine soldiers sweeping through the corridors. Filing cabinets torn open and case notes scattered. Patients questioned and staff led away. And the windowless interrogation room that awaits you at a police station.

As word of the raid spreads, a fearful mood descends on your wards, where nationalist support is widespread among the staff. You pass hushed conversations in corridors. Nurses arrive for work red-eyed and tearful. Some of the young men say they will go into the mountains and join the FLN. A number of the interns plan to take the same course as Géronimi and flee the country. You have been trying to call Bencherchali but his phone rings out. Maybe he's gone to ground. Or perhaps he's already been arrested.

For some time now you've been considering leaving Blida and going to Tunisia, the FLN's capital in exile, where you can work openly for the nationalist cause. You're tired of creeping around in the shadows. The battle against France is now a revolution. You will fight for it with all you have.

Beyond the hospital walls, the town is in the grip of a nationwide general strike called by the FLN. With the shops and cafes closed, groups of Arab men loiter on the streets, eyes following any unfamiliar people or cars passing through their neighbourhood. In the European section of the town, the settler militias have increased their roadblocks and checkpoints again.

A letter arrives, unsigned, at your house: 'Fanon, you are a traitor to France. We'll string you up. We'll slit your throat and cut off your balls. We're coming for you.'

You are at the hospital later that morning when one of the nurses comes to find you in the day clinic. She is shaking so badly she can hardly speak but you've seen enough people in the same state of shock to have a good idea of what's happened. You run all the way through the grounds, past the tropical gardens and the whitewashed pavilions, until you reach your house. As you suspected, it has been bombed. The front windows are shattered and the walls blackened and chipped with the blast. But the building is still largely intact which means that, rather than a murder attempt, the attack was probably intended as another warning.

The fact of being targeted like this doesn't scare you. You have seen real conflict before in France. You know what it is to fight and even to be wounded in defence of your beliefs. All the same, you feel saddened and dazed as you walk into the living room and look around at the charred furniture and the scorched books. Shattered glass crunching beneath your feet, glimmering like ice, like snow. It's time to go.

Your hand is still trembling when you return to your office and write to the Resident Minister in Algiers.

Monsieur le Ministre

For almost three years, I have put myself totally at the service of this nation and the people who live in it. I have spared neither enthusiasm nor effort. There is not one bit of energy which has not been directed toward the cause of creating a more livable world.

But what matters the enthusiasm and the care of one man if daily the truth is hidden by lies, cowardice, and contempt for mankind? What is the value of good intentions if their realization is made impossible by lack of spirit, sterility of ideas, and hatred for the people?

If psychiatry is a medical technique which aspires to allow man to cease being alienated from his environment, I owe it to myself to assert that the Arab, who is permanently alienated in his own country, lives in a state of absolute depersonalization.

For these reasons, I have the honour of asking you to accept my resignation and to bring my mission in Algeria to an end.

Respectfully

Dr Frantz Fanon

The response comes a week later, marked 'Letter of Expulsion'.

Dr Fanon

In consequence of your status as a foreign resident and your association with undesirable elements within the nation, I write to inform you that you are formally required to depart from the state of Algeria.

In accordance with Prefectoral Decree no. 3734-UR, you have forty-eight hours to leave Algerian territory or face arrest.

Faithfully

Resident Minister

You leave the following morning, packing your clothes and the remaining undamaged books into the boot of the Simca. In advance of the raid which might come at any time – tomorrow, next week, even this afternoon – many of your staff are leaving too, slipping away without announcing their departure. Into the mountains or out of the country. You bid a brief, constrained farewell to Géronimi while one of his cousins hovers impatiently nearby, waiting to drive him to the airport. Then, with a catch in your throat, you say goodbye to Azoulay. He is planning to join you in Tunisia but you are travelling singly to avoid the possibility of being arrested at the same time. You shake his hand and then throw your arm over his shoulder, embracing him tightly, his face stricken as you turn away and head out of the grounds.

The drive east takes you across the same dry land that you travelled through when you first arrived three years ago. Olive trees with their twisted trunks. Mountains rising pale and fine on the horizon. It strikes you how little of this country you've seen during your time here. Yet you are prepared to risk arrest and even death for it. It is not the place but the people and the principle they're fighting for that has captivated you. The freedom not to be a prisoner of history. In France, in Martinique, to be a coloured man is to be heir to the inevitable truth of your own inferiority. Here, in a country that remains foreign to you in many ways, you've discovered the lie in that notion. Freedom can be seized. The way ahead is mutable. You turn on the wipers to clear the dust and insects from the windscreen. Through the smeared glass, the low orange light of the afternoon sun fills the car. Roll down the window a notch. Let a breeze in. The dust motes stir. In front of you, all is unfolding. All is in motion. That which seems solid might melt into air.

There Are Other Worlds

When I was two years old, my family moved from London, where I was born, to Accra, Ghana. We lived there for three years – not very long – but enough time for Ghana, through my child's eyes, to take on the heightened reality of a dream. Even today I think of the huge jars of palm nut oil, glowing cadmium orange, sold by women at the side of the road. And the open drains at the edge of the pavement, their entropic scent and the terror of falling into the stream of iridescent green slurry that ran through them. The moon after dark, large and low, brilliant as a star, its light reflecting in our eyes, turning our pupils silver, bright and glowing. At dusk one evening I looked up and saw a bat flying overhead. I spotted another, and more, and then the sky was filled with them, flapping ungainly, swarming into the gathering darkness to feed on heedless insects.

Returning to London was disconcerting. It was the mid-1970s and Britain seemed to be living in the past, fixated on memories of war and empire. The Africa that existed on TV shows and in playground games was nowhere I recognized. It was the imperial continent of H. Rider Haggard, Edgar Rice Burroughs and Michael Caine in *Zulu*: perpetually savage and primitive, untouched by progress, the antithesis of Western civilization. Everyone was watching *Roots*, and the mornings after each new episode in the playground were filled with shouts of 'Kunta Kinte!' As the historian Hugh Trevor-Roper had written a decade earlier, 'Perhaps in the future there will be some African history to teach. But at the present there is none, or very little; there is only the history of Europeans in Africa. The rest is largely darkness . . . The unedifying gyrations of barbarous tribes in picturesque but irrelevant corners of the globe.'

It was superheroes that came to my rescue. The British-made comics at my local newsagent were dour fare, war stories printed on coarse paper with names like *Death Patrol* and *Fight or Die!* By comparison, the American superhero comic books I loved were slick to the touch and audaciously imaginative. They were also master-classes in social allegory, and though I wouldn't have put it in those terms at the time, I had already started reading them with that per-spective in mind. For instance, the members of the X-Men were gifted with fantastic powers. They could read minds or walk through walls or call lightning down from the skies. But as mutants, a genetic race apart from ordinary humans, they were feared and despised by the very people they sought to protect. The X-Men were born dif-ferent. Prejudice made them outsiders. In their experience of the world, I saw something of my own.

By eight years old, my bedroom floor was piled deep with copies of Marvel comic books: *Moon Knight*, *Warlock*, *Star-Lord*, *Ghost Rider*. And most of all, *The Black Panther*. I first discovered him in a reprint of *Fantastic Four* #52, the July 1966 issue in which he made his debut. The Fantastic Four are invited to visit the isolated African kingdom of Wakanda by T'Challa, the nation's young prince. The country proves to be an African Shangri-La, where science and spirituality comfort-ably coexist, with T'challa the heir to powers of superhuman strength and agility conferred by his ancestral connection to Bast, the powerful panther god. T'Challa cuts a cosmopolitan figure. He has the looks of Sidney Poitier, the erudition of a man schooled at 'the best universities of both hemispheres', and a sensualist's eye for interior decor. Invited into his groovy bachelor apartment, the Four can only gape: 'Wow! Wotta pad! I'll bet even Hugh Hefner couldn't improve on this layout!'

The apparent paradox of a hyper-advanced nation in 'the heart of the jungle' baffles the group. 'How does some refugee from a Tarzan movie lay his hands on this kinda gizmo?' they ask, when T'Challa gives them a ride in a noiseless Wakandan aircraft powered by magnetic waves. Marvel superheroes tended to have a signal vulnerability. Iron Man's impenetrable armour shielded a weak heart. The Hulk was a scientist given to transforming into an uncontrollable id monster. The Fantastic Four were an extended family whose bonds were weakened by constant bickering. The Black Panther was different. What should have been his biggest weakness – his origin in a seemingly backward country – was his greatest strength. And where many comics offered sympathetic allegories about prejudice and otherness, the Panther storylines often dispensed with subtext altogether. T'Challa's enemies were colonialists and racist mercenaries. He even travelled to the Deep South and fought the Ku Klux Klan in a memorable story arc that reached its climax with the hero bound to a burning cross.

Over time, my exposure to the Panther comics emboldened me. Amid the pervasive racism of the 1970s, being Black could often feel like a burden. The Panther showed the opposite was true.

That's not to say the comics were above criticism. The Black Panther was created by Marvel Comics visionaries Stan Lee and Jack Kirby, the prolific writer–artist duo responsible for the likes of Iron Man, the Hulk, the Avengers and the X-Men. It was Lee and Kirby who introduced to comics the premise of the hero as flawed outsider – an idea that may have been inspired by their own background as the Depression-era children of Jewish immigrants. With their eyes on the turbulent social currents of the 1960s, the duo also pioneered a character-driven, naturalistic style that revolutionized comics by addressing contemporary topics such as drugs and the Vietnam War. But they were less sure-footed on the subject of race.

The Panther's first appearance came at the height of the civil rights struggle, just one year on from the Selma Marches and the signing of the Voting Rights Act in 1965. Four months after the character's debut, Bobby Seale and Huey Newton formed the Black Panther Party. The choice of name was coincidental but Lee and Kirby were anxious to avoid any connection to radical politics. Their hero was briefly renamed the Black Leopard, with T'Challa offering an awkward justification for the change: 'I neither condemn nor condone those who have taken up the name – but T'Challa is a law unto himself.' Later the Panther, his original name restored, was given a solo comic with the ill-judged title of *Jungle Action*. His nemesis in this series was a bestial Wakandan in a gorilla suit called Man-Ape.

Despite these missteps, the Panther comics had a particular timeliness. T'Challa's glorious homeland of Wakanda – a nation of wealth and learning that had never been colonized – spoke to the fascination with, and longing for, independence-era Africa shared by a generation of African American artists and activists in the 1960s, including Nina Simone, Maya Angelou, Eldridge Cleaver and W. E. B. Du Bois, all of whom emigrated to the continent during that decade. Kirby drew Wakanda as a dazzling vista of soaring towers and glass domes, but also a place that remained tied to its spiritual roots. His images recall the paintings of Aaron Douglas, the leading visual artist of the Harlem Renaissance, who conjured a stylized, romantic Africa of regal sphinxes and elegant pyramids. An Africa of beauty and boundless possibility: 'Transcendentally material, mystically objective. Earthy. Spiritually earthy. Dynamic.'

The Panther was the first Black superhero to be featured in a mainstream American comic. Others followed through the 1970s, although none possessed the inventiveness of T'Challa. Most either came with laboured reference to their racial identity – Black Lightning, Black Goliath, Black Racer – or else they were stuck fighting jive-talking drug-pushers in the ghetto, like Luke Cage and the Falcon. As an African, rather than an American, the Panther was allowed to transcend the urban everyday and to embrace instead the speculative and the mythic. By the late 1970s, his adventures had become wildly cosmic. He fought time travellers and aliens and went on a quest to find the lost treasure of King Solomon. In a vision, he journeyed into outer space, watching in awe as 'galaxies drift like cosmic ghosts, and stars and planets wheel in lonely majesty'.

The Panther walked between the worlds of realism and fantasy with an ease that confounded even his own creators – and which spoke to W. E. B. Du Bois's powerful notion of 'double consciousness'. Du Bois, the great civil rights scholar and activist, had coined the term more than half a century earlier to describe the disquieting experience of living as a Black person physically within and psychologically outside white society. 'It is a peculiar sensation, this sense of always looking at one's self through the eyes of others, of measuring one's soul by the tape of a world that looks on in amused contempt and pity.' For Du Bois, writing in 1897, double consciousness was bitter proof that Black people were doomed to spend their lives in embodied alienation. The Panther showed how the idea could also be understood as a gift – a superpower of sorts – that enables Black people to move freely between parallel, coexisting truths and realities. It was a prompt for us to imagine ourselves on our own terms, with all the fierce dreaming we might summon to that task.

It can be argued here that the Panther's journey into increasingly esoteric territory represented a step back from the grappling with racism which had made the comic so special. But it seems to me that Kirby's change of direction didn't mark a retreat from questions of race. Rather, it offered a thrilling vindication of the fantastical as a site of liberation. An embrace of the possibility of alternative worlds. A territory within which Black people can assert the simple and fraught nature of their aliveness.

—

The Black Panther's forays into the other-worldly put him into unanticipated company with Sun Ra, the mystic jazz musician and self-styled 'traveller of the spaceways'. Ra was born Herman Poole Blount, in 1914, Birmingham, Alabama, named after Black Herman, a vaude-ville performer who billed himself as the 'world's greatest Negro magician'. A gifted pianist from childhood, he was composing his own music by the age of eleven and was playing with adult bands in his teens. Jailed for being a conscientious objector during the Second World War, he was told by the judge at his trial, 'I've never seen a nigger like you before.' Blount replied, 'No, and you never will again.'

In the early 1950s, Blount sequestered himself in Chicago with a huge library of books on magic, the occult and Egyptology. By the time he emerged, he had changed his name to Le Sony'r Ra, or Sun Ra for short, after the Egyptian god of the sun, and claimed to have been abducted from Earth as a child and raised by aliens on Saturn.

Ra's decades-long adherence to this personal mythology, along with his air of serene bemusement and his extravagant robes and headdresses, led to his popular image as a colourful eccentric. But it's more instructive to set him within a lineage of self-fashioned African American seers dating back to the nineteenth century. Fig-ures like Jarena Lee, the first Black female preacher in the United

States, who was said to have gifts of healing and clairvoyance. Or Rebecca Cox Jackson, the Shaker mystic, who left her husband and six children after a religious awakening, becoming an itinerant preacher and eventually the leader of her own sisterhood of Black Shakers. In her spiritual autobiography, *Gifts of Power*, Jackson described developing extraordinary skills, including the ability to read minds, divine the future and travel 'between the living and the dead'. Or the author and folklorist Zora Neale Hurston, who travelled to Haiti in the 1930s and was initiated into the religious practices of Vodou. Undergoing secret rites, Hurston had a vision in which, as she wrote, 'I strode across the heavens with lightning flashing from under my feet, and grumbling thunder following in my wake.'

Whether Sun Ra's claim to alien abduction was fabulism or extraordinary fact, it enabled him to look, with an outsider's perspective, on an America warped by racial division and the tensions of the Cold War. 'I am strange,' he wrote in a poem. 'I am not a part of the world which hates / and the world which destroys.' In the 1960s, as America and the Soviets competed to put a man on the moon, Ra argued that Black people should leave behind the corrupt terrain of planet Earth and embrace an 'altered destiny' in the stars. The theme of interstellar escape ran consistently through his songs: 'Astro Black', 'Door of the Cosmos', 'Next Stop Mars', 'We Travel the Space Ways'. The mysterious synthesizer sounds and swirling violins on 'There Are Other Worlds (They Have Not Told You Of)' suggest celestial searching, celestial yearning. Amid an orchestral swell, voices chant in whispers: 'There are other worlds they haven't told you of.' Then the chanting grows louder and more insistent: 'They wish to speak to you.'

Ra's faith in cosmic travel put him at odds with other prominent African American figures of the period, who saw the space race as a distraction from the more urgent struggles of the civil rights era.

The day before the Apollo 11 moon launch on 16 July 1969, Ralph Abernathy, Martin Luther King's successor as head of the Southern Christian Leadership Conference, led a march of poor Black families, complete with wagons drawn by mules, to the fence of Cape Kennedy in Florida. Carrying signs that read 'Rockets or Rickets' and 'Moonshots Breed Malnutrition', the marchers had gathered, said Abernathy, to protest against the 'distorted sense of national priorities' behind the $25 billion moon programme. With the giant Saturn V rocket looming behind him, Abernathy addressed the march. 'We may go on from this day to Mars and to Jupiter and even to the heavens beyond, but as long as racism, poverty and hunger and war prevail on the Earth, we as a civilized nation have failed.'

Others concurred. At a Stevie Wonder concert in Harlem the next day, mention of the lunar module brought boos from the crowd. Activist poet Amiri Baraka decried the Western technology that took humans into space even as it 'kills both plants & animals, poisons the air & degenerates or enslaves man'. Singer Gil Scott-Heron was equally scathing on his track 'Whitey on the Moon': 'The man just upped my rent last night / Cause whitey's on the moon / No hot water, no toilets, no lights / But whitey's on the moon.'

Ra, who'd grown up amid the poverty and discrimination of the Jim Crow South, shared the goals of the civil rights movement. But he continued to keep his head turned skyward. In the 1974 science fiction film *Space is the Place*, he starred as an extraterrestrial prophet come to lead America's Black people away from Earth. Stepping down from his spaceship in Oakland to recruit volunteers, his character is initially met with scepticism. 'How do we know you for real?' scoff the kids at a youth centre, taking in his shimmering robe and gold platform boots. But Ra sets them right. 'I'm not real, I'm just like you. You don't exist in this society. If you did, your people wouldn't be seeking equal rights. You're not real. If you were, you'd have some status among the nations of the world. So we're both myths. I do not come to you as a reality, I come to you as a myth because that's what Black people are, myths.' In the film's closing scene, Ra and a group of teenagers fly off in his spaceship. Behind them, the Earth, fatally riven by conflict and prejudice, finally explodes, its shattered pieces spinning into space, until all that remains is darkness.

Despite the film's apocalyptic ending, Ra's broader message was an optimistic one. For Black people, the future lay beyond West or East, beyond science and technology and myths of progress. Look up and see. Other worlds are waiting.

———

Long before Herman Blount reinvented himself as Sun Ra, Black people were already devising means of escape from America. Under chattel slavery, the search for freedom took many forms, not all of them literal. Enslaved people challenged their captivity through myriad acts of trickery, evasion and spiritual invocation. Some practised strategies of quiet refusal: feigning illness, misplacing tools, killing livestock or poisoning crops. Others found strength in the pursuit of forbidden spiritual beliefs, invoking ancient gods through secret signs and symbols. Quilts were stitched in red-and-white thread in praise of Shango, the powerful Yoruba deity of thunder and lightning. Or decorated with snake motifs for Damballah, the Vodou god of fertility. Double meanings were smuggled into spirituals: ostensibly Christian narratives of suffering and redemption, like 'Wade in the Water' and 'Steal Away Jesus', instructed listeners to stay alert for how or when to flee the plantation: 'Steal away, steal away, steal away to Jesus! / Steal away, steal away home, I ain't got long to stay here.'

Many tried to physically flee, devising ingenious means to confound their captors. They crossed rivers to put the dogs off their scent, or sprinkled black pepper in their socks and ran without their shoes to make the animals sneeze. Some fugitives spent years hiding out close to the very plantations they'd escaped from – in tracts of uncultivated land like the Great Dismal Swamp which ran through Virginia and North Carolina – where thousands of runaways sought shelter during the decades before abolition in 1865.

There were those, too, that hid in plain sight. Escape could be a matter of performance, an illusion of dress and deportment. One runaway from North Carolina, who looked like 'a white man . . . His eyes are blue, his hair very straight', escaped to Washington where he sought 'to pass as a free man'. Even dark-skinned people could pull off this trick. It was just a matter of dressing the part. Sam, 'an artful fellow', managed to walk free from Livingston, Alabama, by exchanging drab cottons for a black cashmere overcoat and silver huntsman's watch worn with a swaggering air of self-confidence. In 1848, Ellen and William Craft, an enslaved couple from Macon, Georgia, travelled north by train and steamboat all the way to freedom in Philadelphia, with the light-skinned Ellen passing as a white man, in top hat and trousers, her face partially obscured by bandages, and William posing as her enslaved valet.

Escape could also be a conjuring act. In March 1849, Henry Brown, an enslaved man in Richmond, Virginia, had himself mailed to freedom. His audacious scheme was born of despair. Brown had worked for eighteen years in a tobacco factory, supervised by a violent and vindictive overseer. In 1848, his pregnant wife and three children were sold to a plantation in North Carolina. With nothing to lose, Brown conceived his plan. As he wrote later, 'The idea suddenly flashed across my mind of shutting myself up in a box, and getting myself conveyed as dry goods to a free state.'

With the help of a free Black man and a sympathetic white shoe-maker, Brown was nailed into a pine crate measuring '3 feet long, 2 ft 8 inches deep, and 23½ inches wide'. It was marked as dry goods and addressed to the Pennsylvania Anti-Slavery Society office in Philadelphia. The box was lined with baize and Brown squeezed inside it, carrying only a bladder of water and a few biscuits. He travelled 350 miles across country by wagon, train, steamboat and ferry. The journey was hazardous. On several occasions the crate was left turned upside down, causing the blood to pool in Brown's head, his eyes 'swelling as if they would burst from their sockets'. At another staging point, it was tossed off a wagon: landing headfirst, Brown felt his neck 'give a crack, as if it had been snapped asunder'. Eventually, after twenty-seven hours in transit, he was delivered to safety. To the group of four abolitionists anxiously clustered around the crate, he managed a debonair greeting: 'How'd you do, gentlemen?'

By accomplishing one of the most spectacular escapes in the era of slavery, Brown became a celebrated figure in abolitionist circles. Leaving America for England and eventually settling in Canada, he found fame as a popular entertainer, taking on the roles of singer, actor, playwright, magician, mesmerist and escapologist under the stage name Henry 'Box' Brown. He became an artist of the self, free to shift his form at will, constrained only by the limits of his imagination.

———

At the stroke of midnight on 24 October 1964, a soldier lit a huge copper torch in Lusaka's Independence Stadium to celebrate the birth of the newly independent nation of Zambia. The Union Jack was lowered, bringing British rule of Northern Rhodesia to an end, and ceding power to the republic under its first leader, President Kenneth Kaunda. Fireworks exploded overhead. Cheers filled the crowded arena. Interviewed outside the stadium by *TIME* magazine, Edward Mukuka Nkoloso, a 45-year-old high-school physics teacher, was in a less celebratory mood. 'If I had had my way,' he said, 'Zambia would have been born with the blast of a rocket being launched into space.'

Nkoloso was the director of his own, self-titled National Academy of Science, Space Research and Philosophy. The space race between America and the Soviets was accelerating, and he insisted it was time for Africa to enter the fray. 'My spacemen are ready. I'll have my first Zambian astronaut on the moon by 1965.'

For the international press, gathered in Lusaka to cover the independence ceremony, Nkoloso and his amateur space programme made for a bizarre, comic side-story. 'Nkoloso is training twelve Zambian astronauts, including a curvaceous 16-year-old girl, by spinning them around a tree in an oil drum and teaching them to walk on their hands, "the only way humans can walk on the moon," ' said *TIME*. At the academy's training facility, an abandoned farmhouse seven miles outside Lusaka, Reuters filmed Nkoloso drilling the young recruits he had named his 'afronauts'. In the film, he wears a shirt and tie, a British Army-style battle helmet and a dark cape with gilt piping. The afronauts jump up and down on the spot. They march in a line and perform sit-ups. One of them is squeezed into a forty-gallon oil drum and rolled down a hill. 'This gives them the feeling of rushing through space,' Nkoloso tells the camera. In an exercise meant to simulate a watery landing, the same oil drum is pushed into a river while the unhappy-looking afronaut inside tries to remain afloat.

The NASSRP's rocket was a ten-foot-long cylinder made of

aluminium and copper. It had a round viewing hole in one side and no obvious means of propulsion. Nkoloso maintained he had devised his own 'Mulolo' launch system, in place of a conventional engine. 'Mulolo is the word for swinging. We have tied ropes to tall trees and then swung our astronauts slowly out into space.' So far, he admitted, they had achieved a distance of ten yards. By lengthening the rope, they planned to go further. Another, more sophisticated power system was also in development but its details were under wraps. 'Turbulent propulsion! Yes please, I can say no more at the present time. National prestige is involved. We must beat Russia and America to the moon. What they can do, we can do also.'

Nkoloso's star recruit was Matha Mwamba, the 'curvaceous 16-year-old' of the *TIME* report. She also featured in the Reuters interview, dressed in an army fatigue jacket and patterned skirt. Mwamba was training for a solo trip to Mars, to be accompanied on the flight by her ten cats. 'Partly, they are to provide her with companionship on the long journey. But primarily they are technological accessories,' explained Nkoloso. 'When she arrives on Mars she will open the door of the rocket and drop the cats on the ground. If they survive, she will then see that Mars is fit for human habitation.' Throughout the interview, Nkoloso seemed preoccupied by the threat of foreign forces at work within the country. 'I have known for a long time that Russian spies are operating in Zambia. Yes, and American spies are all over town too. They are all trying to capture Matha and the cats. They want our space secrets. I feel the Zambian government should help now if we are to become controllers of the Seventh Heaven.'

On camera, Nkoloso appears painfully oblivious to the Reuters reporter's condescending manner. Behind him, in the supposed hub of the Zambian space programme, a woman ambles by carrying a shopping bag. Children play in the shade of the farmhouse roof. A VW Beetle loiters beneath a tree. 'What do you think the reaction of the superpowers will be to Zambia joining the space race?' asks the reporter. And he replies, 'Yes please. They'll only be surprised. They will underestimate our resources and intelligence. I am sure we are catching them.' After the interview ends, the journalist speaks directly to camera, with Nkoloso blinking beside him. 'To most Zambians, these people are just a bunch of crackpots. And from what I've seen here, I'm inclined to agree.'

Unsurprisingly, Nkoloso's rocket never got off the ground. Government indifference, a lack of funding, and presumably the failure to devise a breakthrough propulsion system, all stymied the project. Even Nkoloso's afronauts abandoned him. Two of his recruits disappeared after a drinking spree. Matha Mwamba got pregnant and dropped out. 'They won't concentrate on space flight; there's too much love-making when they should be studying the moon,' lamented Nkoloso. The failure of the space programme was evidence, in the eyes of the press, of Africans' inability to make sense of advanced technology. It was proof of their essentially childlike nature. Nkoloso himself was a 'court jester'. He was 'Zambia's village idiot', an 'amiable lunatic'. Even today, you can go online and find footage of Nkoloso and his afronauts practising their star jumps on YouTube, their efforts framed in the same derisive tone as the 1964 reports: 'Zambia's Laughable Space Program' and 'The Most Insane Space Program. Ever!' Few people, then or now, appear to have looked further than a sensational headline. If they had, they might have discovered an altogether different, and more complex, story.

Nkoloso was born in 1919 in the north-east of Northern Rhodesia. He studied Latin, French and theology at a seminary with the aim of becoming a priest. Instead, the Second World War broke out and Nkoloso was drafted into the Signal Corps of the colonial army. He fought in Burma and Abyssinia and was promoted to sergeant. After the war, he became a government translator in Lusaka and seemed content to join the ranks of the Évolués, the city's European-ized urban elite. But a series of clashes with the colonial authorities over the following years precipitated a dramatic change in his outlook.

Shortly after settling in Lusaka, Nkoloso applied to open his own school, envisaging an academy that would specialize in science and equip pupils to meet the sophisticated challenges of the post-war era. His permit was turned down. He opened his institution anyway. He was prosecuted and the school was ordered shut.

In the mid-1950s, he became a travelling salesman for a pharmaceutical company. The job took him to Ndola, the heart of Northern Rhodesia's Copperbelt mining district, where Western companies exercised power over the territory with virtual impunity. He discovered that the graves of local people were being secretly dug up and moved to make space for mining operations. Appalled by what he saw, Nkoloso joined the United National Independence Party led by Kenneth Kaunda, the future president, and became known to the regional government as an agitator. After organizing a succession of strikes and walkouts among African workers, Nkoloso was jailed and tortured by the Northern Rhodesian police.

Prison only radicalized him further. The brutality of colonial rule demanded commensurate acts of shocking, provocative violence, he argued. Shortly before independence, in 1964, he broke into a mortuary with some UNIP comrades and stole the corpse of a white woman. Smearing the body with goat's blood, he dumped it on the floor of the whites-only bar of the Ridgeway Hotel in Lusaka and shouted at the horrified crowd, 'White men, your time is limited!

We have killed the wife of Prime Minister Welensky and we shall soon pounce on you!'

With his surreal act of protest, Nkoloso showed himself willing to go to startlingly transgressive lengths to bring attention to his goals. After independence, he was appointed President Kaunda's special representative at the African Liberation Centre, an office providing support to rebel organizations in neighbouring countries still under colonial rule, where he was welcomed as a respected veteran activist. His background as a seditionary raises the question of whether the space programme was also a kind of performance. One that was intended to disorient Western onlookers as he pursued more consequential ambitions.

A perceptive *New Yorker* essay by the Lusaka-born author Namwali Serpell suggests that, as well as rolling his afronauts down hills, Nkoloso was also drilling them in making bombs and preparing Molotov cocktails, as insurgents for UNIP. His recruits may, in some way, have been involved in the gruesome 1960 murder of a white British expatriate, Lilian Margaret Burton, whose car was stoned and set on fire by UNIP youth-wing activists while she was still behind the wheel.

Does this mean the space programme was straightforwardly a deception? An elaborate cover to recruit young fighters into the anti-colonialism movement? Possibly. But I suspect the truth is more nuanced.

Writing in the 1980s, the scholar Henry Louis Gates coined the term 'signifyin'' to describe the African American verbal strategy of subversive wordplay and indirect communication. To signify means to seem to speak about one thing while conveying a hidden meaning or subtext about another. It means parody and misdirection, the blurring of distinction between the literal and the metaphorical.

Gates traces the symbolic origins of signifyin' to the figure of the trickster, a recurring character in African mythology. The trickster is Esu-Elegbara in Yoruba belief; Legba in Benin; Anansi in Ghana. From Africa, the trickster was brought to the New World by enslaved people, where he took on many forms including the wise-cracking Br'er Rabbit and the sly and satiric Pompey, playing dumb to his (white) master in nineteenth-century folk tales:

Pompey, how do I look? the master asked.
O massa, mighty. You looks mighty.
What do you mean 'mighty', Pompey?
Why, massa, you looks noble.
What do you mean by 'noble'?
Why, suh, you looks just like a lion.
Why, Pompey, where have you ever seen a lion?
I saw one down in yonder field the other day, massa.
Pompey, you foolish fellow, that was a jackass.
Was it, massa? Well, suh, you looks just like him.

At its core, signifyin' is a form of resistance. Under colonialism in Africa or as enslaved people in the New World, Africans fought against their subjugation by mastering the master's tongue, turning it against him through folk tales and wordplay and, in the process, affirming their autonomy and their continued humanity.

Understood through the prism of signifyin', Nkoloso's space programme takes on a new resonance. In Zambia, the trickster is a wily hare called Kalulu, who delights in skewering the vanity of Lion and the pomposity of Elephant, his jungle peers. Kalulu is also a messenger deity, who stands at the spiritual crossroads between the worlds of gods and humans. He is always elusive, always on the move between the margins and the centre, adopting multiple identities and testing the social order through wit and cunning. Nkoloso is a Kalulu-like figure if there ever was one. His space programme cannot be ascribed to binary interpretation: politics versus play, a covert mission or an elaborate exercise in wishful thinking. It was both at once. Everything and more. An idealistic dream, an absurdist fantasy, a piece of performance art, a statement of Pan-African pride, a riposte to colonial power and a skewering of Western hubris.

In 1970, Nkoloso caught the attention of the foreign media again. An Associated Press report announced: 'The man who aspired to put Zambian astronauts on the moon has a new cause. He says African witch doctors deserve government support and should be encouraged to take their rightful place beside modern physicians. Mukuka Nkoloso does not practise witchcraft himself, although he admits having "a mystic vision" whenever he ponders the subject.'

The story was presented as more amiable irrationality. It was headlined: 'Support Your Witch Doctor, Zambian Says'. But read as another form of signifyin', Nkoloso's assertions reveal themselves as an argument for a decentring of knowledge. He rejects the correlation between Western science as progress and African spiritual practice as superstition. He makes a case for Africans to be seen not as figures outside history, but as heirs to a rich cosmology of myths and beliefs.

The same tactic was surely at play with the space programme. Nkoloso never had the means to reach the moon or Mars. But through his poly-vocal, many-faced performance, he insisted nevertheless on the freedom to imagine himself beyond the terrestrial. And on the right of Africans to have a voice in the space race and the fortunes of the planet. In the process, he highlighted the Western inability to conceive of African people as equals in matters of ambition and invention. He demonstrated that it was Western not African minds that were closed to new visions of progress and possibility.

———

Before European colonization, the various kingdoms of West and Central Africa were cosmopolitan cultures of wealth, artistry and sophistication. Some states, like Benin, were known for the dazzling skill of their craftspeople. Others, such as the Mali Empire, were famed for their wealth. When Mansa Musa, ruler of Mali, made a pilgrimage to Mecca in the 1320s, he did so with a lavishness that remains unsurpassed to this day. His caravan included sixty thousand attendants dressed in brocade and Persian silk, and eighty camels, each bearing three hundred pounds of gold, which he distributed to the poor along the course of his two-year journey.

African nations were not untroubled paradises. They were often highly stratified caste-based societies, whose wealth depended in part on the capture and enslavement of rival peoples. Imagine, nevertheless, the sense of loss at being seized from the continent and transported across the ocean to the New World. How great the depth of your sorrow must have been in knowing neither you, nor your descendants, would ever go home.

This yawning sense of loss became the catalyst for new myths across the African diaspora – stories of return and restitution in response to collective grief. One such is the legend of the flying Africans. In May 1803, seventy-five enslaved Africans, many of them belonging to the Igbo people of present-day Nigeria, staged a revolt on the schooner *York* as it neared America. The ship was bound for St Simons Island, on the south-east coast of Georgia. As it approached its destination, the captives rose up against the crew, killing some, forcing the rest overboard, and then running the vessel aground. Once on land, the Igbos were said by one eyewitness to have 'taken to the swamp'. Rather than risk being returned to captivity, they joined hands and walked into the water together in an act of mass suicide. But other accounts tell a different story. Instead of drowning themselves, it is said the Igbos raised up their arms, invoked their gods and took to the sky, soaring back home over the ocean.

In the wake of that original 1803 revolt, the tale of the flying Africans has been retold by generations of Black communities across the southern states of America and the Caribbean. Ceasar Grant, a former enslaved man from South Carolina, interviewed in the early 1900s, described seeing a group of Africans on a plantation who 'leaped up into the air with a great shout; and in a moment were gone, flying, like a flock of crows, over the field, over the fence, and over the top of the wood until they passed beyond the last rim of the world and disappeared in the sky like a handful of leaves'.

In 1980s Jamaica, Ishmael Webster, a descendant of enslaved Africans, told a researcher a story that had been handed down to him about escapees from a plantation: 'They couldn't stand the work when the taskmaster them flog them; and they get up and they just sing their language, and they clapping their hands – so – and they just stretch out, and them gone – so – right back. And they never come back.'

In the 1990s, the Detroit techno duo Drexciya conceived an alternative mythology around the Middle Passage. The duo, James Stinson and Gerald Donald, cultivated an air of mystery as musicians, concealing their own identities throughout the decade when they were actively releasing music. They rarely gave interviews. They never played live. And the records they produced together mapped out a compelling, mythic territory that merged the legacy of slavery and colonialism with the fable of a Black Atlantis.

Across a string of haunting concept albums, with titles like *Neptune's Lair* and *Harnessed the Storm*, they imagined a submarine realm populated by the descendants of pregnant African women thrown overboard from slave ships. The story was based on factual antecedents, like the case of the *Zong*, an eighteenth-century British slave ship whose captain had 132 sick or dying Africans thrown overboard so that he could collect the insurance money for 'property lost at sea'. What if, said the musicians, those murdered women's foetuses had learned to breathe through the embryonic fluid of their mothers' wombs, and were born adapted to life underwater? What if they survived and thrived, under the sea, and their children's children's children lived there still? Stinson and Donald imagined a sovereign state on the floor of the Atlantic Ocean, peopled by those water-breathing descendants – a glorious vision of how Black life might have flourished in Africa without the depredations of slavery.

In Derek Walcott's 'The Sea is History', the Atlantic seabed is a burial ground for lives lost during the slave trade. 'Exodus. / Bone soldered by coral to bone, / mosaics / mantled by the benediction of the shark's shadow.' But the same poem closes on an affirmatory note, envisaging the water as the site of life starting anew: 'and in the salt chuckle of rocks / with their sea pools, there was the sound / like a rumour without any echo / of History, really beginning.' Similarly, Drexciya grappled with the horror of the Middle Passage and found, on the seafloor, amid nautilus shells and corals, and the memory of the shackled and the drowned, the space to imagine new configurations of Black life and resistance.

For the most part, stories of Africans who can fly or breathe underwater are understood as folklore or fantasy: poetic evocations of the desire to escape from a state of oppression. But suppose instead these stories are more than just fiction. More than just superstition, or any of the other names used to dismiss beliefs that fall outside narratives of order, progress and science. Not fact exactly. But a form of refusal of the narrow parameters of Western rationalism. Even if they're not literally true, the power and the persistence of such legends come from the dazzling act of signifyin' that lies at their heart. The process of reaching. Of envisaging. The articulation of unbounded imagination and invention that is, in itself, an act of liberation. Here is inversion. Here is metamorphosis. The shackled take flight. A dream has the intensity to outshine waking life.

4

Malcolm X

I

Accra, Ghana, 10 May 1964

How will they come for you, you wonder, as the airplane touches down in Accra. Bullet, knife or bomb? Since you split from the Nation of Islam in March, the Messenger and his men have only grown more determined to take revenge. James 3X Shabazz calls you a hypocrite who deserves to die. Captain Joseph, at your own Temple No. 7 in Harlem, has ordered his men to bomb you in your car.

The plane door swings open on to cloying heat and the smell of fecundity. Picture gaudy flowers. Picture rich black earth. Walk across the baking tarmac into the terminal building crowded with people pushing trolleys teetering with suitcases, children at their feet, ceiling fans pushing ineffectually against the heat. Somehow, Julian Mayfield finds you amid the throng and guides you outside, past the gaggle of unlicensed taxi drivers calling for your custom. He stows your luggage in the boot of his yellow convertible Sprite and you drive together into the city, Julian pointing out the sights of the city with the pride of a local – Flagstaff House, Black Star Square, James-town Lighthouse – the roads gradually clogging up with traffic as you edge closer to the centre, women weaving between the becalmed cars carrying trays of deep-fried fish and plantain for sale.

Julian is an author and actor, and the unofficial leader of the small community of black Americans that have settled in Ghana since the country won independence seven years ago. As more countries in Africa gain their freedom, Kwame Nkrumah, the Ghanaian presi-dent, envisages nations coming together from across the continent to form a United States of Africa, a new global superpower. For Julian and his fellow exiles that's a more enticing prospect than staying in America, where all the marches and rallies and sit-ins of the past years have brought little change for black people.

Your eyes slide shut as Julian talks, absorbed in his own account of émigré life in Accra. You have been on the move for the past month, from Mecca to Nigeria and now Ghana, and you are bone-tired. These trips are supposed to be about building your future after the Nation. But it's also a way to keep moving ahead of the death threats that hound you.

Just a few months ago the idea that anyone in the Nation, let alone the Messenger himself, would be conspiring against you would have seemed inconceivable. Even after you were suspended and stripped of your duties, you were convinced you'd be back at Temple No. 7 as soon as you'd served your time. James 67X, your most trusted lieutenant at the mosque, was the one who set you straight. He called the house one evening, defying the Messenger's order for all Muslims to shun you. On the phone, a husky voice, and Betty passing the receiver to you, saying she couldn't make out who it was. You arranged to meet him later that night in the dark, picking him up in your Oldsmobile and driving out to Morningside Park. You did most of the talking, saying how you regretted the distance between you and Elijah Muhammad and what you'd do to set things right once you returned. James looked at you, shocked, from the passenger seat. 'Malcolm, you were seen in favour by Mr Muhammad. And I hope you will return to his favour,' he said. 'But no, you're not going back in the Nation. People are talking about killing you.'

Evening coming on. Sunlight plunging precipitously into equatorial night. You take a taxi to Julian's house, where he's holding a party in your honour. You are dressed casually in a white short-sleeved shirt and grey slacks, still sporting the goatee beard you grew in Mecca. Some forty American exiles, or 'Afros' as they call themselves, are crowded into the living room, talking animatedly, while a Miles album plays in the background. Julian lights up when he sees you. He shakes your hand vigorously and leads you to a nearby group of guests.

They are deep in a conversation about W. E. B. Du Bois, the great scholar, who died last year in Accra. He and Shirley, his wife, moved here in 1961 at the invitation of Nkrumah, says Julian, establishing the path from America to Africa that most of the folks at this party have subsequently followed. 'How many of us are out here now?' you ask Julian, the conversation stilling as the guests turn their attention in your direction. 'About two hundred,' he replies. 'Beautiful,' you say. 'That's beautiful. What are we doing?' Julian looks around at the watching faces. 'We're trying to help the president. We have different levels of involvement but between us we are represented in most institutions in the country.' You sip your club soda, weighing his words. 'That's what I call making a real revolution.' And a murmur of appreciation ripples through the group.

The room gradually returns to its hum of conversations. You listen and nod as the men and women around you speak in turn. Robert Lee, a dentist who has emigrated to Ghana from South Carolina, mentions your friend, the heavyweight champion Cassius Clay, who has scandalized America by announcing himself a member of the Nation of Islam. Cassius is like a brother, you say, and you couldn't be prouder of him. Your paths have diverged since you left the Nation and he chose to stay, but you still follow every one of his fights. He still has your heart.

A woman in a dazzling red, yellow and green kente-cloth dress crosses the room, calling to you, 'Malcolm, it's Maya!' She envelops you in a hug, wooden bangles clattering on her wrists. You first met Maya Angelou three years ago in New York, when she was acting in an off-Broadway production of Jean Genet's *The Blacks* alongside James Earl Jones, Cicely Tyson and Abbey Lincoln. At the time she was leading a demonstration outside the United Nations building against the murder by CIA-backed mercenaries of the Congolese leader Patrice Lumumba. She came to see you, looking for the Nation of Islam to join the protest. You met her eagerness by parroting the Messenger's disdain for organized politics. 'Carrying placards will not win freedom for anyone, nor will it keep the white devils from killing another African leader.' To your embarrassment, you can still picture the crestfallen expression on her face as she left the meeting. But here she is now, eager and garrulous, leading you round the room without any ill feeling, introducing you to her friends: Alice Windon, a sociologist working in Accra as a secondary school teacher; Leslie Lacy, a graduate student at the University of Ghana; and Julia Wright, daughter of the author Richard Wright. With a half-smile, Maya says they have formed themselves into a group, self-titled the Malcolm X Committee, to arrange your schedule in Accra. They weren't sure when you were arriving so the whole bunch of them have been camping out at Julian's house for days, in a state of excitement that edged increasingly into anxiety with each flight that landed without you. At least one person was convinced you'd been kidnapped by the CIA.

Listening to them talk, you become aware of a nervous undercurrent running beneath their lives in Ghana. Most of the Afros came to Accra expecting to be welcomed as honoured relatives, the vanguard of a new era of American-African kinship. But their arrival has coincided with a period of heightened tension in the country. In January, an assassination attempt was made on Nkrumah by a police constable stationed at Flagstaff House, the president's official residence. In its aftermath, a mood of suspicion reigns. Rumours of spies and foreign plots abound. Instead of being embraced, the Afros now find themselves denounced by the Ghanaian press as neo-colonial stooges. 'Beware, brother! Especially of these American-Negro rascals! Beware, brother, for there is an enemy at your doorstep.' They're looking to you to lift their spirits and reassure them that they haven't made a terrible mistake in coming to Africa. As Leslie says, 'Although we're here to serve President Nkrumah, our real leader is the tall red man from Harlem.'

The Afros' regard for you is bittersweet. It reminds you of how the brothers and sisters of the Nation used to sit rapt, taking in your every word, when you were preaching. How quickly things changed. Even before you announced your departure, the leadership in Chicago had started whispering against you, calling you traitor, spreading the lie that you'd betrayed the Messenger. In January, walking down 130th Street, huddled in your coat against the cold, you ran into a young brother, a teenager, new to the movement, who must have swallowed whole the stories about you. He glared at you with such naked animosity that you physically recoiled. Against such a hostile backdrop, perhaps you need the Afros' support as much as they need yours.

Past midnight, when you've all fed on the plates of rice and curried goat that Julian's wife, Ana Livia, brought from the kitchen, and most of the guests have talked themselves out and gone home, you sit with the members of your self-appointed committee, who are still too excited by your presence to let you leave. Leslie Lacy stands up and delivers a free verse poem over the music, letting the words come to him in the moment. 'We laughed, slapped hands, listened to Bessie Smith. Talked some more, ate Ana Livia's curried goat. Looked at Malcolm and *felt good*. Looked at each other and *felt good*. Listened to Miles and *felt good*. And talked about Harlem, West Oakland, Chicago. Ate some more. And, after all that soul, talked to our leader. And it was the best of nights.'

When the party is finally done, Leslie and Maya drive you back to the hotel. No one speaks, content to ride together in companionable silence. The stillness inside the car contrasts with the activity outside. Even in the middle of the night, the roadsides are busy with people lying on mats, too hot to sleep inside, or walking through the unlit streets, coming from their villages to sell yam or cassava at the market in the morning. Two women stand over a brazier, cooking food, the embers from the charcoal fire spitting into the night air, glowing brilliantly and then evaporating into the darkness.

11 May

Breakfast at the Ambassador Hotel. At eight in the morning the dining room is populated with white businessmen. Two men at the table next to yours are loudly discussing Africa's 'untapped wealth', oblivious to the Africans serving them coffee and scrambled eggs. One of the men glances in your direction and then does a double take with a look of startled recognition. He reaches over. 'Mr X, I've truly admired you.' You shake his hand but, even as you do so, you can't help thinking of how these men, whose forefathers arrived in ships to capture and enslave Africa's sons and daughters, are still scheming to exploit the land. You ask him, so friendly over breakfast, if he'd have shaken your hand back home. He looks confused and then angry, blustering something about how you're both Americans and can't a fellow be civil, before pushing back his chair and walking out, his food unfinished on the table and his companion scurrying after him.

The Afros have arranged a frenetic round of meetings and receptions for the week, like you're a visiting ambassador. Which in a way you are: the official representative of the benighted states of Afro-America. The densely packed schedule feels familiar from your days as chief spokesman for the Nation, when you were constantly on the go, travelling from city to city giving speeches, lectures and interviews. The media wanted to paint you as a demon of hate and the best way to counter their lies, you believed, was to engage with friends and strangers alike. With the help of the committee, you plan to follow the same approach in Accra.

Noon. Ana Livia drives you to the Kenyan Embassy, where you receive a generous welcome. Then, at 3 p.m., you visit Kwaku Boateng, the quick-witted Minister of Education, followed by a visit to Kofi Baako, the Minister of Defence, at his house. Several other ministers are present and the conversation is lively and informed. When you are leaving, Ana Livia's car stalls and Baako has to use his car to get you started. Ana Livia is mortified but you reassure her. There are worse calamities that might befall a person.

In between meetings, you go looking for 16mm film for your movie camera. After trying several places, you find three rolls to buy at $15 apiece from a hotel. You set the camera whirring. Watch the people walking, shouting, gossiping through the viewfinder. A policeman directing traffic at a junction, wearing white gloves and standing on a white box. Billboards for Castle Milk Stout and Henkes Schnapps, 'Ghana's favourite since 1870'. Three girls, dressed in white tunics, stand in the open doorway of All's Well Beauty Saloon, their heads turning one after another towards you, as they register the camera. And then a car lying in the road, flipped over on to its roof, no driver in sight, just a crowd of onlookers gathered around the vehicle, amused and baffled.

In the evening, as you are drinking a glass of lemonade in your hotel lobby, a young black man stops and asks if you are Malcolm X. He is from Louisiana and has spent five years in Africa with the Peace Corps. His white companion is a recent graduate of Columbia, here in Ghana representing the World Bank. He studied African Affairs and is supposedly a specialist in determining the political stability of African countries applying for a loan. He doesn't seem to be twenty-five years old, yet he is in a position to say which African nation is or isn't qualified for aid. His arrogance leaves you fuming and you have already broken off the conversation in disgust by the time Julian arrives. You sit gratefully with Julian talking animatedly until one in the morning and you are the only two guests left in the lobby.

12 May

Wake up feeling worn out. It is early in the day and the heat is already intense. After breakfast, Maya takes you to meet Nana Kobina Nketsia, the Minister of Culture, a good friend of hers. He is very friendly and relaxed, laughing and joking a lot.

Lunch with Ras T. Makonnen, from British Guiana, one of the architects of the great Manchester Pan-African Congress of 1945. This man brought together a future generation of African leaders: Nkrumah, Malawi's Hastings Banda, Jomo Kenyatta of Kenya. He is an acute thinker. Even two decades ago he could see the shape of a new Africa rising into view.

After you leave Makonnen, you walk for several blocks trying to get a cab in the hot sun. Return to the hotel feeling light-headed and exhausted. Take a long nap with your bedroom windows open. All you can face for dinner is a bowl of hot consommé, for fear your food will come up. You are lying on the bed fully dressed, staring blankly at the ceiling, when the phone rings. It's New York on the line – Mal Goode calling from the American Broadcasting Company.

Goode was the first black reporter on network TV. He's interviewed you a bunch of times and you normally enjoy talking to him. But now they've got him on some fool story unworthy of his talent. 'What's your involvement with the Blood Brothers in Harlem?' he says, as if you're supposed to know what he's talking about. It turns out the Blood Brothers case has been the big story while you've been away. An elderly white couple, the owners of a second-hand clothing shop on 125th Street and Fifth Avenue, were attacked in their store by a group of black teenagers. The wife, stabbed thirteen times, died from her injuries. The boys arrested by the police said they were innocent and have been targeted unfairly. All they've done is form a group, the Blood Brothers, inspired by your teaching on black resistance. Since then the newspapers have been full of stories about black hate groups out to maim and kill whites.

'Mal,' you say, 'you as a journalist can't be surprised when violence breaks out in the ghetto. Every day black people are penned in and brutalized by white America. It's inevitable that they will lash out against the system at some point. If you spend time out there in the street with people, listening to what they have to say, what you'll hear is that they're dissatisfied, they're disillusioned and fed up. They're getting to the point of frustration where they feel: what do we have to lose? And that creates a dangerously explosive atmosphere. This is what's happening now. This gang is not a hate gang or an anti-white gang, it's an anti-oppression gang. It's an anti-frustration gang. The idea that any single man is responsible for their actions is a fantasy.'

On the other end of the line Goode sounds embarrassed but you are too wiped out to say you don't blame him personally for the ginned-up story. He's just a reminder of how America consumes its own. Taking its black folk and turning them against each other. You return the receiver to its cradle and lie on your back, looking up at the fan clacking in the ceiling.

In your diary, you scribble questions to which you have no answers. 'Can the Negro really become economically independent simply by controlling the retail stores in his community? Who would control the wholesale houses from which he would buy his goods? Move the family out of America? May be good for us personally, but bad politically?'

13 May

You wake from a long sleep, feeling restored.

In the hotel lobby, a lady from Colorado asks to take a picture with you. While her friend is fussing with the camera, she starts to talk about the race problem and how she hopes that this trip will make you see it in a new non-violent light. 'Look at all the progress your people are making . . . You shouldn't go back and stir things up . . . You are a great leader' – and all that bunk. But she does seem sincere.

Maya and Alice take you out to Tema, about an hour west of Accra. It's a new industrial city founded by Nkrumah: modern housing, advanced factories and a deep-water port. Tremendously impressive.

Lunch with Alhaji Isa Wali, the Nigerian High Commissioner, still accompanied by Maya and Alice. Mr Wali once lived in DC and is well versed in American current affairs. Like everyone else you meet at the moment, he wants to know about the situation with the Nation. Why did you split from Elijah Muhammad? You skirt the issue, saying only that the differences between you are political not personal. You are grateful for the Nation as a source of moral reform in America and to Elijah Muhammad himself for lifting you up when you were lost. But you are on your own journey. Your visit to Mecca has opened your eyes to a much bigger perspective on Islam than you were able to explore with him.

When everyone has finished eating and the plates have been cleared, Mr Wali presents you with a woven smock, the same sort he's dressed in, which, he explains, is traditionally worn by Muslim men in the north of Ghana. Alice makes you all line up on the verandah for photos. You pull the smock on over your shirt for the picture and then, a moment later, you're all laughing uncontrollably. The High Commissioner is a small man, his voluminous smock reaching down to his knees. But you are more than a foot taller than Mr Wali and, when you put your smock on, it only just comes past your waist.

After lunch, you go wandering through Jamestown with Maya. It is one of the oldest and poorest neighbourhoods in the city, a warren of dense streets and crumbling colonial buildings. At a photography studio whose sign says it's been here since 1920, you manage to buy another roll of Tri-X film. The walls of the studio are lined with portraits of upper-class Ghanaian families, the women in voluminous dresses and the men in stiff-collared shirts and dark suits, alongside pictures of colonial administrators in pith helmets and knee-length shorts. You follow Maya back into the streets, the camera to your eye. Women are washing clothes in shallow tin pans at the front of their houses. A dog dozes in the shade, a litter of puppies nuzzling at her belly. Children are running through the alleyways, groups of them jumping up and down to attract your attention. 'We make a pretty pair of tourists,' jokes Maya, both of you conspicuously tall and dressed in Western clothes.

You stroll through the streets remembering Richard Wright, who visited Jamestown a decade ago and hated it, perplexed by the people and the poverty. 'Africa in all its squalor, vitality and fantastic disorder . . . The early morning stench of homemade soap, the noon-hour cooking smells, and the vapours of excrement drifting into the hotel from the open drainage ditches outside . . . And almost always one could hear the continuous and mysterious beating of drums deep in the maze of the streets.'

Probably not much has changed since then but the dynamism of the streets belies Wright's pessimistic description. Turning a corner into a small square, you come to a market, stacks of goods laid out on flagstones: eggplants and large ripe plum tomatoes, tins of Carnation milk, mounds of yam and sweet potato and loaves of kenkey, fermented white corn wrapped in banana leaves. Across the square, the sound of highlife, Ghana's exuberant band music, is spilling out from the open doorway of a tiny record store, the owner bent over a turntable, a crate of records at his feet and the sleeves of albums and singles stapled to the walls all around him. Alongside the Ghanaian and Nigerian records on the walls there are some familiar names: Sam Cooke; Ike & Tina; James Brown, *Live at the Apollo*. The music takes you back to the clubs and late-night dives of your youth, back when you were Detroit Red. You smile and nod at the owner. You swore off dancing years ago, when you became a Muslim – just another vice to distract you from Allah. Still, when Maya catches your eye in delight at this small marvel of a place, you can't resist smiling back at her, and for one minute at least, you let the euphoric music lift you up out of yourself and into communion with the thrum of the Jamestown streets.

An evening lecture at the University of Ghana, arranged by Leslie. When you arrive, the Great Hall is packed with students and faculty, along with plenty of whites who have come on to campus hoping, as Leslie says, for some entertainment. A rumour is flying round that fifty CIA agents have infiltrated the crowd although no one has yet spotted any likely candidates for that role.

From behind the lectern you gaze out at the students below, in the academic gowns which they are required to wear to lectures due to an archaic rule from the colonial era, and begin your speech. You stand before them, you say, as the product of a morally bankrupt country. A country that oppresses its own while lecturing the rest of the world on justice and equality. To come of age under independence in Ghana, as you students have, to be able to fully exercise your freedom as a citizen; this is something that no black person in American history has ever experienced. Already their lives are radically different to your own.

You were born in 1925, you tell them, and grew up in Lansing, Michigan, the fourth of eight children. Your father, the Reverend Earl Little, was an itinerant Baptist minister, going from church to church, preaching the gospel in return for the meagre sum of collection money raised by each congregation. Your mother, Louise, spent her days cooking, washing, cleaning, and chasing after you and your seven siblings. She was very light-skinned, and you inherited her complexion more than the other kids, although your reddish hair was yours alone. Blacks in America are taught that having light skin is something to be proud of, you tell the room ruefully. You used to believe that too until you were old enough to know better.

The constant rows between your parents over lack of money and stymied opportunities. Earl was tall and muscular, knotted up with anger at his treatment by white folks – this was the height of Jim

Crow – and he would whip your older brothers till they were pleading for mercy. Never you, though. Maybe because he'd been so taught to admire light skin he couldn't bear to raise his hand to you. Although that didn't stop him beating your mother when the mood took him. Whatever the reason, you were his favourite.

Both your parents were local leaders of Marcus Garvey's Universal Negro Improvement Association – an organization that argued for black economic and political independence from white America and believed that the future for blacks ultimately lay in returning to Africa. Your father liked to take you with him in his old Ford sedan to UNIA meetings around the county. There'd be maybe a dozen or so people, sitting in someone's living room, but the mood was always intense and focused. And you, aged six, sitting among the strangers, as your father described the day when Africa and its people around the world would cast off the white man and claim their destiny. 'No one knows when the hour of redemption cometh. It is in the wind. It is coming. One day, like a storm, it will be here.'

In the minds of white folks, Earl's proselytizing made him a troublemaker. To them he was an 'uppity nigger'. You had to watch out when whites took against you. Three of Earl's brothers had been killed by white men, including one who was lynched. In Lansing, you had the Black Legion, a Klan-like organization that wore black robes instead of white. They patrolled the district after dark and would give any Negro they found a beating, or tar and feather them, or worse.

One night you were woken from sleep by shouting. There was smoke in the air and all the kids were yelling and running back and forth. Amid the commotion it took you some time to realize the house was on fire. Your parents were trying to round everybody up and get them outside. The smoke stung your eyes. It choked your breath. You stumbled on to the porch and out into the yard to find your mother screaming, trying to get back into the house even as the flames intensified. She had lost sight of your baby sister, Yvonne.

Then, from amongst a pile of quilts dumped in the yard, Yvonne started crying. The fact that she was safe was the only moment of respite that whole awful night. Soon after, the house collapsed in on itself, showering sparks and fragments of charred wood. You and the other kids huddled together in the cold, terrified and crying, while your father lifted his pistol and fired shots into the dark, saying he'd seen somebody running from the house. No firemen arrived to put out the flames.

Even worse was to come. Two years later, Earl was out one evening on the north side of Lansing. Hours after he should have returned, there was a rapid knocking at the front door. It was a Michigan state policeman. Earl had been run over by a streetcar, his head crushed and his left leg almost severed. By the time your mother could get to him, he was dead. The police said he must have slipped and fallen on to the tracks. But to the family it seemed more likely that Earl was the victim of the Black Legion, his body laid in front of the streetcar afterwards to make it look like an accident. Why else would they have found him with a gag in his mouth?

You don't remember much about the days that followed. Your mother crying hysterically in the bedroom. The house full of people and you, six years old, feeling empty and alone among all the visitors. At the funeral, a big black fly landed on your father's face in the casket. Wilfred stood up to shoo it away and came to sit back down with tears streaming down his cheeks.

Left to look after eight children on her own, your mother found it impossible to cope. She suffered a nervous breakdown and was committed to the State Mental Hospital at Kalamazoo. You kids wanted to stay together with Wilfred and Hilda, the eldest siblings, looking after the younger ones. But the welfare people wouldn't listen. They split you up and sent you to different foster homes around Lansing. They destroyed the family. You all kept in touch as best you could but, to this day, you're still bitter about the authorities' carelessness, their disregard for your pain.

You look down at the lectern, collecting your thoughts. The truth is, you say, there's no condition on Earth more deplorable than the plight of the twenty-two million black people in America. If your people still have to beg and crawl just to get a chance to drink a cup of coffee, in a country with so much wealth, then the condition is deplorable indeed. By contrast, you say, raising your head, Africa is the most beautiful continent you've ever seen. You don't feel that you have to beg in Ghana. You feel that you are at home. You feel that you are free. You've been away for four hundred years but not of your own volition. And now you're home and it's wonderful.

As you finish, the hall erupts with cheers. The students chant, 'Brother Malcolm! Brother Malcolm!' The force of their reaction is overwhelming. One student is in tears. Others are taking off the academic gowns and stamping on them. To see these young people, so elated, so proud and beautiful, it's enough to bring you to tears yourself.

'The Ghanaians are by far the most progressive and independent-minded in Africa,' you write in your diary back at the hotel. 'Even their laughter is tinged always with an ominous note of seriousness. They laugh and joke with each other almost constantly but it is not the same type of laughter, or jokes, found among other Africans. The country is seething with serious awareness of itself, its potential wealth and power, and the role it seems destined to play.'

14 May

Breakfast with the Algerian ambassador, who describes to you how his people rose up against the French and drove them out of the country. It is exhilarating to hear him speak.

From there, Maya takes you in her Fiat to the Cuban Embassy. The ambassador is down-to-earth and friendly. 'We must have a party in your honour,' he says. 'We will organize this before you leave. It must happen.'

To Julian's then for lunch with the Malcolm X Committee. Everyone is in high spirits. Julian: 'Man, we ought to pay you for this visit. You've given this poor group of black exiles some status. Man! We were living here before, but now we have really arrived.'

In the afternoon, a visit to Christiansborg Castle with Maya. The castle is a former Danish colonial fort, built on the seafront overlooking the Atlantic. Since the assassination attempt at Flagstaff House, Nkrumah has used Christiansborg as his main residence. Your deepest hope during this visit is to sit down with the president, but so far Julian's attempts to arrange a meeting have failed. For now, there's Christiansborg itself, a large, whitewashed building dating from the seventeenth century. The castle is one of over two dozen forts and lodges strung along the Ghanaian coast, remnants from centuries of European exploitation. In the broad courtyard, Maya points out the storerooms to the right, which were used as warehouses for elephant tusks and liquor. On the left, the dungeons which lead through to the Door of No Return, from where human captives were ferried by boat to slave ships and then transported to the Danish Antilles in the Caribbean. You picture, in the wake of the ships, a graveyard of bones at the bottom of the sea.

Bodies cast overboard, sometimes living, sometimes dead. Bodies decaying on the seafloor. Once-living things turning infinitesimally into sand.

Below the castle walls, fishermen are fixing their nets and preparing their boats to go back out on to the water early tomorrow morning. A transistor radio, its long silver aerial gleaming in the sunlight, blares highlife songs, and two boys and a girl, dressed in outsize, ragged T-shirts, are practising a dance routine. The sight of them reminds you of kids dancing on the sidewalk in Harlem. It is a glimpse of a possible world, where black people gathering, at churches, on street corners or on protest marches, is not a catalyst for white violence – but is nothing more or less than an assertion of kinship and love.

On the battlements of the fort, a salt-scented breeze blowing in off the sea, you talk to Maya about your youth. Back then, aged eighteen, you expected to die at any moment. You even welcomed the prospect. You kept three guns on you at all times: one at your waist, another in a shoulder holster, a third strapped to your leg. For a while you even had a machine gun on hand. This was after you'd left Lansing and were hustling in New York. Running numbers and selling weed to musicians in jazz clubs. Your light skin and copper hair earning you the name Detroit Red. A kind of spiritual zombie-hood which only Elijah Muhammad was able to save you from in the end.

You had a gang. You, your buddy Shorty, your white girlfriend Bea, and her sister who was going with Shorty. The four of you specialized in burgling the homes of rich white folks. The girls could case a house in a wealthy neighbourhood without attracting attention. You and Shorty would do the job. In and out in ten minutes. At your first meeting, you're all sitting about in an apartment, shooting the breeze, when you pull out a gun, shake out the five bullets it holds and push one of them back into a chamber. You twirl the cylinder, put the muzzle to your head and say, 'Now, let's see how much guts all of you have.' Everyone freezes, hardly daring to breathe. With a smile on your face, you pull the trigger. There's a loud click. The chamber is empty. At this point everyone goes crazy. Shorty's begging you to stop. The girls are in tears. You raise the gun to your head again. Pull the trigger again. The hammer clicks on another empty chamber. The girls are screaming and Shorty's yelling, 'Red, Red, cut it out, man!' The gun returns to your head. You pull the trigger. The chamber echoes empty. You bring the gun down, let it rest in your lap, your fingers still curled around the handle. That's to show you're not afraid to die, you say, the three of them looking back at you aghast. You meant it too. What was there to live for? What was there to believe in? All you had was your anger.

Maya starts to reply, maybe to offer something about her own past. But then she seems to think better of it and falls silent. The two of you stand side by side on the battlements, watching the waves meet the shore, the water intermittently green then blue then clear. Foam soaking into sand. In the shared silence between you, only the sea is voluble. The sound of waves dragging over shingle like a whisper or a moan.

Night-time. On the darkened terrace of the Ambassador Hotel. Writing postcards by lamplight to escape the oppressive heat in your room, while trying to ignore the mosquitoes darting at your neck, your ankles.

On the back of a picture of Akosombo Dam, Nkrumah's grand hydroelectricity project in south-east Ghana, you jot a message to Gloria Owens, the sister of Maceo X Owens, a former lieutenant of yours at Temple No. 7: 'Greetings from an ancient land that is fast leaping out of the past and into the future even ahead of us.'

To Redd Foxx, the comedian, a card with a photo of a chimpanzee: 'One hundred years have passed since the Civil War, and these chimpanzees get more recognition, respect & freedom in America than our people do, because even the monkeys that lead them have more sense than the monkeys that lead us.'

You choose a postcard for Betty next, but as you write her name, it occurs to you that you don't know what to say. For so long your words, even your thoughts, were dictated by Elijah Muhammad. How you dressed, what you ate, the way you walked. Even now you've left, it's hard at times to express yourself freely.

You put down the pen and peer into the dark of the unlit hotel garden, scratching at your ankle. For twelve years, everything you did within the movement felt as rational as it now does aberrant. Like you, many brothers and sisters came to the Nation the hard way, through prison or drugs or both. Each of you carried more anger than affection and the result was an organization that spoke of love but was full of spite. The Fruit of Islam, the Nation's 'security wing', marched in formation, trained in martial arts and close combat. Austere mosques and the expectation of an unblinking adherence to the movement's many strict rules. A minor violation – being caught cursing or drinking – would incur a ban from the mosque for several weeks. More serious transgressors, such as adulterers, were 'silenced': cast out for ninety days or longer, exiled from the companionship of their Muslim brothers and sisters. Some temples also operated secret punishment units, 'pipe squads' staffed by the Fruit of Islam. The pipe squads fancied themselves as enforcers of discipline against the so-called 'hypocrites' who brought shame on the Nation. A brother caught smoking might be thrown down a flight of stairs. An adulterer, even one who had already been publicly sentenced, could receive a follow-up call from the squad in the form of a brutal beating.

All this – the zealotry, the suppressed rage – it suited you at the time. Somewhere to put all the pain and fear and resentment. White people were the enemy and you were the blazing truth. Brother Malcolm, so severe, so righteous, his finger stabbing the air, the most dangerous man in America, and the audience clapping and calling out at your speeches, 'Yes, Brother Malcolm! Tell it like it is!'

In the midst of it, you met Betty. She was a nursing student in Brooklyn, twenty-two years old, visiting Temple No. 7 with a friend who was already a member. Betty was raised a Methodist and not looking to change faiths. But the friend insisted, so she came to the mosque anyway, and you noticed her right away. Feeling drawn to her, you were confused about what to do. According to Elijah Muhammad, women were a weak species that required control and protection by their men. You personally had always insisted you had no intention of getting married; you wanted to dedicate your life to helping black people. On the other hand, a minister must set a good example to his flock, including perhaps through marriage.

You proceeded cautiously. One-on-one dates were not permitted between Nation members. You invited Betty on group outings to the Hayden Planetarium or the Museum of Natural History; you sat near her during the community's weekly Sunday dinner at the Nation-owned restaurant near the mosque. Finally you told yourself, if you were getting married after all, you'd do it without any of that Hollywood stuff that women had filled their heads with. If Betty was expecting bouquets and kissing and being swept off her feet like Cinderella, then she was looking at the wrong man.

You were in Detroit one January morning when you figured, if you were going to do something, it was best to get on with it. You stopped at a gas station, fed a couple of quarters into a payphone and dialled her number at the hospital dorm. And what you said was,

'Are you ready to make that move?' Like you were back in your hustling days, making a deal. Betty screeched in delight and said yes, yes. Her parents were horrified at the idea of her marrying a black Muslim and converting to Islam but the two of you did it anyway, moving into a house in Queens, divided into small apartments, which you shared with three other Nation couples.

Of course you insisted she give up nursing to stay home. She was the wife of a minister and it was the proper thing to do. This while you were away for weeks or sometimes months at a stretch, and rarely back for more than a few days in between. Boston, Miami, Philadelphia, Los Angeles: awakening the brainwashed black man was a full-time job. On the days that you were home, you insisted on quiet and order. Plain meals, eaten slowly and in silence. Most evenings you read or worked on a lecture. You were aware that your strictures did not suit her. But you thought of how your father had imposed his will on your mother. And Elijah Muhammad said that a man must be master of his household. In this, as with all else, you followed his teaching. Sometimes Betty would beg you, 'Please, I want to work. I want to work,' and then get mad and call you selfish and a monster. But you didn't want her to socialize with the other sisters because gossiping would inevitably follow and you hated gossip. It was a truism among the brothers: 'Telling a woman not to talk too much is like telling Jesse James not to carry a gun or telling a hen not to cackle.'

Once she gave birth to Attallah, the friction between you increased. She complained of feeling trapped in the tiny apartment. She said she missed the world. When Attallah was a few months old, you returned home from a lecture in Albany to find the apartment empty. Betty had left with the baby and gone to stay with her cousin in Brooklyn. You waited two days, then drove round and told her to get into the car. She came readily enough.

After that you did let her run classes for the sisters at the mosque so she'd have some company. But the marital tension continued to grow. You tried to keep your voice level and reasonable during the arguments, asking her to consider how undignified it was that the other couples in the building could hear everything. That only made her more mad. She mocked you sexually, said you were impotent and incapable of meeting her needs, and if you weren't careful she'd seek satisfaction elsewhere. It got to be that you preferred to stay out on the road than come back to more fighting.

You look back now with some shame at those early days. You trying so hard to be a man you couldn't respect her on her own terms. Over time you found your way to tenderness. You were able to see her for the woman she was, not the figure you wanted her to represent. You loved her for her clear brown skin. For her shining eyes and gleaming dark hair. Her black beauty and beautiful mind. You still went away for long trips, but you'd hide money in different places around the house for her to find. You would leave a note that said: 'Look in the top desk drawer in the back. There's some cash there for you to buy something, and a love letter too.' She would go look and sometimes there would just be money and sometimes there really would be a love letter. It got so that as soon as you were out the front door, she would start hunting around the apartment, but she'd never found anything. A few days later, you'd send the letter telling her where to look. You made sure it was never in a place you'd used before.

In Accra, the fathomless night wrapped around you, you realize what you can write to your wife. The postcard shows an illustration of a Ghana Airways passenger jet flying over Africa. On the reverse, you say that you were dreadfully afraid of planes until you made your first trip by air. Since then you've found it is the best method of travel. Your marriage to her is the same way. It is the best thing for you.

15 May

To an evening reception at the Ghana Press Club. Every few months the local journalists meet and talk over calabashes of palm wine. Today you are the guest speaker, although according to Julian, who belongs to the club, some members opposed the invitation. Most journalists here consider it their role to support, not critique, the government. The editors of all the main newspapers meet daily at Flagstaff House to receive an official briefing on what stories to cover. To many of them you represent a reputational danger for the government: 'a racist always talking about white devils'.

No doubt they expected you to arrive today spitting fire, you say, to the seventy or so journalists, sitting in twos or threes around cocktail tables facing you. And yes, you might have done so in the past. But last month you were blessed to visit the Holy City of Mecca and complete the hajj. And having done so, you would rather talk today about beauty than rage. To the listening journalists, you paint a picture of streets filled with people of all nations, all colours. Hundreds of thousands converging by car, bus, camel, donkey and foot in a city that has witnessed the same sight every year since the days of Abraham. Mecca is surrounded by mountains, you say. The cruellest-looking mountains you've ever seen. Black, and no vegetation on them at all. But the spirit of brotherhood is everywhere and practised sincerely by everyone you meet.

Whenever they see you resting, someone offers you mint tea or iced water. Everyone shares what they have. You stayed in a spacious tent with brothers you met along the way. Eating from a common dish, drinking without hesitation from the same glass, washing with the same pitcher. One night, sleeping out with eight or ten others on a mat, nothing but the sky overhead, you lay listening to the snoring

248

pilgrims from every land, and concluded that when it comes to sleeping, everyone speaks the same language.

You tell the journalists about circling the Kaaba, the huge square building of black stone in the middle of the Great Mosque. The largest crowd you had ever seen, ever been a part of, and everyone in white, wearing the two-piece ihram, with the right shoulder bare. Every nation on Earth represented there, together in devotion. It was a wonder to behold.

When you belonged to the Nation of Islam, you were told to regard whites as blue-eyed devils, the enemies of black people. Integration between the races was impossible and anyone who suggested as much was a shucking and jiving Uncle Tom. And yet, during your fortnight in the Muslim world, you shared food and slept on the same rug with Muslims whose eyes were the bluest of blue and whose skin was the whitest of white. Their belief in one God had removed the white from their minds, their behaviour, their attitude. You were truly all brothers. The journey has convinced you that perhaps American whites can be cured of the racism which infects them. Now, standing here, you can no longer subscribe to the sweeping indictment of one race. In honesty and sincerity, you wish nothing but freedom, justice and equality for all people. You bow your head and leave the podium.

Lunch at a restaurant: fufu and palm nut soup with Leslie and Julian. Watching the afternoon traffic stream by beneath the balcony, you are struck by the powerful urge to describe your impressions of Accra to Elijah Muhammad. Even now, after breaking with him, the need to speak with the Messenger persists; to hear his voice, as you have done through almost all of your adult life.

Later, walking back to the hotel alone along crowded sidewalks, the Messenger is still on your mind. Perhaps you might send him a postcard when you reach the Ambassador, you think. You were in your early twenties when you first wrote to him, already in prison, doing an eight-to-ten stretch for burglary. The sentence was much longer than the average penalty for a first offence – the judge added extra time as punishment for running with a white girl and turning her into your 'love slave'. In prison, you got to thinking on how you and the other black inmates were victims of a white social system, notwithstanding any of the crimes you'd committed. All of the hustlers you'd known back home: the cat burglars, pickpockets, numbers runners. All of you might have become scientists or businessmen but were instead reduced to living by cunning. The awareness of how you'd been denied your chance in the world made you furious. You spent your days getting high on ground nutmeg, cursing out the guards, pacing up and down in solitary talking to yourself for hours on end, so unhinged the other inmates named you 'Satan'.

Elijah Muhammad was the first person to show you how to use that anger. Two years into your sentence, your older brother Philbert wrote to you about the Nation of Islam. He said it was 'the natural religion for the black man'. Initially you were sceptical. Philbert was always after joining something so it was hard to take his enthusiasms seriously. But when Wilfred and Hilda backed him up, you started to pay more attention. That was the beginning. The moment when you felt your consciousness expanding. The birth of a new awareness in yourself.

You started learning about the Nation's history. Its founder, Wallace D. Fard, had been sent by Allah to redeem the 'Original People of the Earth' from the 'white race of devils' and reconnect them to their true Muslim culture. The Nation was now run by his successor, Elijah Muhammad, a former Garveyite and the 'Messenger of Allah'. One night in your cell, you had a vision of a man beside you.

He wore a dark suit and had oily black hair, his skin colour neither black nor white. You looked into his face and knew you weren't dreaming. It was Fard. He had shown himself to you as a sign to trust in the Messenger. From then on you wrote to Elijah Muhammad every day, describing the disarray of your life so far and pledging your faithfulness to him and the Nation.

In 1952 you were released from prison. Free after six and a half years of incarceration, you travelled with Wilfred and Philbert to hear the Messenger at the Nation's headquarters in Chicago. You took your seat among two hundred congregants. Elijah Muhammad entered from the rear of the hall and walked slowly to the platform, dwarfed by the imposing Fruit of Islam guards who flanked him on either side. He was a slight figure with delicate, birdlike features and a gold-embroidered fez that sparkled under the house lights. The Dear Holy Apostle, the Exalted One, the Divine Warner. And to your surprise, he knew you. From the stage, Elijah Muhammad called out your name and made you stand up. 'Brother Malcolm has just come out of prison,' he said in his high, frail voice. 'And every day he wrote to me, pouring forth all his fears and all his hopes. Now that he's out of jail, the devils will try to tempt him back to drinking and smoking and crime. But this one is strong. He is faithful. He is true.'

Elijah Muhammad gave you the surname X, 'in place of your slave name'. In return you became his most devoted follower and, eventually, the Nation's principal spokesman. In all you did, you gave praise to the Messenger. Your mind, your body, your voice were his. He was your guide. Your father. In return, you called yourself his slave, his servant, his son. Twelve years of devotion. What would you say to him if he were here now?

A state dinner at the Chinese Embassy. The Afros also present. The ambassador, Huang Hua, is extremely shrewd and discerning.

Once the dinner is over, he screens a Chinese-made documentary film about the black liberation struggle in the United States. Its many scenes of police brutality are a dispiriting reminder of what waits for you back home, and you are talking despondently with Julian when Shirley Graham Du Bois arrives. You feel a tug of excitement at the sight of her. You have always revered W. E. B. Du Bois as one of the most important black thinkers of the twentieth century. Julian sees the direction of your gaze. 'Even after her husband's passing last year, Shirley remains close to Nkrumah,' he whispers. 'She telephones him every night at bedtime, advising him on his health and diet and the day's politics. Nkrumah calls her "Little Mother".' You are about to go and introduce yourself when Mrs Graham Du Bois crosses the room herself, her bearing stately, takes you by the arm and leads you to a couch.

As she talks about her late husband and their life together, it's easy to see why Nkrumah is devoted to her. At the age of sixty-seven she has led an exhilarating life, a pioneering composer and playwright, travelling across Europe, Africa, China and the Soviet Union. Even now she's breaking new ground as the first director of television in Ghana, a role to which she was personally appointed by Nkrumah. She seems similarly taken with you. 'I must admit when you first arrived in Accra, I was wary,' she says. Leaning close. 'I didn't know anything about the Nation of Islam except what I'd seen in the press, which was all negative. I understood you wanted to meet the president but I said to myself, I'm not going to take just any old riff-raff to see him. I realize now I was in error.' Mrs Graham Du Bois stands up and announces across the room, 'This man is brilliant. I am taking him for my son. He must meet Kwame. They have too much in common not to meet.' Tomorrow, 9 a.m., she says, present yourself at Flagstaff House. She will make the arrangements.

The news pitches the committee into a frenzy of excitement. Later that night, at a hastily convened gathering at Julian's house, opinions are divided. Julian, a devoted supporter of the president, is enthusiastic. Others are more cautious. Nkrumah is not the man he was, warns Leslie. When Ghana first gained independence, he was hailed as Africa's most dynamic leader. To his people he was Osagyefo, the Redeemer. Surveying the continent, he styled himself as 'the Voice of Africa', a role he had coveted since he was a student dreaming of Pan-Africanism. Seven years on from the advent of self-rule, the vision has soured. Grand projects like the Akosombo Dam, intended to provide an abundance of cheap electricity for the country, have proved costly and cumbersome. Representatives of the US-controlled International Monetary Fund are coming to Ghana to discuss the nation's mounting debt crisis. And as the economy has faltered, Nkrumah has retreated into authoritarianism.

Earlier this year, he sacked the Chief Justice and gave himself the power to reverse High Court verdicts. Ghana is now a one-party state. The national flag has been changed from red, gold and green to red, white and green – the colours of Nkrumah's Convention People's Party. Nkrumah's illiberalism has been exacerbated by the assassination attempt against him in January. The attack came much closer to success than was reported. His assailant managed to fire all five shots from his rifle at the president. Once the gun was spent, he chased Nkrumah into the kitchen of Flagstaff House. They were grappling on the floor, the president fighting for his life, when the guards came to rescue him.

Shaken by the close call, Nkrumah is increasingly paranoid. Brooding on the assassination of his friend Patrice Lumumba by Western agents, he's convinced the CIA was behind the Flagstaff House attack and is plotting against him. And, as Leslie points out, it's not just the immigrant Afros who are classed as 'deceivers and betrayers of the people' in this new climate of paranoia. Ghanaian politicians, judges, civil servants and university lecturers have been caught up in a wave of firings and imprisonments, as CPP loyalists call for a 'ruthless purge' of 'anti-progressive' elements in the nation. Under the current mood of anti-Western hostility, it's hard to know if you will be received as an ally or an enemy, and risky to guess wrong.

The discussion goes on into the night as Leslie and Julian argue back and forth. Finally you stand up. It's late and you're tired. And what you have to say to Nkrumah is too important to forgo. Tomorrow, for better or worse, you'll meet the president.

16 May

Nkrumah's office at Christiansborg Castle. The president rises from behind a large teak desk. He grips you by the forearm and pulls you into an embrace. 'Mr Malcolm X. I'm very glad to finally meet you. I've admired you for a long time.'

An aide in a dark suit pours two glasses of iced water, puts the carafe on the desk and backs out of the room. Nkrumah shows you to a couch and sits beside you.

The office looks out past the walls of Christiansborg to the open sky. Framed by the window, a gull hovers in the air, wings outstretched, and then banks out of sight to leave an empty square of blue. Nkrumah presses you on the details of your trip, nodding with satisfaction as you describe the past few days of receptions and dinners and the students' reaction to your speech at the university. You perch on the edge of the seat, gathering your thoughts. Then you begin to speak your mind.

'Mr President, the contrast between the joy of your people here and how black folks are living in America is stark. You have lived in the States. You're familiar with the plight of our people. You know that when we protest our men, women and children are beaten by police and savaged by their dogs. The spray of water cannon rips the clothes from our bodies. We are at the mercy of racists who murder us for no reason other than we are black and of African descent. America talks of integration while practising segregation. It talks of equality but enacts oppression. America is cunning like a fox, friendly and smiling, but more vicious and deadly than the wolf.

'This is what I want to discuss with you today. Being in Ghana, the fountainhead of Pan-Africanism, has made it clear to me that black Americans must "return" to Africa philosophically and culturally. We must be a part of Pan-Africanism.'

Nkrumah nods gently as you speak, his high forehead shining.

'For the so-called leader of the free world to be engaged in the dehumanization of twenty-two million of its own people is a moral question of global consequence. Our quest as black people is about more than a domestic struggle for civil rights. It is, in fact, an international battle that needs to be understood in the same way as the fight against apartheid. Mr President,' you say, 'we hope that you and your brother nations in Africa will come to our aid. We African Americans are marooned in a strange land that has rejected us, and, like the prodigal son, we are turning to our elder brothers for help. We beseech you to recommend an immediate investigation into our problem by the United Nations Commission on Human Rights. Will you act for us?'

Nkrumah gazes out of the window at the cloudless sky, apparently absorbed in the view. The question hangs in the air long enough for you to wonder if he has heard you. 'Mr Malcolm X,' he finally replies. 'You see this scar?' He points to a pale line running along his cheek. 'I received this trying to fight off the man who tried to kill me. I don't know how I lived. It was a miracle of God.' He shakes his head with a faint smile as if he's summoning a fond memory. 'This is how the imperialists work. They turn your people against you and come after you in your home. When I first mooted the idea of African unity, the West laughed it off. But when they saw the idea germinating, gripping the minds of other African leaders, the CIA employees were summoned to the White House. The British intelligence agency staff were called to Buckingham Palace and directed to act. They killed Lumumba for the same reasons. Now their local agents in Ghana are pursuing me. They want to silence Osagyefo.'

Nkrumah rises from the sofa, fetches the carafe and refills your glass and his. A scowl crosses his face and for a second his genial manner evaporates, a sudden glimpse of the paranoid autocrat you've heard about. 'Tell me, why did you separate from Elijah Muhammad?' he asks. 'Who are you, in fact, Mr Malcolm X?' This last question is asked slowly, with an edge of animosity. Does he really imagine you to be another imperialist agent? You feel your fingertips prickle with sweat. Here, in this one-party state, even the international celebrity who has spent the week dining with ambassadors and diplomats is never truly safe.

Instead of talking about the Messenger, you tell Nkrumah about making the hajj and discovering that a common good, a common goal, might unite people of all cultures and colours. He likes this. The mood in the room lifts. He reaches over, shakes your hand again and walks you to the door, as affable as when you first arrived.

The meeting leaves you rattled. That flash of suspicion on his face. 'Who are you, in fact, Mr Malcolm X?' The way he ignored your question about the UN, leaving you now with the sense that he was looking past you, deliberately putting you in your place. And his final words as you left his office. Gripping your hand, Nkrumah leaned close and whispered, 'Be careful, Mr Malcolm X. When you return home, your life will be in danger.'

You stare out of the window of Julian's car, letting the streets slide by. In the moment, you assumed he was imagining phantom imperialist agents again. As the city unfurls past the windscreen, past the half-finished buildings that signal the country's faltering economic fortunes, it occurs to you that perhaps it was a more direct reference. Nkrumah knows what it is to exercise power. He knows vengeance. Maybe, even from Accra, he knows what Elijah Muhammad is capable of doing.

Julian's car is caught between a battered truck with 'Jesus is Saviour' written across the back, and a tro-tro, a minibus, packed to overflowing with passengers. As the car crawls forward, your thoughts run backward, replaying the circumstances of your break with the Messenger.

On 22 November last year, President Kennedy was shot dead while riding in a motorcade through Dealey Plaza in Dallas. In the aftermath of the assassination, Elijah Muhammad ordered Nation leaders to avoid controversy by making no comment on the killing. A month later, in December, you gave a lecture in midtown Manhattan, the audience mostly made up of brothers and sisters from Temple No. 7. The speech was fiery. 'White America is doomed,' you told the crowd. 'The West is a wicked world, ruled by a race of devils, that preaches falsehood, practises slavery, and thrives on indecency and immorality.' It was a world that rewarded racists and made victims of the virtuous and the innocent. Medgar Evers in Mississippi, Patrice Lumumba in Congo, the four girls bombed in a Birmingham church. Surely, soon, it would collapse under its own corruption.

The speech made no mention of Kennedy but afterwards, as you took questions from the press, you mused that his killing was a case of the chickens coming home to roost. A proof that the white world, in its wickedness, would even turn against its own. Being an old farm boy, you quipped, chickens coming home to roost never did make you sad. They always made you glad. There were gasps, but also laughter and loud applause from the audience.

The comment was a throwaway one and you thought little of it at the time. But looking back now, you can see it clearly as a symptom of your disenchantment with Elijah Muhammad, which had been quietly growing for a year or more. In April 1962, the LAPD raided Mosque No. 27 during a confrontation between police and members of the Nation. Seven brothers were shot. One was paralysed for life. Another, Ronald Stokes, a friend of yours, was killed as he tried to surrender, his hands already up. Enraged, you wanted to strike back, to send a Fruit of Islam squad out from Harlem to target the LA officers. But Elijah Muhammad vetoed a counter-attack, sticking to his principle that the Nation should stay out of worldly affairs. This response was almost as maddening to you as the raid itself. At a time when black people were raising their voices like never before, and Martin Luther King and his allies were staging sit-ins, marches and boycotts in the South, the Nation refused to take an active part in the civil rights struggle. Elijah Muhammad said that the ultimate goal of the movement was the creation of a separate black state. But it was no closer to that goal than when you'd joined over a decade ago. And you were getting sick of waiting.

Perhaps it was awareness of your waning faith that prompted the Messenger to confront you the way he did following your comment about Kennedy. A few days after the speech, you received an angry call from him summoning you to Chicago. The meeting was brutally short. You'd made 'a very bad statement' that had directly contravened his instructions and hurt the reputation of the Nation. As punishment, you were to be silenced for ninety days: stripped of your duties, banned from speaking in public, and forbidden from associating with any other member of the movement.

You flew back to Harlem, churned up with conflicting emotions. Stunned and ashamed at your suspension. And also furious that after twelve years working harder than anyone in the Nation, you could be treated with such disregard. To begin with, you imagined serving your time and then being welcomed back into Elijah Muhammad's good graces. Others had transgressed and returned. You yourself had suspended Captain Joseph, leader of the Fruit of Islam in Harlem, for beating his wife. After his punishment was complete, he returned and, in accordance with Muslim rules, his offence was never mentioned again.

But it was a hard sentence to endure. January 1963, a month into the suspension, was dark and cold. Cooped up in the house in Elmhurst, the kids running everywhere, the phone ringing incessantly with the press wanting interviews, and Betty alternately furious at you and fearful of the family's predicament, you felt besieged. The suspension had also placed you in a precarious financial position. You normally received a monthly $150 stipend from the Nation. In lieu of those payments, you had no savings to fall back on, no pension or life insurance. As the days of isolation stretched on, you considered appealing the sentence. Yet it began to dawn on you how few friends you had in the upper tiers of the movement. Much of the Chicago leadership was made up of Elijah Muhammad's extended family. And the other senior figures had always been jealous of your public profile and your proximity to him. With your position now weakened, they were the ones gleefully spreading stories that you were a traitor. You imagined pleading your case directly to the Messenger. In your journal, late at night, half-formed thoughts addressed to him: 'Had no bad motive. Had good intention. Feeling innocent, have felt extremely persecuted. Have felt lied about. Unjustly and unnecessarily. Made a serious mistake by not coming straight to you – and that mistake led to others. Am sincerely sorry and pray to Allah for forgiveness.'

In February you took Betty and the children to stay with Cassius in Miami Beach. He had a title fight coming up against Sonny Liston, the world heavyweight champion, and he wanted your spiritual advice as he prepared for the match. At the time, no one knew he had converted to Islam, not even his training team. It was the first vacation you and Betty had ever taken together, and you tried to forget your troubles and enjoy playing with the girls in the hotel pool and strolling along the beach with your wife in the evening cool.

By the end of the month, you were back in Queens and ready to work. But the suspension deadline approached, then passed, and still no word from Elijah Muhammad. And then the conversation with James 67X, hunkered in the dark in your Oldsmobile. 'People are talking about killing you.' That's when you realized. Any threat involving death could only have come from the very top of the Nation. Not from jealous lieutenants, not from Elijah Muhammad's relatives, but from the Messenger himself.

Julian's car pulls up at the Ambassador. A porter hurries over and opens the passenger door. Inside, the lobby is busy with the usual noisy breed of white businessman. The terrace at the back of the hotel is quieter and less hectic, with only a few tables occupied. You sink heavily into a seat, wincing at the headache that's been building at the front of your skull since you left Christiansborg. Two workmen dressed in white overalls make their slow progress across the lawn, backs bent, hacking at weeds with machetes. Tomorrow morning you leave Ghana for Morocco and then Algeria. Then home. The prospect of returning to the United States fills you with dread.

Once they were seeded, your doubts about Elijah Muhammad kept growing. A few months after the LA raid, you learned about his custom of hiring young, unmarried girls as his secretaries. Secretaries who fell pregnant mysteriously, one after the other, and were expelled from the Nation in disgrace. The rumour was that Elijah Muhammad had fathered the children. Initially you'd refused to accept the gossip, and indeed had flown out to see him to discuss how to quell the fallacious stories. You'd imagined he might be angry or embarrassed to be having such an intimate conversation. Instead, his demeanour was serene. He didn't even bother denying the rumours. It was just part of God's plan, he said. 'Malcolm, you always have had such a good understanding of prophecy and of spiritual things. You should understand then that these affairs are simply part of the path that I'm compelled to follow as God's divine prophet. When you read about Lot, who went and lay with his own daughters, or how David took another man's wife, I'm that David.' You left him, lost for words. Gasping for air.

After you found out about the assassination order, the last of your illusions collapsed. Elijah Muhammad was not interested in Muslims but only in personal gain. His promise of salvation was a lie. You had spent years living modestly in a two-bedroom house in East Elmhurst, its title deeds held by the Nation, while Elijah Muhammad owned an eighteen-room Victorian mansion near the University of Chicago. Betty had begged you to put some money aside for the family but each month the stipend was swallowed up in household expenses. You had told her, don't worry. If anything happens, Elijah Muhammad will ensure the family is looked after. He was Allah's Messenger. God's disciple on Earth. You just had to trust in him and all would be well.

On 8 March, you quit the Nation. You would build a new organization based on black nationalism. You told the press that you had no desire for turmoil. Members should stay in the movement and continue to follow Elijah Muhammad, even though you had chosen another path. But you knew that, however diplomatically you framed your departure, there was no easy escape. Your profile was too high for Elijah Muhammad to let you go. He couldn't risk the competition, especially given the damaging information you knew about him. You were a danger to the movement and sooner or later he would have to act. Out in the street. In a store. From a passing car. A brother coming towards you with a gun in his hand. And the Messenger would be the one who'd sent him after you.

It is noon in Accra. A rust-coloured lizard skitters across the paving stones of the terrace. The white-overalled gardeners make their slow passage over the lawn. You should start packing. There are more postcards to write. Phone calls to be made. Any minute Julian will arrive, voluble as usual, to drive you to your afternoon meeting with the ambassador of Senegal. Yet you can't face moving. Just a moment before getting up. One moment more before meeting the future.

17 May

Last morning in Ghana. You wake at dawn to pray and then put on the same long white robe that you wore on the hajj. Julian, Maya and Leslie arrive to drive you to the airport. As you gather outside the hotel, a convoy of limousines draws up. Alhaji Isa Wali, the Nigerian High Commissioner, emerges from a black Mercedes. He has also come to escort you to the airport, as have the ambassadors of Mali, Yugoslavia, China, Guinea, Cuba, Algeria, Egypt. It is an unexpected and generous gesture, and for a few minutes there is a cheerful confusion of people getting in and out of cars and handshakes and embraces.

You are standing with Maya, the diplomats waiting in their cars and the whole convoy ready to get moving, when you hear a loud, familiar voice behind you. Cassius strides out of the hotel, surrounded by his training team and a big group of fans. He has a different name now – he changed it right after he beat Sonny Liston to become world champion. You were elated when he won, overcome with emotion. To crown his victory, he publicly announced himself a Muslim and was given a new name by the Messenger. Muhammad Ali. You haven't seen him since then. You want to run over, shake his hand and tell him how proud you are of your little brother. But you hold back. Muhammad catches sight of you now across the front lot. You lock eyes briefly, and then he turns away and continues walking towards a row of waiting cars. For a moment you stand frozen, unsure, but then you follow him, calling his name. He turns again, looks hard at you, and walks on, addressing his entourage at theatrical volume. 'Man, did you get a look at Malcolm? Dressed in that funny white robe and wearing a beard and walking with that cane that looked like a prophet's stick? Man, he's gone. He's gone so far out he's out completely.' Loud laughter from the fans. 'Doesn't that just go to show that Elijah is the most powerful? Nobody listens to that Malcolm any more.'

Watching Muhammad's car roar away, you know it's not possible for real love to disappear, even in the heat of betrayal. Rather, you feel it all the more clearly in moments like this. You want to reach out to Muhammad, so young and so sure of himself, and tell him that even if he turns away the next time you meet, nothing will change for you. He is still a friend. He is still a brother.

2

New York

20 May 1964

Dear Brother Malcolm

You are residing in a building purchased for the inhabitant to undertake his solemn duties as a minister of the Nation of Islam, by the grace of the Honourable Elijah Muhammad. Since you no longer hold this position, we request you vacate the premises immediately.

Yours sincerely

Captain Joseph

—

A hypocrite is a person who is disliked by everyone. You can never trust hypocrites. They are liars, the most hated of all people . . . There is no help for the hypocrites. They are very deceitful and must be opposed by all means.

Elijah Muhammad, *Muhammad Speaks*, 12 June 1964

—

Fiery Malcolm X went into temporary hiding fearing for his life late Tuesday night as police averted a shooting war between rival Muslim factions by arresting six of Malcolm's followers at 116th and Lenox Avenue, who police say were armed with guns and ammunition and ready to make war on the Muslim followers of Elijah Muhammad. Police said the men were obviously concerned with the welfare of Malcolm X and a showdown appeared imminent between the two Muslim factions. Malcolm's bitterness appeared to stem mainly from the attempt to evict him from his home in East Elmhurst. The court hearing in that case this week ended with a judge reserving a decision. As Malcolm appeared in court, police received reports of attempts to assassinate him and the Queens courthouse became an armed camp as armed cops guarded him in addition to some of his followers bearing firearms.

Amsterdam News, 20 June 1964

—

The Negro leader of one of two feuding Negro extremist groups here yesterday called on his rival to make peace and work with other Negro leaders in the civil rights struggle. Malcolm X urged in an open letter to Elijah Muhammad, the Black Muslim leader: 'Instead of wasting all of this energy fighting each other, we should be working in unity and harmony with other leaders and organizations in an effort to solve the very serious problems facing all Afro-Americans. Historians would then credit us with intelligence and sincerity.'

New York Times, 27 June 1964

—

I see my brother pursue a dangerous course which parallels that of Judas, Brutus, Benedict Arnold and others who betrayed the fiduciary relationship between them and their leaders . . .

I am aware of the great mental illness which beset my mother whom I love and which may now have taken another victim, my brother Malcolm.

Philbert X, Muhammad Speaks, 10 August 1964

—

Malcolm X is a red, no-good dog. He will be killed by a Muslim or a white devil. If we decide to kill Malcolm, no one can help him. All you have to do is go there and clap on the walls until the walls come down and then cut out the nigger's tongue and put it in an envelope and send it to me. And I'll stamp it 'approved' and give it to the Messenger.

Elijah Muhammad Jr, New York, September 1964

—

Malcolm X has renounced the philosophy of black racism and denounced Elijah Muhammad, leader of the Black Muslims, as a religious 'faker'. Malcolm said: 'For 12 long years I lived within the narrow-minded confines of the "strait-jacket world" created by my strong belief that Elijah Muhammad was a messenger direct from God Himself, and my faith in what I now see to be a pseudo-religious philosophy that he preaches. But as his then most faithful disciple, I represented and defended him at all levels . . . And in most instances, even beyond the level of intellect and reason. I shall never rest until I have undone the harm I did to so many well-meaning, innocent Negroes who through my own evangelistic zeal now believe in him even more fanatically and more blindly than I did. I totally reject Elijah Muhammad's racist philosophy, which he has labeled "Islam" only to fool and misuse gullible people, as he fooled and misused me. But I blame only myself, and no one else, for the fool that I was, and the harm that my foolishness in his behalf has done to others.'

New York Times, 4 October 1964

The mud is flying thick and heavy in all-out war between Malcolm X and his former leader, Elijah Muhammad, and police authorities are beginning to wonder if New York is big enough for both of them. They're silently hoping that both leave town – as fast as possible!

The most recent outburst finds Malcolm accusing Mr Muhammad with allegedly seducing several girls in his Muslim movement and allegedly fathering almost a dozen illegitimate children. This bitter diatribe was unleashed in court following Mr Muhammad's attempt to oust Malcolm from his New York home. Mr Muhammad contends that Malcolm's home, in Queens, belongs to the Black Muslim sect. Malcolm, in explosive testimony that shocked the courtroom audience, said that Mr Muhammad allegedly impregnated two girls from prominent Philadelphia families and four others of his corps of 18 'private secretaries'. Malcolm said 11 children were the result of this 'divine intercourse', as he said Mr Muhammad termed it.

Pittsburgh Courier, 7 November 1964

—

The die is set, and Malcolm shall not escape, especially after such evil, foolish talk. Such a man as Malcolm is worthy of death.

Minister Louis X, *Muhammad Speaks*, 4 December 1964

—

The former press secretary of Heavyweight Champion Muhammad Ali (Cassius Clay) told the *Amsterdam News* Tuesday that Malcolm X had been marked for death by his former associates. He added that orders were issued by the Muslims last October calling for all Muslims who followed Malcolm X to be killed or maimed. The charges were made by Leon Ameer, 31, who until last December was a captain in the Muslim order of Elijah Muhammad, assigned as the press secretary to Cassius Clay whose Muslim name is Muhammad Ali. He was severely beaten in the lobby of the Biltmore Hotel in Boston. Police said he was beaten by his fellow Muslims. Hospitalized for 15 days with fractured skull, broken ribs and a ruptured eardrum, Ameer said that a recent shooting of a Corrections Officer in the Bronx was tied up with the war among Muslims created by the defection of Malcolm X from the Elijah Muhammad forces.

Amsterdam News, 16 January 1965

—

Minister Malcolm X this week charged that 'my death has been ordered by higher-ups in the Black Muslim movement'. He alleged that an attempt was made on him last week in Los Angeles as he was leaving a hotel and at his home here in East Elmhurst on January 22nd.

'They came at me three seconds too soon and I was able to rush back into the house and call the police. I came out with my walking stick and the men were gone.'

Malcolm denied reports that he travels with a bodyguard, declaring that 'my alertness is my bodyguard'.

Amsterdam News, 6 February 1965

3

Smethwick, England, 12 February 1965

Three days in Britain. Yesterday, a speech at the London School of Economics. Tomorrow, Birmingham University. This morning a trip to Smethwick, a town four miles outside Birmingham.

From the train station you walk down cobbled streets, past a tired-looking pub and a giant bingo hall, to meet Avtar Singh Jouhl, the energetic leader of the Indian Workers' Association, a local group campaigning against an anti-immigrant fervour that's taken hold of Smethwick. Jouhl leads you through the town, his breath forming steaming clouds in the cold air, as he describes how burgeoning job opportunities in Smethwick's factories and car plants during the 1950s drew thousands of young men from India and the Caribbean. And how, in turn, they received a harsh welcome from locals in the town which was once the constituency of Oswald Mosley, founder of the

British Union of Fascists. Landlords wouldn't rent to them, said Jouhl. Pubs wouldn't serve them. In the factories, they were given the dirtiest and most dangerous jobs. Last year, Britain held a general election. In Smethwick, the contest took place between a sitting Labour MP and Peter Griffiths, the Conservative candidate, a supporter of apartheid who ran on the slogan, 'If you want a nigger for a neighbour, vote Labour.' Griffiths won the seat. At the announcement of the vote, Tory supporters heckled the defeated Labour politician, shouting: 'Where are your niggers now?'

Listening to Jouhl, you think immediately of growing up in Lansing, and how the white folks, even the well-meaning ones, couldn't conceive of black people as anything other than an inferior species. You remember doing some yard work for an elderly white couple who always treated you well, and hearing the husband say to the wife that he couldn't understand how Negroes could be happy living in poverty like they did. And her replying with a shrug, 'Niggers are just that way.' Black people might be with them in the same town but they were never considered *of* them. Smethwick today is no different to Lansing then. You feel the same disgust and anger here as you did there.

A freezing rain blows through the streets and, in the silvery light of its aftermath, the sun a glowing disc behind a thin sheet of cloud, the red-brick terraces that line the roads take on a brighter hue. You notice the varying shades of the brickwork, a spectrum of auburns, ochres and maroons. On a wall a sprig of weed pushes out from a gap in the mortar, straining towards the light.

Jouhl walks alongside you, describing the increasingly tense atmosphere in the town created by Griffiths's victory. Gun pellets were fired through his living-room window, he says. He and his friends were chased through town by white youths. A branch of the

National Socialist Movement has been founded in the area. And Griffiths is backing a plan by the Conservative-run Smethwick Council to buy up properties on Marshall Street, a row of run-down houses that blacks and Asians have recently been moving into. The plan is to rent the houses exclusively to white people to stop the street from becoming what Griffiths calls 'a coloured ghetto'. Marshall Street is where Jouhl is leading you.

You arrive to a hectic scene. A mass of newspaper reporters and a BBC TV crew are clustered in the road, waiting to interview you. On the pavement beside them, a clutch of white residents, mostly women in housecoats, some of them toting small children, look on, arms folded, muttering sceptically among themselves. Griffiths is also here. He's already talking to the press, from amongst a group of aides, his finger indignantly stabbing the air. 'It makes my blood boil that Malcolm X should be allowed into this country,' he is saying. 'The whole news-gathering side of the English world is trying to turn Smethwick into something it's not. This is Birming-ham, England, not Birmingham, Alabama.'

All your life you've known these men, who think their whiteness gives them the right to deny coloured people their respect as a human being. He's no different from the men who killed your father, or the judge who inflated your prison sentence for having a white girlfriend. The sight of him, thin-lipped, red-cheeked, fills you with abrupt contempt. But as you approach the scrum of reporters, you are cool. The reporters spot you and begin shouting questions. 'Malcolm, why are you in Smethwick? What's your message for people here?' Across the street, the local residents start to shout too, hurling abuse at you. How many times in your life, you wonder, will you face white people to insist on your right to existence?

'The worst form of human being is one who judges another

human being by the colour of their skin,' you say to the reporters. From what you understand, Peter Griffiths can strut up and down the streets of Smethwick, preaching *If you want a nigger for a neighbour vote Labour*, and that's all right. As long as it's the far right and the fascists and the Nazis, no problem. But when you, Malcolm, come to Smethwick, there are protests.

As you speak, Griffiths looks on from the side, seething. He tries to interject but you raise your voice and carry on speaking. You will not debate with Peter Griffiths on the streets of this town, you say. He is beneath debate because his kind doesn't accept the basic rules of a civilized society. Britain has a colour problem and people like him would rather object to your presence than address the real issues at hand. From what you've seen today, the situation in Smethwick is as bad as it is back home. Coloured people here are being treated in the same way as the Negroes are treated in Alabama, when all they want is to be respected for their humanity.

Without waiting for any reply from Griffiths, you walk away from the reporters. For a moment you feel overwhelmed by the endless, tidal nature of the struggle. Both with Elijah Muhammad and now on your own, you have fought for black people and you hope to have been of some service through your actions. But it's never enough. The attacks keep coming.

A photographer trails after you, insisting on a photo by the Marshall Street sign. You wonder what expression he'll capture on your face. The resolution of a leader, or a man searching for the strength to keep going?

On the train back to London, the winter fields lying plain and clodded beyond the window. Birmingham, England. Birmingham, Alabama. The issue is not which one is worse than the other but how, in all these places, the same madness prevails. The British in

Africa and American settlers in the New World. Each of them promised to bring civilization and order to the conquered. But all that follows is disorder and violence. The sickness they have sown in its many forms.

Queens, New York, 14 February

Yesterday, you arrived home from Britain to two pieces of news: one unexpected, the other unwelcome. Firstly, Betty is pregnant again. This time with twins, she says. So whether boys or girls, there will soon be six children in the family. Secondly, a final stay of execution on the eviction notice has failed. You will have to move out of the house in a week's time.

The irony of losing this house is that it's barely been a home to you anyway – just the place where you return exhausted from another trip, too tired and tense to spend time with the kids or Betty, retreating instead to your study in the attic to work on your next speech. When you look back now, you realize how little you've been a part of the family. When your girls came, yes, you experienced the shock and joy of becoming a father – you felt that every time. Attallah, then Qubilah, then Ilyasah, then Gamilah. You adored the idea that Allah had enabled you and Betty to create these new human beings that were part of you both. And it has been a beautiful surprise to see each of them taking form, from squalling babies into mercurial children, wild and wilful, sometimes sombre, occasionally profound. You see yourself in each of them.

But what you missed in your many absences. On Sundays, after mosque, going out to eat dim sum or Indian or Ethiopian, and then a show, the Alvin Ailey Company performing *Blues Suite*, setting black life in motion as a kind of magic. What you missed. The kids at the beach, playing in the water, playing in the sand. What you missed. Reading them stories. Sending them drifting into sleep. Attallah and Qubilah back to back in the same bed, their faces so soft, their breathing so gentle.

When you returned from Africa last year, Qubilah had left a little passage on your desk, something she'd read out in school. It was written in pencil in big awkward letters, the spelling haphazard. She'd propped it by your typewriter so you couldn't miss it, and you've kept it there since then. 'Malcolm X, A Black Leader,' it read. 'Malcolm X is a brave leader, he fights for all black people. His words are in everybody's heart. When he preaches, people are listening instead of falling asleep. Listening to his black word.'

—

It is some time past two in the morning and you are asleep at your desk when you hear a crash downstairs. It sounds like breaking glass, a window shattering. You rush out on to the landing to find black smoke billowing up the stairs. Another crash. This time from the master bedroom, where Betty's sleeping. By now you can see that the front of the house is on fire and you're running from room to room, Betty is up too, and you're gathering up the screaming girls and trying to escape through the smoke and heat and the scent of gasoline. In the back yard, near the window of the rear bedroom where Attallah and Qubilah sleep, you find a broken bottle and a burned-out wick. The arsonists must have come from both sides, the front and the back of the house, to hurl their flaming bottles through the windows. To set the whole place alight and trap you inside. But it looks like the guy at the back messed up and dropped his bottle before he could throw it.

Thirty-five years ago, in Lansing, you stood in the early-morning dark, watching your family's house go up in flames. You can picture that scene as clearly as the one before you now. The raw heat and your terrified brothers and sisters, wailing and coughing from the smoke. The creaking of the house as the rafters gave way and the building collapsed into itself. The past and present blur, and you stand like a man on the deck of a ship in a storm, the floor beneath you treacherous and the horizon elusive, and your thoughts and memories jumble together with the smell of smoke, and you feel Ilyasah's hand gripping yours tight, her fingernails digging into your palm.

You can hear your mother crying after they found your father on the tracks. She was inconsolable. All you kids cowed into silence, stuffing down the hurt, while she wandered from room to room, screaming, her mind broken. And then at the funeral, Wilfred standing to shoo a fly away and returning to his seat weeping because he'd done what none of the rest of you could bear to do, and looked into the casket, and seen the caved-in facsimile of Earl's face.

No doubt Elijah Muhammad and his people will be laughing at the sight of you out here in your pyjamas. For a second, you feel a catch in your throat, the intimation of tears, at the thought of your study gone up in flames. All your books – the complete works of Shakespeare, Baldwin, Herodotus, Du Bois, histories of the Moors and the Mali Empire, books on botany and astronomy and Chinese philosophy. The Messenger will take this as a victory. But ultimately this is no more than a setback. In the morning, once the fire brigade has put out the last flames and the police have come and shrugged their shoulders because black folks trying to murder black folks is no business of theirs, you'll fly to Detroit, even if the only suit you can find is stinking of smoke, and you will give a speech. Then on Sunday, a lecture at the Audubon Ballroom, and afterwards Los Angeles.

You think of the first time you met Maya Angelou, when she came to see you about the protest for Patrice Lumumba. She wanted you to join them. You told her there wasn't a ghost of a chance. Muslims had no faith in organized politics, you said. Carrying placards wouldn't win freedom for anyone. She went away crushed. Even after you got to know her properly in Ghana, you never told her how ashamed you were to have treated her that way. The blindness of that time. You're glad to be free of it. You were a zombie, only capable of following orders, and it cost you twelve years of your life. Even if death comes for you tomorrow, you're more alive now than you ever were then.

Black smoke churning into a black sky. A red glow at the centre of the house. Silvery ash drifting to the ground. It comes to you with an abrupt clarity that the path you're on is the same one you've followed since the Garvey meetings that your father held, driving round the county in his Ford, you beside him as the favoured child. Only a handful of people in a room but the mood righteous and true. Earl raising up his arms as if Africa was just there. A black world within reach. 'No one knows when the hour of redemption cometh. It is in the wind. It is coming. One day, like a storm, it will be here.'

In the 1990s, I worked as a magazine journalist. I often travelled to New York to interview hip hop artists. During that time, much of America was gripped by a moral panic about gangsta rap. This was the era when West Coast artists such as NWA and Snoop Dogg and East Coast hardcore acts like Wu-Tang Clan and Mobb Deep were accused of making music that glorified 'rape, murder and even necrophilia', as one writer put it. For its critics, hardcore hip hop represented a profound break with a tradition of Black music as a medium of kinship and connection, stretching from gospel and blues to R&B and soul. In the words of historian Mark Naison, gangsta rap was 'a sad commentary on the decline of humanistic values in African-American communities and in American society as a whole'.

'It is difficult to convey just how debased rap is,' wrote music critic Stanley Crouch. 'The obscenity of thought and word is staggering.' In New York, the Reverend Calvin O. Butts III was so disgusted by the 'vile, ugly, low, abusive' music form that he piled hundreds of rap CDs on the street outside his church in Harlem and drove over them with a steamroller.

This music was predominantly made by artists who came up amid the fallout of the crack epidemic, in a physical environment typified by poor housing and schooling, inadequate welfare programmes and mass incarceration. And what its critics overlooked is the way these musicians used the genre to express some of the most poignant reflections on male lived experience of their generation. Hip hop was where the dynamic tension between street authenticity and hypermasculinity on one hand, and emotional complexity and male vulnerability on the other, was at its most acute. This is how it seemed to me anyway, when I met and spent time with those rappers. Ice Cube, Dr Dre, the Wu-Tang Clan: onstage, they were larger-than-life characters. But in the relative intimacy of an interview setting, they were more introspective, and it was easier to see them as the poets and artists that they were – creatures of sensitivity as much as bravado.

Take the album *Illmatic*, by Nas, for example. The record was released in 1994 and its ten tracks explore coming of age in the bleak aftermath of the crack epidemic. Nas, pictured at the age of seven, stares out from the cover. His eyes are wary. His mouth turned down. He seems to be watching us watching him. His portrait is superimposed over a picture of the monolithic housing projects in Queensbridge where he grew up. The image fixes him as a product of his environment. Its similarity to a mugshot is an ominous foreshadowing of the way Black boys are transformed by the popular imagination into brute, lawless thugs. The names of innocents so carelessly defined as aggressors spring easily to mind. Tamir, Trayvon, Michael. Or think of Ralph Ellison's fictional, unnamed protagonist in *Invisible Man*, grappling with the racialized denial of his personhood: 'I am invisible, understand, simply because people refuse to see me. When they approach me they see only my surroundings, themselves or figments of their imagination – indeed, everything and anything except me.'

Nas was twenty at the time of *Illmatic*'s release but his writing has the circumspection of someone who's seen too much too young. As he recounts on 'Memory Lane (Sittin' in da Park)', 'My window faces shootouts, drug overdoses / Live amongst no roses, only the drama.' *Illmatic* is peppered with references to Willie 'Ill Will' Graham, Nas's best friend, who was shot dead in the same Queensbridge project pictured on the record sleeve. His evident sorrow at Graham's passing turns the record into an elegy, and a testament to life as delicate and precious, even when it's spent in feuds and shootouts over corner spots.

Mobb Deep's 1995 record, *The Infamous*, is another striking document of young masculinity in Queensbridge. The album details the tense, claustrophobic environment of the public housing projects in which the duo, Prodigy and Havoc, grew up, where ordinary life was overshadowed by endemic gun violence and the constant proximity of the carceral state. *The Infamous*, Prodigy reflected afterwards, was an unblinking account of that daily reality. 'We were letting people know, "Dog, this is what it is. This is how we get down."'

But rappers are poets as much as they are documentarians. For all Mobb Deep's emphasis on reality, the record also conjures a strange, swirling, hallucinatory terrain replete with operatic sound effects and lyrics of baroque menace: 'Rock you in your face, stab your brain with your nose bone.' This strand of the album seems to owe as much to Prodigy's inner struggles as to the group's disenchantment with their physical surroundings. We know now that he suffered from the debilitating genetic condition sickle cell anaemia, which caused him to attempt suicide at thirteen, and eventually contributed to his death at the age of forty-two. Personal trauma blended with the pain he saw on the streets around him to create a torturous sense of melancholy: 'I'd be in the hospital . . . Feeling like I ain't gonna make it. When Havoc would make these dark-ass beats, that's exactly how I felt inside. It matched my moods and attitude. That's the attitude I had about life. I didn't give a fuck. I'm going to die anyway.'

The Infamous is certainly *real*. But instead of an album of uncomplicated authenticity, it summons the notion of 'dilated realism' that Ellison described in 1948, when he published an early excerpt from *Invisible Man* in a magazine. Asked by confused readers whether his richly fantastical depiction of Black life was a work of truth or fiction, his response was testy. 'The facts themselves are of no moment. The aim is a realism dilated to deal with the almost surreal state of our everyday American life.'

—

In 1992, the hip hop star Tupac Shakur got a new tattoo. Tupac was a regular visitor to Dago's Tattoo and Piercing Studio, where he had previously received designs including an image of Queen Nefertiti on the left side of his chest above the words '2 DIE 4'. The new tattoo was his most arresting yet. Inscribed across his torso in three-inch-high letters were the words 'Thug Life', the 'i' formed by a bullet. Tupac was twenty-one, improbably beautiful, with high, slanting cheekbones and dark, long-lashed eyes, and the slogan was a telling summation of his conflicted life to date.

Tupac Amaru Shakur was born in East Harlem on 16 June 1971. His mother, Afeni, named him after an eighteenth-century Peruvian revolutionary leader who was executed by Spanish colonizers in gruesome fashion (they had him drawn apart by horses). Afeni was one of the Panther 21, a group of Black Panther Party activists tried for plotting to blow up several New York department stores in the late 1960s. Prosecutors said the group had been intent on 'overthrowing the government by force and violence'. Afeni represented herself in court, while pregnant with the child who would become Tupac. Mounting a brilliant cross-examination of a key prosecution witness, subsequently revealed as an undercover government agent, she won an acquittal for herself and thirteen of her co-defendants.

After this success, Afeni was feted in New York liberal circles – there were invitations to speak at Yale and Harvard, and a subsidized apartment on the Upper West Side. But by the late 1970s, the Panthers' cause had fallen out of fashion, interest in Afeni had waned and the family was struggling. At the age of ten, Tupac had already moved apartments at least eighteen times, including spells in homeless shelters. Sensitive and artistically inclined, he kept a diary, wrote poetry, and involved himself in local community theatre. But he was wracked by insecurity: painfully aware of his family's poverty, embarrassed by his delicate, 'pretty' features, and desperately lonely. 'My major thing growing up was I couldn't fit in,' he recalled in an interview later. 'Because I was from everywhere, I didn't have no buddies that I grew up with . . . Hell, I felt like my life could be destroyed at any moment.'

As he hit adolescence, he was bitterly aware of the absence of a father figure. Afeni had never known who her son's biological father was. When she became pregnant, she had been dating two men: one a fellow Panther and the other a low-level gangster, 'Legs', who worked for heroin kingpin Nicky Barnes in Harlem. At the time, neither had claimed paternity. So the male role models in Tupac's childhood were his stepfather, Mutulu Shakur, and his godfather, Geronimo Pratt, another prominent Black Panther. By the time Tupac was thirteen, Geronimo was in jail and Mutulu was on the FBI Ten Most Wanted list for his part in a violent armed robbery. 'In my family every black male with the last name of Shakur that ever passed the age of fifteen has either been killed or put in jail,' Tupac said later. 'There are no Shakurs, black male Shakurs [. . .] breathing, without bullet holes in them or cuffs on his hands. None.' The lack of a male presence rankled.

It was around that time that Legs came back into the picture. Tupac was pleased to have him in the house. Sometimes he called him 'Daddy'. Legs moved in with the family in the early 1980s and immediately introduced Afeni to crack. 'That was our way of socializing,' she said. 'He would come home late at night and stick a pipe in my mouth.' Legs stayed around for a couple of years before Afeni separated from him. Tupac was fifteen when the news came that Legs had died of a crack-induced heart attack. The loss struck him hard. 'That fucked me up. I couldn't even cry. I felt I needed a daddy to show me the ropes, and I didn't have one.'

In search of a new start, Afeni moved the family to Baltimore. Tupac won a place at the prestigious Baltimore School for the Arts, where he thrived. For a kid from the ghetto, he said, the school was heaven. He majored in drama, studied poetry and Shakespeare, and learned ballet, performing as the Mouse King in *The Nutcracker*. Under the name MC New York, he also started to rap. 'It was the freest I ever felt in my life,' he said. 'There was no gangs. I was an artist.'

The pleasure he felt at school stood in contrast to worsening conditions at home. Hooked on crack and unable to pay the rent, Afeni was unravelling. In 1988, she moved the family to Marin City, Northern California, across the bay from Oakland. The town was an anomaly, the only poor Black neighbourhood in California's richest county. Dominated by a sprawling public housing project, it had few amenities and just one store. To locals, it was known as 'the Jungle'.

Seventeen-year-old Tupac, distraught at leaving Baltimore, found himself the outsider once more: bullied for his appearance, his gaucheness, his lack of street awareness. In an effort to ingratiate himself with the local criminals, he tried selling drugs, but he proved so inept at the job that the dealer demanded his product back. 'They used to diss me. I got love but the kind of love you would give a dog or a neighbourhood crack fiend. They liked me because I was at the bottom.' At home he watched his mother succumb to addiction, becoming lost to herself and her son. Their relationship fell apart, and eventually he cut off contact with her, moving into an abandoned apartment with a group of boys and dropping out of school just before graduation. He continued to write poetry, expressing his forlorn state of mind in poems like 'I Cry':

> The tears I cry are bitter and warm.
> They flow with life but take no form.
> I cry because my heart is torn.
> I find it difficult to carry on.

A few months later, Tupac took a risk. The underground hip hop scene in Northern California was flourishing and his own skills as a poet were developing rapidly. He had heard about an up-and-coming group from Oakland called Digital Underground, known for their sprawling line-up and goofball style. Setting aside the fear of another rejection, he auditioned for the band and was taken on as a roadie and back-up dancer. The work was sometimes demeaning. His duties included simulating coitus onstage with an inflatable sex doll. But he felt at home within the camaraderie of the band and he was inside the music world for the first time, touring with the group and hanging out in the recording studio. He began working on his own music, crafting songs that merged the introspection of his poetry with the painful consciousness of inequality he'd been carrying since childhood.

By 1991, Tupac was ready to release his own debut album, *2Pacalypse Now*. On the record he styled himself as an abrasive, profane gangsta rapper – 'hard like an erection', as he put it on 'Young Black Male'. But his belligerence was intertwined with moments of affecting sensitivity. The poignant track 'Brenda's Got a Baby', for example, was based on the true story of a teenage girl raped by her cousin who threw her newborn baby into an incinerator. *2Pacalypse Now*, he said, was a portrait of a Black generation adrift in America. It was a plea for empathy. 'Before you can understand what I mean, you have to know how I lived or how the people I'm talking to live . . . Compassion, you have to show compassion.'

Further albums followed, each of which sold over a million copies, along with lead roles in major movies. In just a few years, the bullied and friendless teenager had transformed himself into a platinum-selling rapper and film star.

Success put Tupac in company with West Coast hip hop artists such as Ice-T, Scarface, Dr Dre and Ice Cube, whose self-consciously menacing public image played up to the fear and fascination with young Black men that was such a prevalent aspect of 1990s America. This was the age of the 'hoodlum' and the 'thug', a decade characterized by the demonization of young Black men, as typified by the case of Rodney King. In 1991, 25-year-old King was pulled over for speeding in Los Angeles and brutally beaten by four policemen. He suffered a concussion, a broken leg, nine skull fractures, a shattered eye socket, and nerve damage that left his face partly paralysed. In court on charges of using excessive force, the policemen described King as dangerously bestial. He was 'buffed-out', 'bear-like', 'Hulk-like'. He was like 'a wounded animal', 'a mean dog', 'a monster'. They were acquitted of his assault. Afterwards, a member of the jury told the press: 'The police department had no alternative.

He was obviously a dangerous person . . . Mr King was controlling the whole show with his actions.'

Alongside cases like King's came a succession of well-publicized scandals that seemed to further confirm Black men as an inherently criminal element of American society: the O. J. Simpson case, Mike Tyson's rape trial, the sexual harassment allegations against Clarence Thomas during his appointment hearing to the Supreme Court, former Washington DC mayor Marion Barry caught on camera smoking crack. And into this environment of cultivated moral panic arrived a new word: 'superpredator'.

The term was coined in 1995 by an influential political scientist, John Dilulio, who wrote, 'America is now home to thickening ranks of juvenile "superpredators" – radically impulsive, brutally remorseless youngsters, including ever more preteenage boys, who murder, assault, rape, rob, burglarize, deal deadly drugs, join gun-toting gangs and create serious communal disorders.' In the deluge of press stories across the decade that followed Dilulio's report (' "Superpredators" Arrive: Should we cage the new breed of vicious kids?' asked *Newsweek*), Black boys and young men were invariably cast as the perpetrators of violent crime – never, by contrast, as its victims.

Aggressive and nihilistic in persona, gangsta rappers seemed to epitomize this cartoonishly malign figure: Black manhood at its most ruinously miscreant. And none more so than Tupac. He drank to excess, smoked weed heavily, kept a cocked pistol in his waistband and revelled in violent confrontation. 'To the American imagination', said *Spin* magazine, he was 'a gun-toting revolutionary, a sexual dynamo, a loose cannon with a 400-year-old chip on his shoulder'. Yet even while he grew in success and controversy, Tupac continued to make music about what it was to feel stymied and negated while yearning to assert your own presence in the world. He spoke, he said, for 'the have-nots, all the underdogs, all the niggas with no daddies, all the niggas that nobody wants, all the niggas in juvenile hall, in jail and everything. I'm going to remind people how cursed it is out here by being just how I am.'

'The body has a language which "speaks" what it has witnessed,' writes the poet Elizabeth Alexander. In the context of the times, and his own life to date, Tupac's decision to write 'Thug Life' into his skin represented the willed embrace of an outsider status. It was both a symbol of resistance and a mnemonic for anger and shame. According to the film-maker John Singleton, who directed him in the movie *Poetic Justice*, Tupac embodied 'a position that cannot be totally appreciated unless you understand the pathos of being a nigga – that is, a displaced African soul, full of power, pain, and passion'.

For his eloquence in addressing the precarious condition of ordinary Black existence, Tupac is widely considered one of the most influential rappers of all time. He has been the subject of more than a dozen documentaries, plays and books. But I want to dwell here on a period in 1993 when, aged twenty-two, his life began to spiral out of control through one violent, self-destructive incident after another.

In March of that year, Tupac assaulted a limousine driver in a Fox TV parking lot in Hollywood, accusing the chauffeur of speaking to him 'like he was less than a man'. Three weeks later he swung a baseball bat at a local rapper during a concert in Michigan. When the case went to court in September 1994, he was ordered to spend ten days in jail. In April 1993 he attacked the film-maker twins Allen and Albert Hughes after they dropped him from a role in their movie *Menace II Society*. 'That's a fair fight, am I right? Two niggas against me?' he joked before being sent down for fifteen days. Come October, he was arrested again in Atlanta for shooting two off-duty police officers, having gone to the aid of a Black motorist he said was being harassed by the men. One of the officers was hit by a bullet in the abdomen, the other in the buttocks. Tupac was charged with aggravated assault. The case was later dropped when it emerged the policemen had been drinking and had used a racial slur against the motorist, but it played into continued controversy about gangsta rap and the behaviour of its star performers. The day after Tupac's arrest, Flavor Flav of Public Enemy was charged with the attempted murder of a neighbour. This while Snoop Dogg was waiting to stand trial on murder charges in Los Angeles. As the *Washington Post* lamented, 'This brings to three the number of big-name rappers facing gun-related felonies – blurring the lines between the supposed fiction of "gangsta" rap and the reality of today's gun culture.'

A fortnight after the Atlanta shootout, Tupac was in New York. He met a nineteen-year-old woman named Ayanna Jackson and invited her to his suite at the Parker Meridien. When she arrived, Tupac was in the living room of the suite with his road manager and two friends. They were smoking weed and watching TV and Jackson sat with them for a while before Tupac took her hand and led her into the bedroom. They had begun to kiss when the door opened and the three men from the living room entered. Jackson said she tried to leave but Tupac held her down while the other men 'set upon me like animals'.

In Tupac's account of the night, he left when the other men entered and went to sleep on the couch, only waking up when Jackson came back into the living room in tears. 'In my mind I'm thinking, "This motherfucker just raped me, and he's lying up here like a king acting as if nothing happened,"' said Jackson. In the lobby, Jackson told hotel security she had been attacked. Tupac was charged with sodomy, sexual abuse, and an additional count of criminal possession of a weapon after two unlicensed guns were found in the suite. He faced twenty-five years in prison.

The trial opened on 9 November 1994. Outside the courthouse, Tupac was defiant. He spat at the gathered photographers and said of Jackson, 'It was her who sodomized me.' The trial ended on November 30th and the jury retired to deliberate overnight. Just after midnight Tupac and three friends went to a recording studio in Times Square, where he was due to record a verse for a track by the New York rapper Little Shawn. Two men dressed in army fatigues were loitering in the lobby as they entered the building. Despite Tupac's fame, the men looked away, affecting not to notice him. As he waited by the elevator, they looked up, pulled out 9mm pistols and yelled, 'Don't nobody move! Everybody on the floor!' Tupac remained frozen in place while his friends fell to the ground. 'Shoot that motherfucker,' shouted one of the men. A gun fired. Tupac collapsed, wounded. The men tore off his gold chains and a $30,000 diamond ring and fled.

Tupac was rushed to Bellevue Hospital with gunshot injuries to the head, hand and testicle. To the NYPD, the incident was no more than a robbery. But Tupac was convinced the men's real intent was murder. He was sure they'd be back the same night to finish the job. Just hours after emergency surgery, he checked himself out of hospital and moved secretly to the house of his friend, actor Jasmine Guy. The following day he arrived at court in a wheelchair, wearing a bulletproof vest, and bandages round his head. The jury returned its verdict. Tupac was found innocent of the sodomy and weapons charges and guilty of sexual abuse – non-consensual groping and touching. He was sentenced to eighteen months to four and a half years in jail.

Looking back, it might be said that the trial prompted a kind of reckoning for Tupac. During the month-long court case, he had been finishing the recording of a new album. *Me Against the World* was released in March 1995, one month into his incarceration, making him the first recording artist in history to reach number one in the album chart from prison. A tone of weariness pervaded the record, characterized by songs with titles like 'Lord Knows, It Ain't Easy' and 'So Many Tears'. The album mourned the passing of friends and lamented the numbing allure of sex and weed. Thoughts of death formed a running motif. In its more tender moments, it paid affecting tribute to Afeni, affirming his love for her through the bleakest times: 'And even as a crack fiend, Mama / You always was a black queen, Mama.' *Me Against the World*, as Tupac described it, was 'a blues record. It was down-home. It was all my fears, all the things I just couldn't sleep about . . . My inner-most, darkest secrets.'

Locked in his cell for hours on end, unable to drink or smoke, Tupac's manic energy, which had possessed him for years, began to melt away. Becoming calmer and more reflective, he was writing songs and reading 'whole books in a day': Machiavelli's *The Prince*, Sun Tzu's *The Art of War*, the poetry of Nikki Giovanni. He realized that he had been trapped within a persona, forcing himself to play the thug or the gangsta at the cost of losing touch with his sense of self. 'I wasn't happy at all on the streets. Nobody could say they saw me happy. Emotionally it was like I didn't know myself.' Shortly after being sentenced, he sat for an interview with *Vibe*, the music magazine. Throughout his trial he had refused to accept responsibility for Jackson's assault. But in a drab white room in Rikers Island he acknowledged some culpability for the first time. 'Even though I'm innocent of the charge they gave me, I'm not innocent in terms of the way I was acting,' he said. 'I feel ashamed – because I wanted to be accepted and because I didn't want no harm done to me – I didn't say nothing. I'm just as guilty for not doing nothing as I am for doing things.' He was tired of running from the reality of his actions, he said. It was time to grow up. 'The excuse-maker in Tupac is dead. The Tupac that would stand by and let dishonourable things happen is dead.'

A year later, on 7 September 1996, Tupac was killed in a drive-by shooting in Las Vegas. Despite his insistence otherwise, he had returned to a chaotic and violent lifestyle after his release and this had led, with alarming speed, to his death. To my mind, the fact that he fell back into self-destructive behaviour doesn't invalidate the sincerity of his *Vibe* interview. For at least that moment, irrespective of what had taken him to prison or was yet to come, he spoke with the candour of the man he might have been. 'When you do rap albums, you got to constantly be in character. I wanted to keep it real, and that's what I thought I was doing. But now that shit is dead. That thug-life shit . . . Let somebody else represent it. I represented it too much. I *was* thug life.'

———

Interviewed in the *New York Times* in 2017, Jay-Z reflected on how growing up in Brooklyn's Marcy Houses during the same period as Nas and Mobb Deep had left him numbed and cut off from his own feelings. Scarred by the absence of his father, and the chaos and violence caused by endemic drug addiction, he retreated behind a carapace of masculinity. 'You have to survive. So you go into survival mode, and when you go into survival mode what happen? You shut down all emotions. So even with women, you gonna shut down emotionally, so you can't connect.'

Earlier in his career, songs like 'Big Pimpin' had offered a persona of swaggering hypermasculinity. But even in that era, he released tracks like 2001's semi-autobiographical 'Song Cry', which paints a picture of a man trapped within a fixed idea of maleness, hobbled by a fear of intimacy and unable to hold on to the woman he loves. By 2017, he was taking this vulnerability much further. The nakedly confessional '4:44' is an open letter to his wife Beyoncé, pleading forgiveness for infidelity and positing a direct connection between his crippled emotional state and his unfaithfulness as a husband. In baring such private feelings, Jay-Z confronts the constricted notion of masculinity that has defined his life along with many other Black men like him. He rejects the idea that displaying stereotypically 'feminine' characteristics – acknowledging vulnerability, crying, learning to listen – is equivalent to a denial of maleness. He seems instead to channel the spirit of James Baldwin, who observed, 'There is a man in every woman and a woman in every man.'

The previous year, Jay-Z's wife had poured her hurt and anger at his womanizing into an album, *Lemonade*. The suite of videos that accompanied the record, threaded together by verses by the poet Warsan Shire, extended its narrative arc of grief and healing into a richer, more expansive exploration of Black feminism and spirituality. In response, the extraordinary video for '4:44', made by TNEG (a film production company founded by Elissa Blount Moorhead, Arthur Jafa and Malik Hassan Sayeed), takes a similarly collage-like approach.

The central skein of the video is provided by Storyboard P and Okwui Okpokwasili, two virtuoso dancers, who perform in tandem, flowing and flexing with a compelling sinuousness. Instructed to dance without hearing the song, they move together but apart, in a duet of tension and tenderness that mirrors the precarious dynamics of a romantic relationship. Around this recurrent motif, the directors weave an array of found footage and archive interviews into a tapestry of Black life and Black love, figured as alternately fraught and fragile and wondrous. A boy performs an exquisite rendition of Nina Simone's 'Feelin' Good'. Eartha Kitt expounds on the drama of falling in love. A car careers through a parking lot and deliberately rams a bystander. Two women brawl in the street. An enslaved boy stands on an auction block in a scene from *Birth of a Nation*. The scholar Saidiyah Hartman wanders by, caught in half-light, deep in thought. A young man describes hearing the voice of God after being shot in the stomach. For most of the video, we do not see Jay-Z himself. But the candour of his words ('I promised, I cried, I couldn't hold / I suck at love') produces an effect of dramatic self-exposure. This is the artist revealing himself.

The emotional climax of the video comes with a slowed-down clip of Jay-Z and Beyoncé onstage, singing and dancing together, as Al Green whispers his ballad of desire and devotion, 'Judy'. The romantic longing of the scene mirrors Jay-Z's lyrics at their most yearning: 'We're supposed to laugh 'til our heart stops / And then meet in a space where the dark stop / And let love light the way.' Here, symbolically, is the final disavowal of the shell of unfeeling masculinity Jay-Z has carried through his life. In place of hardness there is intimacy and ardour, an open embrace of vulnerability, a reckoning with love as the signal marker of Black humanness. Emerging with quiet force from TNEG's visual mosaic of Black life, the scene lands with striking emotional power that brings to mind Lucille Clifton's deeply affecting poem, 'reply'. The poem begins with an excerpt from a letter to W. E. B. Du Bois in 1905, asking him 'whether the Negro sheds tears'. Clifton writes in response:

he do
she do
they live
they love
they try
they tire
they flee
they fight
they bleed
they break
they mourn
they weep
they die
they do
they do
they do

Justin Fashanu

Wood Green, London, 1967

Often, you are awake before the other boys in the dormitory. You lie in bed listening to them turn and sigh in their sleep, the windows steamed up by their breath. There are six of you in the room. Six boys each in the other rooms along the corridor too, and the same with the girls on the floor above. An acrid scent reaches your nostrils. Someone has wet their bed. The rest of you will pretend not to notice because to do so is to admit that you are as lonely and frightened as him. All the beds have rubber sheets in case of accidents.

The home is a place of order and cruelty. Breakfast at the bell. Room inspections, kitchen chores, schooltime, dinnertime, bedtime. If you are naughty, the staff send you to bed with bread and a glass of water. For more serious offences like stealing, or as one boy did last week, throwing a can of Coke at a supervisor, there is the cane. Always the bawl and thunder of kids. Stampeding down corridors. Jostling in the dinner queue. The sound is a constant, like waves dragging over pebbles. It's a sort of comfort. It promises you're not alone.

For all its rules, the home is also an ungoverned environment. At night, after lights out, a gang of older boys go from room to room beating up the younger kids. You lie awake, mouth dry with fear, wondering if tonight it'll be your door that creaks open on their muffled giggles and greasy faces. By day, some of the boys make monkey noises when you enter the room. These are the kids that you eat breakfast and play football with. They make no distinction between black people as a general mass and the particular fact of your presence. Your friend Gary insists it means nothing for you to be called a wog, especially by him. It's a joke. It's a way of getting along together.

Out by the chestnut trees on the edge of the green, you find a slow-worm one evening. Gary dares you to, so you pick it up and wave it in the faces of the watching boys. It is about a foot long, smooth, shiny and silver-grey, a spray of blue spots on its back. The worm writhes in your fist, desperate to escape. The boys jeer and shriek. Someone says, 'Let it go.' Another calls, 'Eat it!' The creature suddenly goes slack in your hand like a piece of rope. Is it dead? Have you killed it? But the worm's black eyes are still moving and its tongue continues to flick in and out. You watch as its tail detaches from the rest of its body and falls to the ground, where it lies wriggling and twisting like it has a life of its own. You drop the worm in disgust and the circle of boys jumps back in terror. It vanishes into the field, leaving its tail end behind, a partial life moving blindly, falling finally still amid the soil and twigs and grass.

The one thing that brings together all the bruised and angry boys is football. They play whenever they get the chance, in small groups on the green behind the main building, and occasionally all the different games merge into one huge, sprawling match. (Girls are not allowed. You never know where the girls go, how they spend their time.) You aren't very interested in football yourself. The big matches mostly involve you smaller kids chasing hopelessly after the ball while the older boys run away down the pitch out of your reach. But you play anyway, knowing the game will distract you from the voice in your head asking when Mum will come back.

Gary supports Tottenham Hotspur so you say you do too. Spurs's best player is Jimmy Greaves, a goalscorer of studied ease who can beat three defenders and stroke the ball into the net without breaking a sweat. It's a thrill to watch him play even if you don't care as much as Gary, who actually cried after Greaves scored twice against

Lyon in the European Cup Winners' Cup only for Spurs to be knocked out anyway on the away-goals rule.

Kids at the home come and go without warning. Kevin, a small, wiry boy, announces himself your enemy and says he will fight you on the green. For days you have a knot in your stomach. Then on the day of the fight Kevin disappears. His parents have returned and taken him away. The same can happen to any of you. Cars pull up. Children get in and are never seen again. The tendency towards sudden vanishing renders the home's atmosphere subtly warped, like rays of sun through a glass of water.

Each time Mum comes to visit, you wonder if this will be the time she takes you back with her. You still long for that, even though the family you knew has come apart. Dawn and Philip, your older brother and sister, are still with Mum, but Dad has returned to Nigeria. His departure ruined everything. Mum couldn't cope with four kids on her own. On her last visit she explained to you and John that she has remarried but you won't be meeting her new husband yet. She's still waiting for the right moment to tell him she has two sons in a children's home.

When you first arrived, John was so frightened he developed a stammer and you were the only one who could work out what he was saying. You were his interpreter, guide, protector. Don't let them see you scared, you told him, although the truth was, everyone was afraid. The crime is not to feel it but to show it. That's what prompts the older kids to go marauding room to room at night. They're hunting weakness. You have to pretend that you're a man already, impervious to pain.

Shropham, Norfolk, 1968

After the din of Dr Barnardo's, life at Flint House is like someone's turned the volume down on the world. Betty and Alf speak in soft, slow tones, nothing like the clamour of shouting voices and pounding feet. Alf is a big, sleepy man and Betty teaches piano to local kids. Once a year she holds a recital with her pupils in the church hall and afterwards there is tea and strawberries with cream. You try to look pleased when she says she'll bring you and John this year. You haven't been adopted by them, just fostered. Mrs Scott explained the difference before you left Wood Green, but you already knew it – every child in the home knows the difference. Adoption is forever but if a foster family doesn't like you, they can send you right back.

At the rear of the house there is a garden big enough for a chicken coop, an apple orchard and a vegetable plot full of tomatoes and potatoes and flowering courgette plants. The fence at the bottom gives way to open fields and you realize, when you are gazing at the view, that you've never seen the actual horizon before. Never seen how the sun, shafting through clouds, turns the sky into a waving curtain of light and shade.

In the morning. Up early to walk Bubbles, the black Labrador. Watch her spring across the fields, sending the rabbits dashing for cover, the dew spraying off the wet grass in their wake. A pond turned pale green with algae. The colour is just like the walls of the visitors' room at the home. You met Betty and Alf for the first time in that room. They'd thought of fostering just one child but they couldn't bear the thought of you and John being split up. How humiliating it was to have got dressed up in your best clothes while Mrs Scott asked them if they could take on two coloured boys. You looked up at Betty, making your eyes big and imploring. Like a begging dog.

You're grateful to them for taking you in but you still long to have your own family back as one. Dad returned. Mum squeezing you tight. Dawn and Philip and John all together. But Mum has a new baby to go with the new husband who still might not know you exist. And there's been little word from Dad since he went back to Nigeria.

Nightmares wake you up, thrashing and sobbing in bed. Once you are jolted awake by a cracking sound. You've been sleepwalking and have punched a dent in your bedroom door. You come to in confusion, staring at the door in your pyjamas, then looking around for the intruder in the room.

1972

In Shropham, there is only one football team that counts. Norwich City. To fit in here means dumping Spurs and learning to love the Canaries. And, in equal measure, to loathe Ipswich Town, their local rivals in the neighbouring county of Suffolk. As you've learned, Norwich have had the worse of it between the two clubs in recent years. The team is adrift, searching for direction and hoping for better times. You know the feeling. But Norwich have been fighting back this season, much to the excitement of the local fans. The club has won promotion to the First Division for the first time in its history, which means the whole of Shropham is abuzz whenever a Norwich game makes it on to *Match of the Day*. After the team beats Ipswich 2–1 on the opening day of the season, the town is feverish with joy.

You're finding your feet as a footballer too. At eleven, just starting secondary school, you're already taller and faster than kids two, three years older than you. No trailing at the back of the pack any more. You race past defenders, spreading panic in the opposition box just by your presence alone. You are selected for Attleborough FC, the local youth team, and discover a new pleasure in dominating games as a centre-forward. In the winter months you turn up wearing a bright red woolly hat and mittens that Betty has knitted for you. You look ridiculous but that's OK. The sight of you sets the other team laughing. Who's the coloured clown? But once the match starts, they don't know what's happening. You're so quick they can't keep track of you. There you are, idling by the back post in your red hat while some big defender's calling you a black bastard. Then you've slipped past him and scored before he's even thought of moving. Almost from match to match you can feel yourself becoming more attuned to the rhythm of the game. Nobody can hold you back. One afternoon, Attleborough have three players off injured. You push the other team aside single-handed to score four goals and win the match.

Betty and Alf are only cautiously encouraging of this newfound talent. They don't come to watch you play. Betty says she's proud of you but that she'd prefer you spent more time on your homework than football. You're bright enough to be a doctor or a scientist, she says. You play on anyway, three evenings a week and every Saturday, delighted at how easy it feels to command the pitch. When you write to Mum you say that you're fine and John is fine and then you tell her about your latest match and how many goals you scored. 'Justin is without doubt a strong social leader and remarkably competent in most forms of social intercourse,' says your end-of-year school report. 'He is a sociable and lively member of the class and is very popular.'

In the summer holidays, you and John go beet-picking for pocket money. It's hot, tiring work but you're still kids, full of energy, and you take to racing each other along rows in the field, tugging up the vegetables as fast as you can, until you've left the other pickers far behind. An older man, red-faced in the heat, straightens up, scowling, and shouts towards you, 'Hey, Sambo, get back in bloody line.' The words sting but you slow down until the rest of them catch up. When it's time for a break, someone passes round a bottle of water. Everyone has a swig, holding the bottle away from them and letting the liquid arc into their mouths. By the point it reaches you, the bottle is empty. You and John return to work parched.

Later in the summer, local newspapers report that six servicemen at a US airbase in Lakenheath have been court-martialled for erecting a cross on a football pitch and setting it alight. One of the servicemen made an anonymous call as it blazed, saying, 'This is just the start for the niggers.' When he was caught, he insisted the whole thing was meant as a joke.

Your life here in the countryside has always felt fragile, contingent, but this summer as you walk along the lane, past hedges of sweet briar and bushes drooping with blackberries and redcurrants, you wonder – will there be a cross round the next bend, burning in the field, flames leaping in the breeze, waiting for you? Don't let them win, you tell yourself.

1977

The most exciting team this season is Nottingham Forest. At school, on TV, in the papers, they're the only club anyone is talking about. Norwich have been unremarkable since reaching the First Division. By comparison, Forest's progress has been thrilling to follow. Two years ago the team was floundering mid-table in the Second Division. Then they hired a new manager, Brian Clough. In his first year in charge, Clough got them promoted to the top tier. Now they're on course to win the league. Clough has a long, pointed nose and a distinctive nasal voice that every TV comedian and kid in the playground wants to have a go at imitating. And he's a natural entertainer. One evening you're watching *Parkinson* when Clough turns up as a guest, a mischievous smile on his lips and the audience howling with laughter: 'My wife said to me in bed, "God, your feet are cold." I said, "You can call me Brian in bed, dear."'

The footballing world is not short of showmen and big personalities. You read about them in *Match Weekly*. Put their posters on your wall. Malcolm Macdonald ('Supermac'), Emlyn Hughes ('Crazy Horse'), Ron 'Chopper' Harris, and wayward Charlie George, known for headbutting Kevin Keegan and celebrating a goal against a team by giving the V-sign to a stadiumful of its supporters. This is the world that beckons you. You are sixteen, just out of school, and your starring appearances for Attleborough have earned you a contract with the Norwich City Youth Team.

The apprentice players are the very lowest rung of life at the club. You sweep the litter on the terraces, clean toilets, scour the big communal bath in the dressing room, and pick up the senior players' kit from the floor, sodden with sweat and mud. Still, you stick together. That means pie and chips at the cafe across the road once training's done at midday. Pints on a Saturday night. If it's your birthday, things get boisterous. A lad might get his hair shaved off. Or he'll be shoved naked into the showers and coated in black boot polish.

The atmosphere is much more serious among the First Team. You watch how Duncan Forbes, a brutally combative defender, handles himself. He's had a fractured rib and a punctured lung while taking on opposition forwards, and broken his nose on five separate occasions. You decide you want to be like him. A big player. As fearless in attack as Forbes is in defence. In your first year as an apprentice, you finish the season with forty-three goals and a name for yourself as the club's most compelling new prospect. Already you're playing for the reserves, just one step away from the starting eleven. You overhear John Bond, the manager, talking to the coach about you, praising your aggression on the pitch. 'That boy is unstoppable,' he says. 'In the box he puts himself where angels fear to tread.'

—

You wake to the thump of a crow landing on the roof above your bedroom, its claws tap-tapping across the tiles. It is Wednesday, a day off from training. How rare it is to be alone, no running, no performing. You sit up and catch sight of yourself, stripped to the waist, in the wardrobe mirror opposite. The reflection feels far away, unreachable. It might be a stranger looking back. You watch how his face shifts with the play of light from the window. One moment his eyes are soft, his lips full, a young matinee idol. Now, a tilt of the head, and he's ten years older, stern and firm-jawed. The figure in the mirror stretches out his arms, displaying a sculpted chest, a taut stomach. A thin gold necklace glints against the darkness of his skin. He might be beautiful.

The door creaks and you catch sight of John silently watching you. Hard to know how long he's been standing there. Long enough for you to feel exposed, as though he's caught you wholly naked, stripped inside out. John is tall and muscular now, although in your head he remains the same little brother who followed you around the home. What does he see when he looks at you? Before you can speak, he vanishes from the doorway, as silently as he appeared.

Mid-morning you meet Phil, Dean and Sammy at the snooker hall. Without training, the day stretches long and purposeless before you. The empty hall is suffused with the smell of cigarettes and beer, as though it's full of invisible punters. Sammy racks the balls, takes the first shot and sends the coloured spheres clacking across the baize. Phil and Dean start their own game on the neighbouring table. Sammy is the first to pipe up in the dressing room at half-time if the lads are low and getting beat. The first to get the pints in afterwards, win or lose. And to turn up on Monday with some story from the weekend about shagging a girl in the toilet cubicle at the pub.

You bend over the table. Pot a red. Miss a blue. Sammy is bragging about a girl he scored with last night. 'Playing for Norwich is the greatest thing to ever happen to yours truly,' he says. 'Which bird is gonna look at an ugly cunt like me otherwise?' Sammy pulls a copy of *Razzle* from the back of his jeans and passes it to you. 'Get a look at that horseflesh,' he says. You open the magazine on a woman in a strained pose, skin pallid as moonlight, fingers parting a triangle of pubic hair. Sammy is watching and you try to match the leer of delight on his face, although the splayed woman, the magazine's slick paper, the smell of stale cigarettes in the room, it all stirs up a taste of bile in your throat. You'd rather let the magazine slip to the floor but he's still looking at you so you continue to feign interest, turning the page to the next blank-eyed woman.

In the afternoon, the four of you wander aimlessly along the high street, and Sammy says, 'Let's go to the movies.' You buy tickets for the new James Bond, and take your seats at the back of the cinema, away from the few other scattered punters. During a scene with a Bond girl in a low-cut dress, you hear Sammy stirring beside you. He is slouched down low in his seat, breathing heavily, his hand jerking rhythmically at his crotch. He catches you watching him and looks up with a cackle: 'Don't mind me, I'm just a dirty fucker.' You turn back to the screen, uncomfortably aware of the motion of Sammy's hand, rubbing harder and harder. Finally, he arcs his back with a long, shuddering groan, and then slumps into his seat, wiping his hand on the red velvet covering, and returns his attention to the film. A scent like chlorine hovers in the air, a veil between you and the screen.

You envy Sammy's capacity to behave as he pleases, regardless of the circumstances. He's at home anywhere he goes. The same with the other apprentices. On Saturday nights the boys move as a group, pouring into a club together, drawn by the prospect of girls and alcohol. They sit in a pack sizing up the talent and, by midnight, Sammy'll have his hand up a girl's dress and the rest of them will be on the dance floor trying to pull. You're usually in the midst of it all, two or three girls around you at a table, while the lads look on gleefully, calling you a pimp, a stud. In the late-night miasma, the boys drunk or preoccupied with women, you leave, unnoticed, on your own. As you walk home through the empty streets, you imagine going back to a girl's place. She lets her skirt drop to the floor, unbuttons her blouse, crawls on to the bed, winds herself about you. The softness of her breasts as she unclasps her bra. Her lips parted and the mist of her breath on your face. But this is where your thoughts stall. You watch, as though from a distance, unable to imagine yourself beside her, engulfed in the warmth of her body. A car speeds past, its rear lights glowing like two red eyes, observing you as they recede into the dark.

It's only once you're home that your dreams unfurl themselves. You picture one of the lads in the club, entangled with a girl, his hands searching up and down her body, and you put yourself in her place, his tongue searching the softness of your mouth. Or you imagine yourself the object of Sammy's arousal in the cinema. His voice groaning in your ear, his hand jerking, the sour fragrance of his cum, all of his desire directed at you.

Then, like clockwork, your mind follows the path back to Louis. Betty and Alf's nephew, come from London to stay for the Easter holidays last year. He was eighteen, two years older than you, and due to sit his A levels in May. For the most part Louis kept to himself. At dinner, he wolfed down his food, barely looking up, and then disappeared back into his room. He said he was revising although as far as you can tell he mostly spent the time lying on his bed listening to tapes of punk bands. He paid no attention to you or John. Meet him in the corridor and he'd brush past you, dark hair falling down across his face, with no more than a mumble. Betty and Alf appeared baffled by him. You, in contrast, found it amusing to think of this figure, so self-absorbed, marooned out here in the Norfolk countryside. You tried to match his disregard. But the idea of him in the next room, close enough almost to touch, kept running through your head. At times you couldn't sleep for thinking of him.

Out one evening walking Bubbles, you spotted Louis striding alone ahead of you. The Labrador rushed over excitedly and you fell into step beside him. He didn't speak but neither did he march off, so you walked together in silence through the falling light, pausing to watch the nesting coots scattered along a brook, and then taking the footpath that ran along the side of the fields, Bubbles dashing ahead and then running back to make sure you were keeping up. By the time you were home it was dark. Louis slipped into his room without saying goodbye.

The following evening, he was out again and you fell into the same routine. At the brook he sat down with his back to a tree. You sat beside him. In the twilit silence you studied the eddies on the surface of the stream, the endless, infinitesimal ripples. Without warning, Louis started talking about punk music. It made him feel angry and alive, he said. He reeled off a list of the bands he liked: the Lurkers, the Users, Devo, Suburban Studs. His voice was so soft he might have been talking to himself. The words hung in the air while you considered how to reply. You'd never heard of any of those groups with their vaguely menacing names. You could have told him about hanging around with Sammy and the other apprentices. Wanting to be like them and feeling different. And sometimes feeling happy at that difference and sometimes sad. But all you managed was a nod and a mumbled *yeah*. In the lull he said, 'Silence has its own noise too. The quieter you are, the more you can hear it.' So you sat looking at the water. Listening to the sound of the blood in your ears. You were sitting close enough to Louis for his shoulder to touch yours and you felt his weight increase until he was leaning on you and you were leaning on him. At the base of the tree your hand rested beside his, lightly touching, your palm on the rough surface of a root.

Later that week. Another walk. At the tree your eyes met. He stroked your face, leaned towards you with parted lips. You kissed him. The soft firmness of his hands. His mouth. He unbuttoned the top of your jeans and pushed his hand inside, reaching for your erection. The touch of his fingers made the breath catch in your chest. You leaned your weight on his shoulder, making short, strained gasps until, quite abruptly, you climaxed. The sensation of dizzy release gave way to a plunging shame. 'I'm sorry,' you said. 'I'm . . .' Louis stretched his arms around you. 'For what,' he whispered, his face close to yours. 'There's nothing to be sorry for.'

Norwich, 1979

You make your First Team debut on a viciously cold January afternoon, against West Bromwich Albion, the pitch frozen hard. 'A treacherous surface,' reports the *Sandwell Evening Mail*. 'Four tons of sand had to be spread across it before the match could go ahead.' As well as being your first senior match, the game brings you face to face with the Three Degrees. Alone among leading clubs, West Brom have three black players in their starting line-up: Cyrille Regis, Laurie Cunningham and Brendon Batson, each of them prodigiously talented. Their nickname was coined by their manager, Ron Atkinson, in homage to the glamorous black female pop trio. Black players have been a rarity through the history of British football. The Ghana-born Arthur Wharton, one of Preston North End's season-long-undefeated 'Invincibles' squad in the 1880s, was pretty much unique for decades after his career. But that's starting to change. Today, there are some fifty black players in the top leagues, with Nottingham Forest's Viv Anderson the first to be selected for England. And now here you are, breaking through.

With both teams on the field and the referee about to blow his whistle, you stage an impromptu ceremony, crossing the halfway line and shaking hands theatrically with Regis and Cunningham at the centre circle, marking your meeting with them like it's a moment of football history.

Your first goal of the season comes in a 2–2 draw with Leeds, followed soon after by another in a match away against Nottingham Forest. And then more. You can feel how your game has improved now that you're playing at the top level. With each match you assert yourself anew. You take to the pitch to roaring fans. To the inevitability of another triumphant display. The joy beating inside you each time you take a strike at the goal or wrongfoot some hapless defender. Sometimes the delight is so uncontainable that you pull off your boots at the end of a match and hurl them into the cheering crowd. Then the next day, poring over the match reports in the papers, searching for your name. 'Fashanu is not one of the game's more modest exponents, and possesses a cockiness and sense of fun that is all too rare these days,' says the *Express*. 'He is a member of that rare breed in British football – the character.'

———

The 1979–80 season begins in glorious fashion. You score twice in the opening game to win 4–2 against Everton. And twice again to beat Spurs 4–0 the following week. Norwich go top of the league for the first time in their history and in September you are named Young Player of the Month. You donate the prize money to Dr Barnardo's. A reporter at the *Daily Express* asks what's behind your success. In the past, you say, you'd tried to play like a striker is expected to and that made it easy for opponents. Then it dawned on you that you didn't want to be stereotyped. You're you and nobody else so you started doing your own thing instead. To the sports press you are a rare and unfathomable wonder. Black ace. Coloured prospect. Norwich's new black boy. Black striker of immense promise. Latest coloured starlet to twinkle on the England scene. It will be interesting to see how Justin Fashanu shapes up in the coloured player stakes. Norwich have their own black Flash.

———

February. After the heady start to the season, Norwich have slipped to mid-table. This afternoon you host Liverpool, two-time winners of the European Cup and the team that has replaced you at the top of the league. You are more nervous about today's match than any previous game. Liverpool's starting line-up is full of players you grew up watching on TV. Kenny Dalglish. Graeme Souness. Alan Hansen. To you, they might as well be gods descended from Mount Olympus.

Maybe it's because you're overawed that you start the match so haltingly. It's not just you. It seems like the whole team is off. You're all struggling to get into the game. Something is not clicking. Liverpool are just a smoother, better-organized side and they leave you tattered in their wake. By the second half Norwich are 3–2 down and only just managing to hold their own. Yet the longer the match goes on the more you start to glimpse chances opening up on the pitch. Liverpool are getting too confident. You can see the gaps in their defence. The balance of the game is shifting.

At seventy-four minutes, the ball finds you on the edge of the Liverpool penalty area with your back to the goal. A big opposition defender comes barging forward to claim back possession. You hold him off. At the same time, you flick the ball up with your right foot, spin round to face the goal, and strike it with your left foot. The ball arcs through the air, past the outstretched hand of the leaping goalkeeper, Ray Clemence, and into the top corner of the net. The flawless beauty of the goal draws a collective gasp from the crowd, before the stadium erupts into roaring. Barely deigning to acknowledge the noise, you walk back to the centre circle on your own, one finger pointed to the sky, a mortal challenger to the gods. Footage of your strike makes the *Nine O'Clock News* that night and, at the end of the football year, viewers on *Match of the*

Day vote it Goal of the Season. You are nineteen and, with little prelude, wildly famous.

Bill Bothwell

I read somewhere the other day that Justin Fashanu was the current soccer scene's equivalent of Muhammad Ali. Brian Clough will be livid if he hears that. Justin sounded off in a television interview in a way that conveyed the impression to one and all that not only was he the greatest now, at 19, but that he proposed to become even greater and a millionaire at 26.

From here at the *Liverpool Echo*, I take a proprietary interest in young Fashanu. You see, he was virtually unknown outside reserve football in East Anglia when I first wrote in this column about the breathtaking shooting power of the coloured boy I'd seen a few days earlier. My suggestion that in two years or less the ebony-featured teenager with dynamite in his boots would be a star got the hollow laugh from a First Division manager, who reckoned Justin a nine-days wonder. Well, he knows better now. I hope the increased fame and fortune don't distort the honesty, candour and self-possessed charm of a boy who seemed to me to be restating the truth that it isn't where you start that matters, it's the driving force you generate when you get going.

Norwich, 1981

Bliss it is to be the youthful pride of East Anglia in this new decade. You earn £500 a week and drive a silver Series 5 BMW. You present your own football show, *Fashanu in Focus*, on Radio Norfolk, and write a column for *Match Weekly*. Kids follow you for autographs.

313

Women write you adoring letters. 'Dear Justin, What a great time at Cromwell's nightclub dancing to the Commodores. Every girl wanted to dance with you and your smile was radiant. I think of you every time I smell Paco Rabanne.'

You record a single, 'Do It Cos You Like It'. The sound is pop-soul and on the record sleeve you style yourself like Michael Jackson, with jheri curled hair and jacket and trousers in matching red leather. The lyrics are about appetite, desire, gratification. 'There's no point being cautious / You shouldn't hesitate / Just go out and get it / You've got what it takes.'

BBC Norwich asks you to appear in a documentary series on up-and-coming stars called *The Pace-Setters*. The TV crew trails you from breakfast with Betty and Alf to training in Norwich. Cruising through town in your BMW, you tell the presenter coolly: 'Most people in a village like Shropham associate black people with what they see on the TV, which is muggers and hoodlums and Rastafarians with dreadlocks. But as long as you hold yourself well and don't embarrass people by letting them think, "Oh, he's so thick" or "His ways are so silly," you're all right. You have to have a little bit of presence about you. If you can be just a bit clued-up and you've got a bit of style about you, then you can't go wrong.'

You park the car and as you climb out a swarm of kids surrounds you. 'As far as the fans are concerned, at times they can be a bit of a hassle, when you're not in a good mood and you've got a lot of people around you and they put their fingers on your car which you've just cleaned. But most of the time it's good, because it shows that you're wanted and people love you and it's something which you'll miss when you're not in the limelight.'

'How do you see your life developing over the next ten years?' asks the presenter. You scratch your chin and put on a show of contemplation. Then you gaze up into the camera lights with a broad smile. All you want, you say, is to get more rich and more famous.

At the end of the season, Norwich offer you a new contract which will make you one of the league's highest-paid players. You turn them down, telling reporters you want to move to a big-name team – a glamour club. Manchester City, Liverpool and Newcastle are all fighting for your signature. You are going to be British sport's Muhammad Ali. 'The biggest, the best, the greatest.' It is Nottingham Forest that win the battle to sign you, and even for the biggest manager in English football you come at a price. 'Fashanu Makes It a Million!' runs the headline in the *Eastern Daily Press*. Brian Clough has sent you into the record books as the first £1 million black player in British football history.

Your hunger for attention is so intense it almost hurts. You're reminded of your appetite when you see John trying to follow in your footsteps, eager to grow up. He signs for Norwich apprentices but is soon dropped and then tries out unsuccessfully for a succession of teams. The clubs all expect him to be as good as you were at his age. But at seventeen, you were playing with grown men in their twenties and he's just not at your level yet.

One afternoon you find him waiting for you in the car park after training. A group of boys are clustered around him and he's signing autographs for them. The sight of him feeding on their eagerness enrages you. 'Earn the right to sign your own name,' you say. These kids are only after him because of you, Justin. The level of your anger surprises you but you can't hold it back. You snatch the pen from his hand and snap it in two as the kids scatter and John stands, frozen on the spot, staring at you in dismay.

Sometimes he comes to you saying, 'Help me a bit. Give me a bit of money.'

'John, you've got to work for everything,' you say. 'If you want fame, you've got to work for it.'

When you're out you know that he goes through your suits, looking for spare fivers or tenners you've left loose in the pockets. The gulf is growing between you as your fortunes diverge. He resents your success and in turn you find his neediness embarrassing. You're not in the home any more. What he doesn't understand is that becoming a star means staying in character all the time, always moving ahead, never looking back.

John

Justin has now got to the position where he's so popular in Norwich he can do anything, go anywhere, say anything. He can park his car outside a restaurant on double yellow lines, go in, have a meal and refuse to move it. These are the sort of stubborn, arrogant things that he's getting into now. He's losing his background. He's started to believe in the publicity.

Every day in the papers, he's being hailed as a superstar. Everybody knowing him. Everybody singing his praises. Every day another story about Justin scoring three goals, beating eleven men on his own and putting the ball in the back of their net.

After the Liverpool goal, the endorsements for boots and shirts came pouring in. A lot of money. It became ridiculous. Spending thousands of pounds on clothes and shoes. It's sickening.

——

A Thursday afternoon. Your last few weeks in Norwich. Out shopping for records, you are wandering through the Lanes, the city's historic quarter of narrow cobbled streets and Tudor half-timbered houses. Normally when you're out in public you're conscious of being on display. Fans shout your name or stop you for an autograph. The Lanes feel cut off from the rest of the city. Most passers-by have their heads turned upward, looking at the architecture. They're more interested in the sixteenth-century buildings than the sight of a First Division footballer. That leaves you free to occasionally meet the eye of another man walking past you, his gaze returning yours, looking you up and down without bothering to hide his interest. He walks on and you walk on. But you covet each such exchange, with its discreet erotic charge, and the knowledge that all around you are people shopping and sightseeing while you and these other silent, passing men are engaged in some secret language of desire.

You haven't been close to another man since Louis. Your mind still drifts to him, thinking about what he's doing, which bands he's listening to, where he's living. At the same time you realize you'll probably never see him again. It only happened once – your paths met briefly and then diverged. You can't ask Alf and Betty about him in case they notice a particular tone in your voice. Even if he were suddenly to show up at Flint House again, you can't imagine repeating that evening.

You tell yourself that looking at men out in the street amounts to nothing more than being open-minded. It's different if you decide to act on that desire. The prospect fills you with horror as much as fascination. The gay men on TV are fantastically camp types like Larry Grayson and John Inman. You are nothing like these men, objects of pity and ridicule. Occasionally, a bloke walking down the street holding hands with a woman will pass you with a lingering glance. Sometimes you are that man. You meet girls in pubs, in clubs, on Saturday night after a match. You go back to their place and then you date in a desultory way for a few weeks or a couple of months. Only Steph lasted longer than that.

Steph, who was smart and shy and quite different to the women who are only into you because you're a famous footballer. Steph wanted to be a writer. She gave you books, unintelligible books: *Gravity's Rainbow*, *The Bluest Eye*. 'Hereisthehouseitisgreenand- whiteithasareddooritisveryprettyhereisthefamilymotherfatherdick- andjaneliveinthegreenandwhitehouse . . .' And in return, you played her records that made your heart soar – 'Body Talk' by Imagination, 'London Town' by Light of the World – and tried to explain to her how you loved the sensuality of British soul music, and the fact that these young, black bands were spinning the stuff of their daily life into something unique, just like you running on to a football pitch and striving to conjure a wondrous moment out of the chance pat- terns of a ninety-minute match.

With Steph you came closest to dropping the mask. You told her how much it hurt to be rejected by your parents, and the lone- liness of the home. How you still have nightmares, although their shape is never clear, how you wake to the emptiness and anger. You talked together about getting engaged, getting married. Having children. You saw how you might acquire the certainty you'd never known growing up. Everyone would be happy for you. John, Alf, Betty. Perhaps having your own family would bring you closer to Mum and even Dad in Nigeria. But you also knew that it would be a brittle life. The life of a man hiding from himself. Eventually the surface would crack and give way to desires you couldn't control. In the end you split up with Steph. You sat at her kitchen table while she sobbed opposite you, saying she couldn't understand why it was over. You said nothing. You were sorry to have upset her. But you felt no deeper emotion at that time, other than a sense of relief. You just wanted to be gone, away from the kitchen, away from intimacy.

The curving streets of the Lanes take you finally to your destination, a tiny record store, the only place in Norwich that specializes in soul and funk. Step inside. Shut the door. Let the music sweep over you while you search through the rows of albums, the music holding you close.

———

Before starting the season with Forest, you take a trip to Nigeria with John. You've hardly heard from Dad since he left the family, but now he has been in touch. He is running a law firm in Lagos and has invited you both to visit. As you weave through the crowded airport, your trepidation is mixed with the giddy pleasure of arriving in Africa. For the first time in your life, you are only a face in the crowd, indistinguishable from everyone else.

All around you is the delirious sprawl of Lagos. The roar of cars and mopeds and the ceaseless waves of people. The chaos is alarming. You feel like you might be swept away. Yet at the same time it's intoxicating to be here. Amid the traffic fumes and the scent of spiced roast beef from the street vendors. The market that runs for miles along the tracks of a disused railway line. Throngs of minibuses with hand-painted signs praising Jesus, and the hoardings advertising skin-lightening creams and herbal impotence remedies. When you finally get there, the family house is busy with aunties and cousins and half-siblings. One of them shows you round, pointing out the kitchen, the guest bedroom where you'll sleep, the garden scattered with mangoes fallen straight from the tree, their juice so sweet it's heady like liquor.

On your first night, everyone eats together over dishes of pepper soup and rich, dark goat stew, heaps of jollof rice glimmering with buried pieces of onion, tomato and corn, white and red and yellow. Fireflies glowing in the garden. The earthy taste of eko tutu – steamed, fermented corn pudding – sends you spinning back in time, to before Dad left home and your own family was whole and gathered round a table. It occurs to you with an ache that no matter how many years have gone by since then, a part of you is still imagining the day when the family will be sitting together as one.

You watch carefully how this new family behaves towards Dad. To them he is a Big Man, strong and powerful, demanding of respect, even fear. In the living room, the day after you arrive, you and John sit opposite him, beneath the aggressive whirring of a ceiling fan. He looks the same as you remember. High cheekbones and smooth, dark skin. You are excited and nervous and you talk at him without pause, hoping to impress on him the scale of your success, the Liverpool goal, the size of your transfer fee. Perhaps he will realize how much he's missed since leaving. It's some time before you notice that he is hardly responding, except to nod and smile vaguely. Although you've come all this way to be with him, there's still a gulf between you.

The week is full of food and football games out on the dusty square near the house, where you become a Big Man yourself, invincible ruler of the pitch, amid a trailing mass of cousins and half-brothers. Dad goes to his office every morning and returns home late without paying you much attention, as if you are just another of the many boys in the house. Sometimes your cousins take you out into Lagos and you are mesmerized by the brilliantly dressed men and women in headwraps and embroidered dresses and agbada suits in pink and violet and cornflower blue. But despite the dynamism of city, the days leave you flat and dispirited.

After you return home, you don't hear from Dad again. The visit plays on your mind. What could you have done differently? What kind of man did he want his son to be?

2

Nottingham, 1981

He is, as ever, instantly recognizable. Hazel eyes. Nasal voice. The green sweater and insistently jabbing finger. Everybody knows Brian Clough. When he arrived in 1975, Nottingham Forest was his fourth club in three years. He'd gone from winning the league with Derby and a sojourn at Brighton to a 44-day debacle at Leeds, and there were plenty of people saying he was washed up. At Forest, Clough was reunited with Peter Taylor, his closest friend and long-time assistant, who he'd previously partnered with at Derby. With Clough leading tactics and Taylor as chief scout, Forest followed promotion to the First Division by winning the league title and then, for two successive years, the European Cup. No other British manager has ever achieved so much so fast.

The scale of his accomplishments is matched by his singular manner. The press and public regard him with a mix of reverence, amusement and terror. 'He is a man of extraordinary contradictions,' reports the *Guardian*. 'He can be famously polite or infamously rude, minutely attentive or witheringly dismissive, mean or generous. He does not suffer fools gladly and when he has had enough of someone he will tell them so.'

For all his success, Clough's methods are notoriously unorthodox. He eschews rigorous training or complicated tactical briefings:

'Those who insist that football is intricate and complicated, well, they are too thick to become good managers. Defenders defend, midfield players provide the link and, if you're lucky, strikers score goals. It never ceases to amaze me that so many people make such a simple job so complex.' He insists that a manager's real work is getting his team mentally fit. The night before the 1979 League Cup final at Wembley against Southampton, he gathered the squad in the hotel bar, ordered beers and champagne all round and refused to let them leave until they were blind drunk. The striker Tony Woodcock had to be helped to bed. The hangovers were brutal but Forest won the match, and it was Woodcock who scored the deciding goal. Clough employed a similar tactic before the European Cup semifinal against Ajax in Amsterdam, when he led the team on a walking tour of the red-light district, including a live show in a strip club.

Of all the talents of the most gifted manager of his generation, what stands out is his ability to talk. To listen to Clough is to risk joining the devotees who hover around him, mesmerized by his charisma and cunning wit. For a player, the dream is that Clough might see something special in you, just as he took a gaggle of also-rans and turned them into European champions. The week before you move to Nottingham, he mentions you in his *Daily Express* column. Centre-forward is the most difficult job on a football field, says Clough. 'The No. 9 shirt has gone out of fashion. Even kids have stopped talking about wanting to be centre-forwards. But Justin Fashanu might soon bring it back.'

—

On your first day at Forest, you arrive dressed in a white suit, a gold chain round your neck and a long black wool coat with fur lapels draped off your shoulders. In the car park is a white Toyota Celica sports coupé with 'Justin Fashanu' emblazoned on the side in big letters. A local dealership has given you the vehicle and as a marketing stunt has arranged to put a miniature sticker of a football beside your name for every goal you score.

There are wolf whistles and sarcastic cheers from your new teammates when you enter the dressing room. Someone calls out, 'Bloody hell, who've you come as, Huggy fucking Bear?' You give them a wave and a mock bow. Look and wonder: the Million-Pound Man stands before you. Many of the faces turned towards you are already familiar. There are stars like Viv Anderson and Peter Shilton, widely rated as one of the world's best goalkeepers. And beside them, the players whose lives on and off the pitch have been transformed by Clough. John Robertson, an overweight winger drifting into obsolescence, now the wily intelligence at the centre of the team. Kenny Burns, a brutish centre-forward reborn as a centre-back. John McGovern, the team captain who, according to newspaper stories, Clough told witheringly on first meeting to stand up straight, take his hands out of his pockets and go get a haircut.

Taylor, who first brought you to Clough's attention, leads training. He is shrewd and cerebral where Clough is outspoken and abrasive, yet they share the same footballing philosophy of clarity and simplicity. There is no complicated talk of tactics. No boring drills on the pitch. Training is a light five-a-side game. You're done for the day before you've had a chance to show anyone what you're capable of. Clough turns up only briefly on the touchline, wearing the same green sweater familiar from numerous TV clips, and clutching a squash racquet that he smacks absent-mindedly on his leg as he watches the players. He nods in your direction once, then turns away and walks back inside without speaking.

The first match of the season is at home against Southampton. The fans sing your name to the tune of a British Airways ad: 'We'll take more care of you, Fash-a-nu, Fash-a-nu.' It's a 2–1 win for Forest. Although you come close to scoring, you don't get a goal. Neither do you in the next match. Until now you've played football with an instinctive feel for the game, trusting yourself to read the course of play and know when to make a run, when to feint past a defender or attempt a shot. But now the £1 million price tag hangs heavy on you. There is no room for error. You have to prove you're worth it. For the first time, you are thinking before deciding your next move, and in that gap between intention and action comes a creeping self-doubt. A month into the season there are still no goals. Taylor is sympathetic. 'He can play, he'll come good,' he tells the *Nottingham Evening Post*. Clough remains a remote presence, scowling at you from across the pitch.

The dry spell continues. In October a 3–0 loss to Spurs makes it seven games without a goal. Clough comes into the steam-filled dressing room after the match, red-faced, nose twitching. He pushes a framed black-and-white photo under your face. 'See this, young man, it's what you're supposed to be doing.' It's a picture of him from the 1950s, back when he was a prolific striker for Middlesbrough, 204 goals in 222 matches. In the photo, Clough is holding off a lunging defender and booting the ball emphatically into the net. 'Scoring goals, lad, this is what you have to do. It's as simple as that.' You look down at the floor, burning with embarrassment, the rest of the boys sniggering.

The following afternoon, at McKay's, clustering together at the Formica tables over chip butties and tea, cigarette smoke billowing, John Robertson says, don't take it personally, Clough always gives new recruits a hard time. If he thinks you're too cocky, he'll look to cut you down. All the more so if you're a big-money signing. When Trevor Francis arrived as the first £1 million footballer in the league, Clough had him playing in the Forest reserve team. Peter Ward had it even worse. Returning to Nottingham on the team bus from an away game at night, Ward asked the driver to drop him at a service station where his car was parked. Clough shouted to the driver to keep going. The bus had travelled another mile up the road before Clough relented and allowed him out. Even then he wouldn't let the driver turn round. Ward was left to walk back along the hard shoulder of the motorway through the dark and the rain. Clough's parting words as the bus sped off: 'With a bit of luck the cunt'll get run over.'

Robertson grins and slurps his tea. 'He doesn't want you to get too big for your boots, that's all. He wants you to remember that he could replace you anytime with a better player without blinking an eyelid.'

You smile back at Robbo. Everyone knows there are some players who Clough adores whatever the results of a game, and others he holds in barely concealed contempt. John Robertson is his clear favourite. 'He didn't look anything like a professional athlete when I first clapped eyes on him,' Clough likes to say. 'In fact, there were times he barely resembled a member of the human race.' Clough still affectionately calls him the 'little fat bloke'. He also calls him 'an artist' and 'the Picasso of our game'. Then there are those he takes against. Martin O'Neill is a skilful midfielder who plays opposite Robbo. But O'Neill studied law at Queen's University in Belfast, which to Clough, who failed his eleven-plus, makes him 'a smart-arse'. 'You may have A levels,' Clough bellows across the changing rooms at him every few days, 'but you're thick as a footballer.'

Sometimes in the evenings you call Betty and Alf so they know you're OK. You don't mention the strange feeling of disorientation that accompanies Clough's disdain for you, the constant sickness in your stomach. At night in bed, the fear washes over you.

—

Since moving to Nottingham you've been living in a £500-a-week suite at the Albany, in the centre of the city. Each afternoon when you return from training, a maid has tidied up the clothes you left scattered on the floor, erasing the signs of your presence. The sun pours through the floor-length windows. It's hot and airless. To escape the disconcerting impression of being an insect trapped in a jar, you spend the afternoons in your car, driving without a destination in mind. In the city centre, you notice how the old Victorian red-brick buildings are giving way to glass office blocks and concrete shopping malls. And how, further out, the doors of the houses on the sprawling Clifton estate are turning from municipal-issue green and blue to reds and oranges and purples, as people take the chance to buy up their council homes. These signs of a shifting city fill you with a lurching unease. The sick feeling in your stomach again. Even the buildings of Nottingham are moving forward while you go nowhere.

Your first goal finally comes, ten games into the season, in a 1–1 draw against Middlesbrough. Even this is a pyrrhic triumph. Clough still adores his old club and seems to take the goal against them as further evidence of your unreliability. Later in the week you ask Steve Hodge, a young apprentice, to stay behind after training and help you with extra shooting practice. Hodge looks surprised and pleased that the club's big new signing wants his support. But the session is mortifying. Hodge scores on each attempt while you scuff each shot or send the ball flying high and wide past the net. By the time you finally give up he can hardly look at you.

At year's end there are three more goals but things are still not clicking. There are four football stickers along the side of the Celica. The paltry collection is a daily reminder of your woeful form. In January you accidentally crash the car into a bus and the *Daily Mirror* is quick to pounce: 'Maybe Justin Fashanu should have a bus painted alongside of the footballs to increase his total of hits for the season.'

You call up John. He's finally made it into the Norwich squad although he's yet to join the First Team. However your fortunes have diverged, you're grateful to have him close. You can admit to him that it's been a tough year, and you recount the disorienting methods the club has adopted in order to get you scoring. A visit to a hypnotherapist. An appointment at a nursing home to have an operation on your toes, which, according to Clough, are oddly shaped. John explodes in laughter and it feels good to let go of the tension that seems to exist between you two now. 'You'll come good,' he says. 'It'll be all right.'

It's not only you struggling. It is December, halfway through the season, and Forest are floundering mid-table, with no hope of catching the leading clubs. Off the pitch, money is tight as the club struggles to keep up payments on the new Executive Stand at the City Ground. Almost all of the European Cup-winning players, including Kenny Burns, Trevor Francis and Peter Shilton, are being sold off. The club's future now rests with you and another new million-pound striker, Ian Wallace, who like you has little to show for his hefty price tag so far. This, says the *Mirror*, is 'a season of failure and decline'.

Worse yet, the relationship between Clough and Taylor, the very linchpin of the club's accomplishments, is fracturing. They've known each other since they played together at Middlesbrough, but now the atmosphere between them has turned noxious. The areas of disagreement between them are many and petty. Clough is angry that Taylor has written an autobiography that leans heavily on his relationship with the manager, without giving him a cut of the royalties. Taylor resents being in Clough's shadow and the lack of public recognition he receives as a coach in his own right. More than anything, they're simply worn out after two decades of high-pressure partnership. In the midst of a tough season, they're both so exhausted and resentful they can no longer stand to be in a room together. Clough refers to Taylor as 'the bloke down the corridor'. Taylor is dismissive of Clough's celebrity friends, and the hangers-on who buzz around, vying to fetch him drinks and act as his chauffeur.

In public they maintain a united front. 'There is no rift between us,' Taylor tells reporters. Away from the press, you overhear him complaining to the training staff that Clough has become a monster who 'needs constantly to be number one'. The mood at the club is dismal. With tactics for the next game changing as soon as one man leaves the room and the other enters, the players feel confused and dispirited, fearful that they'll be next to be sold off.

In the absence of direction from either coach, you're a lost figure on the pitch. Where your presence used to trigger panic among opposing defenders, now they can't wait to test you. On the terraces, the fans' affection for you has curdled. To the same British Airways tune, they now sing, 'We're sick and tired of you, Fash-a-nu, Fash-a-nu.' After a rumour that your old club wants to re-sign you, a chant goes round the City Ground: 'He's crap, he's black and Norwich want him back, Fashanu, Fashanu.'

Your managers have always told you to rise above the racial abuse that greets you on the pitch. But no one can prepare you for the physical force of thousands of voices shouting *black bastard*, how it rocks you backwards and brings tears to your eyes. At smaller grounds, the stands reach down to the edge of the pitch, the fans only separated from the players by a low barrier. There's nowhere to escape the spitting and the monkey noises, the bananas flung on the pitch when you take a throw-in from the touchline.

It's a similar story for black players across the league. The Three Degrees have it particularly bad. Laurie Cunningham's house has been petrol-bombed. Brendon Batson describes getting off the bus at away matches to a gauntlet of shouting, spitting opposition fans, the back of his jacket sodden with saliva by the time he reaches the players' entrance. After he is called up to the England team, Cyrille Regis receives a bullet through the post, along with a letter cut out of newspaper headlines: 'If you put a foot on our Wembley turf you'll get one of these through your knees.'

Outside the grounds of Chelsea, West Ham, Leeds and other clubs, you see skinheads from the National Front selling copies of their magazine, *Bulldog*, with its monthly column nominating 'The Most Racist Ground in Britain'. But the dressing room after matches is the worst. Your teammates never mention the insults and the spitting. Don't they notice it, or do they just not care? They talk endlessly about the game and the ref but their silence on this topic is pointed. The experience is yours to bear alone. With each game your confidence dissolves further, washed away amid their indifference.

—

Shortly after lunch on December 28th, Brian Clough goes outside to clear snow from the garden of his house in Derby. He returns a few minutes later, sweating heavily, and collapses into a chair complaining of chest pains. Barbara, his wife, calls an ambulance which drives him to Derby Royal Infirmary with a suspected heart attack. Ordered to take time off, he decamps to his holiday home in Majorca.

In his absence, Taylor is in charge and the atmosphere at the club becomes noticeably lighter. As January progresses, the team plays with a confidence and fluidity it's struggled to find all season. You're still not scoring goals but you feel better, and calmer, and you know your performance is improving.

In a o–o draw with Manchester City you have your best match of the season so far. 'City, it appeared, viewed Fashanu as a moving target,' reports the *Nottingham Evening Post* approvingly. 'This was the Fashanu that Forest paid £1 million for. He proved to be far more mobile and threatening than at almost any other stage this season.'

The respite is only temporary. Clough returns in a poisonous mood, reigniting his feud with Taylor and furious that his first match back is a 2–o defeat to Notts County. The contrast is jarring enough for you to see clearly for the first time where you really stand in the club. For a long while you've understood that you fall into the category of players Clough dislikes. But now you realize that you've become a casualty in his war with Taylor. Clough sees you as overpriced, underperforming evidence of Taylor's failure as a scout. The manager rarely speaks to you face to face but you're painfully aware of how he talks about you behind your back. 'Whenever anyone mentions Justin Fashanu to me, I say one thing. I didn't buy him. It had nowt to do with me. The person who did buy him didn't do his job properly. We signed an idiot.'

Understanding how Clough regards you is its own kind of relief. The whole of Nottingham Forest Football Club exists in the manager's orbit. Players, groundskeepers, the directors, even Taylor; it all revolves around him. There's a yawning pain in knowing you've failed to meet his approval. But you also feel a sense of liberation. You're free to be yourself. You still want to make it, but that's on your terms now, not his. You picture your father commanding his household in Lagos, a sovereign territory of one. You're the villain at the moment, you confide to David Moore, a journalist at the *Daily Mirror*. But if you get a couple of goals in your next match, the whole situation can change.

The next morning, you come to training in a charcoal-grey Armani suit with padded shoulders and single-pleated trousers. You hire a personal coach to work on your fitness and bring him into the dressing room before matches to give you a massage. Even with its paltry four stickers, you drive the Celica around town, leaving it where you please, irrespective of the fistfuls of parking tickets that follow. After a match, you throw your boots into the crowd and raise your arms aloft, soaking up the surge of cheers. None of this behaviour endears you to Clough. But extravagance is a form of assertion. It's a way to stay alive. Fine clothes, fast cars, breaking rules, stirring up the crowd – it's how you keep from drowning.

———

A weekend visit to Alf and Betty. It feels like a lifetime since you were last at Flint House. Ochre walls and paisley-pattern carpet. A round kitchen table laden with fruitcake, scones, cups, saucers, a pot of tea. Betty talking about the latest batch of kids taking piano lessons, Alf nodding absently beside her. You wish John was here too, everything like you'd left it and nothing changed.

The following morning you go for a run over the frosty ground. When you're training, running is a chore. You jog back and forth across the pitch with nothing in your head except waiting for it to be over. But being out in these fields still glimmering with ice is a joyous release. You follow a twisting path that leads you through a copse of trees, the light shafting through the bare branches, and then back out into the open air, the green and silver earth of the fields around you, the hills ahead. The tempo of your breathing loud in your ears, air filling your lungs, lifting you up until your feet are only skimming the grass.

Coming back to Shropham – the sleepy lanes and cottages, Alf and Betty's quiet compassion – you know you are an outsider here now, even more than when you were a kid. You feel the jet lag of travelling between worlds, Norfolk to Nottingham, and all the cities you see from the windows of the team bus, going to and from a match. At least views of black people are changing, even here in Shropham, thanks to you and others in the papers and on television. You, John, the Three Degrees, Imagination, Light of the World. Your success refutes the idea that all black people are muggers and hoodlums, Rastafarians with dreadlocks. You jog past a meadow dotted with winter flowers. Daisy. Yarrow. Chickweed. You travel between identities. Free to bloom otherwise. You are twenty years old, suspended between youth and adulthood. You know both hardness and vulnerability. Blackness and whiteness. Maleness and femaleness. More *and* than *either*.

—

Back when you joined Forest, you'd go out with the rest of the players every Saturday night. First to the King John for a drink, then to a club, the Pepper Mill or Uriah Heep's. And finally, the bar at the Albany Hotel. Someone always joked that you won't have far to go if you pull. It's true there were always girls around, drawn in by the noisy local stars with their aggressive aftershave. You'd buy one a drink. Have a dance. Make a show of kissing her then slip away to your suite by yourself while no one's looking. The novelty of that routine soon wore off. These days you prefer to go out by yourself to Part Two. The venue is a big four-storey converted warehouse that's known for having the best sound system in Nottingham. It's also the only licensed gay members' club in Britain.

The first time you visited, you did so discreetly, coming in by the back entrance and telling yourself it was just somewhere to have a drink where you wouldn't be hassled, because no one there was interested enough in football to recognize you. It made you realize how accustomed you had become to being watched, your shoulders tensed against the gaze of strangers. Over time you have loosened up. The atmosphere at Part Two is carnival-like. Nude mud-wrestling nights, a sauna and a blacked-out sex room at the back. Eartha Kitt dressed in a floor-length mink pulling up in a Rolls-Royce. Sitting at the bar, you can allow your gaze to drift across the crowd, to alight on a figure on the dance floor, catch his eye, both of you holding the look in hungry anticipation. This night-time world is escape. It is magic and fantasy. It is the dream too delicious to wake from.

If you bring a man back to the Albany, you insist that he leaves first thing to avoid the excruciating prospect of the maid barging into the room while he's still there. But after he's gone you lie in bed savouring his scent in the sheets, the memory of his smooth back, the muscles firm to the touch.

At the club you make friends with Peter. He's older than you by ten years and you admire his self-confidence and his quick intelligence. Peter lives in London and you get in the habit of speaking on the phone late at night. You find yourself telling him about your disgust at the prancing queens on TV, and your fear of being seen as less than a man by your teammates. You are afraid too of the 'gay cancer' spreading among men in America. Surely it's only a matter of time before it reaches Britain. After every one-night stand you check your face in the mirror for lesions. You wait with cold dread for a sore throat to get worse. Fear and shame. If this is what it means to be gay, you say, then why would I want that?

The sound of Peter's breathing down the phone fills the space between you, the line crackling softly. He tells you about how, in the 1970s, he was so enraged by the treatment of gay people that he became an activist, staging protests against police harassment and sit-ins at pubs that refused to serve gay customers. Now he's been selected as the prospective Labour candidate for Bermondsey. A parliamentary campaign is still a way off but his new role is already making him a target of abuse. Graffiti sprayed on posters and hoardings around Bermondsey reads 'Tatchell is queer' and 'Tatchell is a communist poof'. When the two of you meet for a drink, Peter often arrives flustered, casting glances around to check if tabloid journalists are following him. It would be better for you, he says, that you aren't seen with him by the press. You insist otherwise. You've never known anyone that views being gay in such straightforward terms, as normal and natural, as he does. You say, you'll take the consequences of being friends, whatever they might be.

You visit Peter in London, following him to parties and West End clubs prowled by paparazzi. With his self-confidence in mind, you arrive boldly at Part Two now, parking the Celica on the double yellow lines out the front, and stopping to talk to the manager before going in. 'You're parking the only white sports Toyota in Nottingham outside the only gay members' club in Britain,' the manager reminds him. 'You might as well wear a pink shirt on the pitch.' On the phone to Peter, you tell him his courage has inspired you. Supposing you stopped hiding, you say. What if you came out to the team and the fans? To Clough? There's a long pause. Peter says, 'You're only twenty. See if you can't square your troubles with Clough first. Don't be in a hurry to say something you can't take back.'

—

Perhaps someone has finally noticed the white Celica outside Part Two. Or they've spotted you sneaking up to your suite with a man in tow. Whatever the cause, rumours about you are seeping through the club, insidious as smoke. Even the most banal talk is laced with innuendo.

You attend the Professional Football Association annual dinner, which takes place at the Grosvenor House Hotel in Park Lane, London, with John. Across the hall, you spot a Queens Park Rangers player. He's laughing and pointing at you with his friends at his table. When he sees you watching him, he mimes a blowjob motion with his hand and his open mouth. John, sitting beside you, stares back furiously. As the player leaves the table to go to the bar, John springs up, ready to follow and teach him a lesson. You pull him back, tell him to sit down.

On a club trip to Spain, you share a room with Viv Anderson. It's some point in the early hours when you open your eyes and discover yourself standing in the dark, at the bathroom basin, the taps running and your hands covered in blood. Viv is in the doorway. He snaps the light on. In the sudden glare, a dazed face, drained of life, looks back at you from the mirror. You turn to Viv, beseeching. 'Sleepwalking,' he says. He'd been asleep and was woken a few minutes ago by a loud banging. He sat up to see a splintered hole right through the door and the sound of sobbing coming from the bathroom. Your eyes were shut and you didn't look up when he entered. You must have smashed the hole in the door and gone to wash your bloodied hands all while sleeping.

You leave the bathroom. Trace a sore hand, with its grazed knuckles, over the gash in the door. All along the corridor, the lads are putting their heads out, half-asleep and demanding to know what's happening. The team doctor arrives, gives you a sedative, and helps you back to bed. You wake up in the morning, confused and mortified. Viv is already out of the room. You catch up with him at breakfast, wanting to say sorry, but he brushes you aside, and turns back to bantering with the other lads. When you return to the room that evening, it's empty. Viv's belongings are all gone. One of the coaches you're friendly with tells you Viv asked to be moved. He called you 'a disturbed individual' and said he wouldn't spend another night in a room with you.

March 1982

A reporter from the *Sunday People* phones. The paper's running a story on what it calls the gay rumours about you. 'Will you end the gossip?' the reporter says, malevolence cloaked in solicitude. 'Tell us if you're gay or not, Justin.'

Your head spins. You try to find the words, any words, in reply. Yes, you say, some of your friends are gay. But as a consequence of being famous you mix in a much wider social world than the average footballer. Men do not figure in your personal life.

The *People* runs a front-page story that Sunday. It describes you 'kicking back against the malicious gossips who have been saying he's homosexual' even as every line insinuates the opposite. Your first thought is, what will John think about this story? Supposing it reaches your father in Lagos? The idea is unbearable. You sue the paper and you win. They apologize in the High Court and print a retraction. 'The reported gossip was malicious and without any foundation. The *Sunday People* did not intend to imply it was true. Any suggestion otherwise is unreservedly withdrawn.'

Victory comes at a steep price. You have sworn under oath that you're not gay. Coming out is now impossible. And despite the court case, the rumours at Forest continue. You wake up knotted with dread at the prospect of training. Driving in one morning, the nausea is so intense that you have to pull over to the side of the road and vomit. How much more can you take? Would it be better to just quit football altogether and escape the smirking faces? Does such a place even exist for you any more? 'He tried to portray the macho image but he's not macho, he's flamboyant,' says Clough in the *Daily Express*. 'He tried to fool me and I saw through his make-believe.'

May 1982

Declaring himself 'mentally and physically drained' by Forest's ragged season, Peter Taylor announces his retirement from football. In departing, he tries to put a gloss on the end of his partnership with Clough. 'There has never been any rift between Brian and myself, although I must admit we've had more ups and downs this year than most others.' You are sorry to see Taylor leave. He was one of the few people at the club who were kind to you. And with him gone, there's no one standing between you and Clough.

Absent Taylor's steadying influence, the manager's behaviour becomes increasingly erratic. The idiosyncrasies that once seemed evidence of genius now ring malign. At training, he leads the players out of the club grounds to run across an open field strewn with cowpats. He gathers you all round a tree and makes you punch the trunk. When he substitutes underperforming players during a match, he gives them an angry punch in the stomach as they come off the pitch.

Then there's the drinking. Clough has always liked the players to have some beers together after a big game, or even before one. Now, he's more likely to be drinking alone in his office. A tumbler of Scotch first thing, to get the morning going. Another with lunch to ease into the afternoon. By the end of the day his eyes are glazed and his face is red and blotchy. His mood oscillates wildly, from shouting abuse at the players to kissing visitors to the club on the lips.

You know you're on borrowed time but the atmosphere is so unpleasant you almost don't care. Almost. Weeks later and without a word to you, Clough puts you on the transfer list. After less than a year at the club he wants you gone. Outwardly, you are defiant. But the chances to turn your fortunes round are shrinking. In a game against Spurs you catch a raking tackle down your calf which puts you out of action for a fortnight. On your return you're sent to the reserves. Instead of playing in a stadium full of fans, you're reduced to scattered crowds at midweek matches with the Second and even the Third Team. Reservists like Steve Hodge are now your teammates. During one match you are so out of sorts that you make a back pass from the halfway line that goes sailing over the head of your keeper towards the net. Only chance sends it wide, preventing the kick from turning into a cruel parody of your famous Liverpool goal. Among the reserves, the joke is that when someone scuffs a kick or mistimes a tackle he is 'doing it the Fashanu way'.

The final day of the season brings a chance at redemption. A string of losses has left Forest in the bottom half of the league. The team is away at Ipswich and desperate for a win. Clough brings you back to the First Team. You are warming up with the rest of the squad an hour before kick-off when there's a stabbing sensation in your calf, a flare-up from your injury earlier in the month. Your leg is so painful you can hardly bend it. You hobble back into the dressing room and tell Clough you can't play. The manager's face flushes red. Shouting obscenities, he cuffs you on the side of the head and tells you to get out of his sight.

Steve Hodge is given his First Team debut as your replacement. He plays well throughout the match and sets up the third goal. With five minutes remaining, Clough substitutes him. As he walks off, Clough jumps up from the bench in delight, gives Hodge a hug that lifts him off the ground, then sits him on the subs bench near you, kneels down and unlaces his boots for him. You look on from the bench, hardly able to believe what you're seeing. The ostentatious fussing over Hodge is a message clearly aimed at you. This is Clough saying, you're disposable. Look how easily you can be replaced.

Clough and the other players are already on board when you get to the bus. As you reach the steps, the manager leans forward to the driver and tells him to shut the door. The bus starts to pull out of the car park without you. 'Let him walk,' you hear Clough say through the window. The bus is halfway down the street before he relents. The door opens. You climb aboard and find a seat by yourself. Nobody talks to you and neither do you turn from the window to speak to them.

August 1982

Clough spends the summer at his house in Majorca. Meanwhile the players are sent on an exhausting tour through Morocco, Kuwait and the Far East, the club desperately trying to raise extra money to meet its debts. The memory of Clough's slap is impossible to get out of your mind. You brood on it for weeks, resenting the contempt in the gesture, the indignity of it, and your powerlessness to retaliate. In that moment he could have said or done anything he wanted and there'd be no way for you to defend yourself. He reminds you of a staff member from the home who would reach out and flick kids on the head for some perceived slighting of the rules. He always knew if you'd complained about him and would make you suffer additional punishments – bread and water for dinner, no TV, no outings – as a consequence.

The fear of being powerless. The fear of being watched and judged. The fear of infection. They blur together. The mysterious American disease has grown larger and more ominous in your imagination as it begins to spread in Britain. The 'gay plague'. Just last month it claimed one of its first official British victims, Terry Higgins, a 37-year-old computer programmer. He collapsed in a nightclub in London and died soon after of parasitic pneumonia. You read about it in the *Mirror* and you kept the paper afterwards, hiding it at the back of your bedside drawer, unable to throw it away.

September 1982

It is the start of the new season and the manager wants you in his office.

Clough is at his desk writing a note as you enter. From his window you can see some of the boys warming up on the pitch. He puts the pen down and leans back in his seat, leaving you standing. 'Young man, I've been getting phone calls telling me you've been frequenting a particular club well known as a meeting place for homosexuals.'

Even though you feel at once both burning hot and frigid with cold, so filled with shame you can't breathe, it's Clough's voice that holds your attention. Today, that familiar nasal drawl, so much parodied by TV comedians that it's almost a punchline in itself, is spare and flat.

'Let me ask you, where do you go if you want a loaf of bread?' says Clough. 'A bakery, I suppose,' you reply, watching the other players trotting up and down outside rather than meet his gaze. 'And where do you go if you want a leg of lamb?' says the manager. 'A butcher,' you say. 'Precisely, young man.' A pause. Three players jog by in unison, their shadows falling in symmetry on the grass. 'So why do you keep going to that bloody poofs' club?' You feel his words punch into your stomach. Tears prickle your eyes. You mumble that you don't know what he's talking about and escape the room as fast as you can.

You stand on the grass, numb to your surroundings and struggling to take in what's happening. Clough leads training today. His voice rings out across the pitch. Even later, alone at the Albany, it still echoes in your head.

October 1982

Peter Taylor's retirement proves short-lived. He has resurfaced as manager of Derby County and he wants you on his team. Derby are the club where Taylor and Clough first made their names together. They are in the Second Division, short of cash and decent players, but Taylor believes that, outside Forest, you can recapture the dynamism of your Norwich days. Your heart leaps at the prospect of playing for a manager who has faith in you. Clough makes no secret of the fact he wants you gone, even if it's to the advantage of Taylor, and a contract is drawn up within the week. Yet something is nagging at you. Sitting with the club secretary in his office, the contract in front of you, it strikes you that agreeing to the transfer would not only mean the end of your career as a top-flight footballer. It would also confirm in their prejudices all those people who say you never belonged at that level, that your face never fitted. You stand up and walk out of the room leaving the contract on the desk, unsigned.

The following week, you turn up for training to find Ron Fenton, Clough's assistant coach, waiting for you with a hangdog expression and a letter in his hand. 'I'm sorry, Fash,' says Ron. 'The boss says you're to go home.' You are suspended for fourteen days and banned from the Forest ground and training facilities. The letter mentions something about instances of indiscipline, but you know the real reason is because you've said no to the Derby transfer. Clough wants to be rid of you and, if you won't leave voluntarily, he's determined to make conditions as humiliating for you as possible. You shove the letter into your back pocket, push past Fenton, and join the team warming up on the pitch.

Ron dashes away in the direction of the manager's office. Fifteen minutes later, Clough comes striding across the pitch in his green sweater. 'Right, you, I want you off our patch,' he shouts. 'You're banned.' The sight of the most powerful figure in British football bearing down upon you is daunting. But you carry on sprinting back and forth at the far end of the field with the rest of the players, as if you can't hear him yelling. At the halfway line Clough abruptly stops and then returns to his office. You think maybe he's had a change of heart. Perhaps a show of quiet resistance has been enough to face down the bully. A half hour later Clough's back, this time trailed by two policemen. You come to a halt with the rest of the players, all of you watching them walking across the pitch, the two police hurrying to keep up with the manager. 'Young man, either get off this pitch or these gentlemen will arrest you,' says Clough. For a moment, you consider standing your ground and saying, do your worst. It goes through your head that you could also just punch Clough and be done with the whole thing. But the sight of the other lads looking on aghast brings home to you the abject nature of this scene. The police look as embarrassed as the players, all of them watching to see how you'll react. The fight drains out of you. Whatever you do, you have already lost.

'It was humiliating,' you tell the *Post* reporter who's got wind of the face-off and come dashing to the City Ground. You're not trying to win or lose a battle with Clough, you say. All you want to do is play football. Clough concocts his own tale for the reporter. 'If this was to be a confrontation in front of the rest of the players, there had to be only one winner. Me.' Clough claims to have given you a kick to the calf when you weren't budging. He claims to have forced you off the pitch in tears. 'He was weeping buckets. He stood his ground at first, but eventually he was led away, protesting. Strange boy.'

Two months later, Forest sell you to Notts County for £150,000.

December 1983

Although they are minnows compared to Forest, you're surprised by how much you've enjoyed playing for County. The team is spirited and pugnacious and holding its own in the league. Last week you scored twice to give County their first draw against Manchester United since 1940, and the fans are hailing you as a hero.

On the last day of the year, the club is playing away to Ipswich Town. It is your first time there since the disastrous bust-up with Clough. Just before half-time against Ipswich, an onrushing opposition defender slides for the ball and catches you on the right side of the knee with his studs. The gash needs four stitches, and a week later your knee swells up like a football. You are taken into hospital. When a specialist examines you, he discovers that the needle used for your stitches hadn't been properly sterilized. An infection has already set in and caused extensive damage. It may be necessary to remove the lining from the inside of your knee. The best-case scenario, says the doctor, is that you're out for the rest of the season. The worst is that you'll never walk properly again.

3

Los Angeles, July 1988

Depending on what mood you're in, coming to Los Angeles seems either like escape or exile or, perhaps, a marvellous act of rebirth. You remember, as a child, how powerfully you were struck by the sight of the unbroken horizon in Shropham, the trees and the sky on an English autumn morning enough to move you to wonder. Here, now, is the same sensation. The late-afternoon light over the city, a haze of soft pink and rich orange, striated with the vapour trails of aeroplanes heading east over the desert and west across the ocean.

A series of expensive operations has drained your savings. But it's been worth it. In Britain every doctor you visited said there was no hope for your knee. Yet the treatment you've received here has worked. Even though you're not back to where you were before the injury, you're fit enough to return to football. You played a few games after surgery for West Ham and Brighton. But rather than scrabble for a permanent team back home, you've secured a contract with the Los Angeles Heat, the leading team on the West Coast. In your debut season you're already the second-highest scorer in the whole Western Soccer Alliance. During the off-season, you'll go north to play for the Hamilton Steelers in Toronto. And you have a plan for the coming years. In 1994, the United States will host the World Cup for the first time. A new national league is set to be in place by 1990, bringing together the best teams from the West and East Coast. You are sure the Heat can spearhead the new league, and you're determined to be there when they do.

Your favourite time of day in LA is late afternoon. After training, you get behind the wheel of your car and lose yourself in the pleasure of motion. A black Mustang convertible with a car phone, the light gleaming off its flanks, and the stereo turned up high on Bobby Brown and New Edition. Swing the car up on to Malibu Canyon Road, following its course as it winds around the mountain, ascending past palm trees and pampas grass and bare rock face. Five miles further and the road opens out on to a plateau and a view of the sky and the city below, arrayed in grid lines, alive with cars and trucks and beautiful strangers.

LA's expat celebrities have taken you in as one of their own. At Rod Stewart's birthday party up in the Hollywood Hills, you get talking to George Michael by the pool. There are two girls in bikinis in the water. As you watch them swimming languidly back and forth, you tell George what a relief it is to be out here beyond the reach of the UK tabloids. All they do is print lies about your sexuality, you say. And George gives you a slow, knowing look and says, 'Relax, you're not a star until they've written a gay story about you.'

News from England comes to you piecemeal. Sometimes a letter from Peter or an imported copy of *The Times* on a news-stand. There's a gay MP in Parliament, and *EastEnders* has screened the first gay kiss on a British soap. Gay pop stars like Jimmy Somerville and Holly Johnson have become gloriously inventive best-selling artists. Thatcher has banned the 'promotion' of homosexuality in schools. A baleful ad featuring icebergs drifting across frozen water and a tombstone chiselled with the word 'Aids' is screening on TV. It's a relief to be out of the country.

Jogging one morning on Malibu beach, a pelican skimming ahead of you over the waves, you realize the knotted feeling in your stomach has disappeared. LA is no provincial town like Nottingham, where a manager makes it his business to know yours. You can play for the Heat and then head to a gay club afterwards without fear of being watched or judged. In footballing terms, LA's nowhere – to the people back home you might as well have vanished into thin air. You tell your friends here that clubs in England are falling over themselves to sign you. Even if that was true, you wouldn't be in a hurry to return. There's no place you'd rather be right now than in the generous warmth of this nation.

In your absence, John's career has flourished and you're glad for him. You know he was jealous of your easy success as a teenager. And you, shamefully, were content to let him struggle, facing rejection from club after club, even though you knew his progress was made more difficult by the comparisons with you. How much of that time, you wonder, fed into the man he's become at Wimbledon? His current club is an assortment of thugs and bullies who call themselves the Crazy Gang. John – 'Fash the Bash' – is at the centre of the team, reigning over an ethos of intimidation. Opposition players are sent limping off the pitch with broken noses and fractured eye sockets. New recruits to the squad face brutal initiation rituals. One lad has dog shit shoved down his back. Another is tied to the roof of a car and driven down the A3.

From a distance, it looks like John's playing a character. When you read about him elbowing the Spurs player Gary Mabbutt so hard in the face that he goes down with a fractured skull, you think of the little brother trailing after you, scared and stammering, at Dr Barnardo's. Maybe it's partly your fault for spurning him when he needed you. The next time you see John you'll say, let's put the past behind us. Let's be brothers not rivals. He can be the Big Man as far as you're concerned. You're content to live free.

Toronto, October 1990

You are in Toronto playing with the Steelers when the phone rings in your hotel room. A voice you don't recognize starts speaking and it takes a few minutes before you realize that this is the moment you've been dreading for the past decade.

The voice belongs to a reporter from a British Sunday newspaper. He has what he calls 'compromising photos' of you in a gay bar and he says the paper is going to run a front-page exposé on you next week. The horror is so all-encompassing you can't bring yourself to ask, which bar? Was it in Nottingham? London? Or have they been trailing you in the States? You feel chilled and shaky as the smirking voice asks if you have any comment, while beyond the plate glass of your hotel window, the traffic flows by soundlessly on the streets below.

You haven't had an agent of your own since you left the country. The only person you can think of to contact is Eric Hall, John's agent. Hall, fast-talking and flamboyantly dressed, is well used to negotiating the murky ways of the tabloids. Instead of letting the paper print their story, he suggests, run your own version instead. He makes some calls and comes back to you soon with a spoiler deal he's organized with the *Sun*. Rather than the original exposé, they will pay £70,000 for an exclusive interview with you as the first professional footballer in the world to come out as gay. The tone will be generally sympathetic and there'll be no lurid nightclub photos. The notion of turning for help from the most malignant tabloid in Britain makes you nauseous. Since the Aids crisis started, the *Sun* has run story after fear-mongering story. 'I'd shoot my son if he had AIDS, says vicar!' Yet what choice do you have?

The paper sends you a ticket and you catch an overnight flight from Toronto to London. Up in the sky, the plane levels off and the stewardess serves drinks and then beef and mushrooms in foil-wrapped trays. The man sitting next to you orders a whiskey and lights a cigarette, absently swilling the ice in the bottom of his plastic glass between sips. Once he's finished the drink and stubbed out the cigarette, his head starts to dip, dozing in the warmth of the dim cabin. You wish you could do the same but you're too agitated. As you stare at the back of the seat in front of you, salvation fantasies circle in your head. Perhaps the whole thing is a case of mistaken identity and it's some other black man at a gay club. Or maybe once you land you'll be able to convince them to drop the article somehow. Or an IRA bomb will explode and drive the story off the front pages. The same thoughts continue to repeat as the plane touches down, even though by then it's long past obvious there will be no reprieve.

London, October 1990

The *Sun* has booked you into a room at the Waldorf Hotel on the Strand. You check in and take a shower but the water doesn't revive you, and you meet the journalist over breakfast feeling dried out and aching all over. The interview is like an interrogation. When did you discover you were gay? Where did you first have sex? Who was it with and how did it feel? You tell him what he wants to hear, nodding along to his leading questions while saying to yourself that none of it matters. The damage is done with the fact of the story itself. Anything else is detail.

Your real concern at this stage isn't the journalist but what you'll say to John before the story is published. You've hardly spoken in the past two years. During that time his status in football has continued to rise as steadily as yours has fallen. He's played for England, become the second-highest goalscorer in the First Division and, last season, the Crazy Gang pulled off the improbable feat of winning the FA Cup final against Liverpool. You ring him after the interview, fingertips damp with sweat as you press the keys on the hotel-room phone.

The call does not go well. John is both furious with you and terrified for himself, immediately calculating how the story will reflect on his hard-man image at Wimbledon. He begs you not to go through with it and, when you tell him it's too late, the interview's done, he slams the phone down.

———

The front page of the *Sun* reads, in mammoth type, '£1m Soccer Star: I Am Gay'. In the photo beside the headline you are looking at the camera with something that can only technically be called a smile. The corners of your mouth are raised but your eyes stare blankly into the distance with no sign of animation on your face. It is a disorienting experience to see yourself in this way, captured through someone else's eyes. Through words that are yours and not yours. 'Soccer star Justin Fashanu confessed last night: "I'm gay – and

I want everyone to know it." . . . As he bids to make a comeback in British football he says he wants to stop "living a lie".'

Now you see the folly of nodding along to the reporter's questions. The paper has spun your life into a confection of improbable 'romps' and 'high jinks'. 'Justin has revealed how he BEDDED a Tory MP and romped with him in the House of Commons. How he SLEPT with top soccer players and stars of TV and pop music. SNEAKED away from his teammates' "bird hunts" after matches to pay secret visits to gay bars. Justin, 29 – who shot to fame with his £1 million transfer – says British soccer is PACKED with gays from dressing room to boardroom.'

The *Sun* has four million readers and you imagine the perverse delight each of them will take in poring over the story. Trapped on the front page, you are an exhibit for their entertainment. Imagine millions of hands gripping your face, plucking at your skin.

And the fallout is hideous. Ken Brown, your old manager at Norwich, is dumbfounded. 'I still can't quite believe it. It just doesn't make sense to me, a fellow like that. Why does it happen? It's a mystery to me.' Mark Ward, a winger at West Ham where you played briefly after Notts County, comes forward to tell a cruel story about avoiding sharing a hotel room with you. 'Being asleep in the bed next to Justin Fashanu? No fucking way!'

The press is also chasing John for a reaction. However annoyed he is, you hope he'll at least be supportive of you in public. A week after the story breaks, the *Voice*, the black newspaper, prints his response along with four other opinion pieces. Each article is excoriating. An editorial headed 'Soccer Star's Own Goal' describes your 'pathetic and unforgivable tawdry revelation', and sets the tone for what's to follow. 'Justin's story should sadden us all,' writes Marcia Dixon, a Christian commentator. Your behaviour is proof that you 'belong to

Satan'. Tony Sewell, the paper's star columnist, argues you deserve no sympathy. Gay people, he says, are their own worst enemies. 'We heteros are sick and tired of tortured queens playing hide and seek around their closets. Homosexuals are the greatest queer-bashers around. No other group of people is so preoccupied with making their own sexuality look dirty.' Most hurtful of all is the interview with John. He says you have shamed the family and the black community. 'If I saw him now, I couldn't be responsible for my actions. I have no wish to contact Justin whatsoever. The real Justin Fashanu can walk into my office any time but this person is not the same person I grew up with. He is a stranger, an utter stranger.'

You read the interview with tears in your eyes. For the first time ever, you wish you were back in the home, where John looked to you to protect him. Where he trusted you and admired you more than you deserved.

Wimbledon play Crystal Palace that Saturday. John is jeered throughout the match, as if his brother being gay is a kind of family disgrace that he now shares. The rest of the Crazy Gang seem uncertain of how to treat him. John scores a thundering goal in the first half but, instead of running over to hug him as normal, the other players just shake his hand. The Palace match seems to harden his attitude to you. 'He's come out publicly and said his sexual preferences. So now he will have to suffer the consequences. I wouldn't like to play or even get changed in the vicinity of him, that's just the way I feel.'

Torquay, 1991

The work has dried up in America. Both the Heat and the Steelers insisted this is nothing to do with the *Sun* story but you don't believe them. So instead of California and Canada you're back in England

351

for the start of the season, aged thirty, a pariah with a weak knee and an unwelcome degree of fame. No First Division club will sign you. They say your fitness is too unreliable. The only club willing to offer you a contract is Torquay United, the bottom team in the Third Division.

You walk to Plainmoor, Torquay's ground, for your first training session, past the seafront villas built during the town's Edwardian heyday as a south-coast holiday resort. Those once-grand buildings are now shabby-looking boarding houses and care homes. On the other side of a public square two men and a woman are perched on a bench, drinking cans of strong beer, while, at their feet, a seagull pecks at greasy chip paper.

Torquay were desperate for a high-profile recruit to bring in the crowds, so you managed to negotiate a fee of £1,000 a week, three times that of the other players, as well as a Jaguar convertible as a signing-on gift. Driving through country lanes after you signed the contract, foot down, feeling the car surge forward, gave you the old thrill. Like you're still somebody. You try and hold on to that good feeling during the various indignities that come, one after the other, once your life with the team begins.

First, there's the club's insistence that you take an HIV test as part of your medical. Apparently you are 'high-risk' due to having had 'multiple partners', although how the club has decided the number and nature of those presumed sexual partners is not made clear to you. Walking into the changing room on your first day, the players grab their arses, presumably to protect themselves from your carnal appetites. It's a joke and they're laughing, looking at you with eager faces to see whether or not you'll play along. When you give them a smile and tell them to fuck off, there's a big cheer all round. Nothing more is said but you get changed by yourself in the referee's room after that.

Your first away match is a game against Fulham. It marks a new low point. As soon as you run on to the pitch, the abuse starts. There are shouts of 'bender' and 'you fucking poof'. When you're near the touchline, the fans spit at you from the stands. They fling bananas at you. Their chanting fills the stadium: 'He's bent, he's queer, he takes it up the rear, Fash-anu, Fash-anu.' All through the game you're under attack with no one coming to your support. It's the same a month later when Torquay are away to West Bromwich Albion. More chanting. More bananas and spitting. This time you can't take it. You go in hard against the West Brom players, making them the target of your anger, raking their shins, elbowing their faces, until the ref shows you a red card, and you walk off to jeers and booing. At the end of the season Torquay are relegated to the Fourth Division. You leave the club soon after, with no idea of what will come next.

—

These are the spinning days. The wandering years. After Torquay, England is over for you. No club will spare you a thought. You head north of the border to play in the minor Scottish leagues: Airdrie-onians; Heart of Midlothian. There's even a spell with a team in provincial Sweden. Every promise of a new start flickers and fades. Sometimes you feel so weighed down you can't get out of bed. It seems easier to stay beneath the covers than to keep trying to move forward. You lie in the dawn light and think of John, of the frightened boy he was. The frightened boys you both were.

Over the Atlantic, 1995

You have been invited to play for the Atlanta Ruckus, a team in the second tier of North American soccer. The flight out of Heathrow is crowded and it takes a half hour of passengers jostling to find space for their bags in the overhead compartments, and then a last-minute wait for a mother and her teenage daughter to come running on to the plane, red-faced and out of breath, before the doors can finally close. As the aircraft takes off, you feel a sense of relief wash over you, to be leaving Britain and returning to America. The plane breaks through the clouds into silver sky. How many new starts can a man have, you wonder, before the fact of starting over, the constant urge to escape, becomes the thing that defines who you are? You close your eyes, try to shut out the roar of the engines, and the chatter of the mother and daughter, who are seated in the row behind you, narrating the drama of their eleventh-hour dash through the airport to each other over and over.

You have been a nomad in your own life this past decade, moving from club to club, country to country, and never staying long enough to put down any roots. At the same time, you've seen your tormentors, men who once seemed your antitheses, come apart too. Brian Clough, his faculties ruined by drink and his reputation tarnished by accusations of bribes, has retired from football. On his last ever game, Forest was relegated from the Premier League. John faced a corruption scandal of his own, with match-fixing allegations that were ultimately unproven. Although you talk occasionally, the two of you are not close. 'He was my shining light,' John said of you to a reporter. 'He became my arch enemy.' You should stop reading his interviews.

Maybe it makes more sense to keep moving. To keep looking ahead to the page not yet written. To a point in time when the name Justin

Fashanu might still stand for something other than scandal. The plane banks to its side and from your window you see the curve of the horizon spread before you. An image comes to mind. You picture yourself sitting with Louis by the brook in Shropham. You haven't thought of that evening for years but now you see it as vivid as life. Sitting beside him, your hand touches his accidentally. You let it linger there, knowing that in the next instant he might move away. You imagine that you can feel the whole warmth of his body through that touch. In a minute you will be kissing but you don't know that yet. All you have is this intimacy, so delicate it might evaporate.

In hindsight this is what you remember most about that evening. Just the fact of sitting beside him without talking. The tree at your back and the water in front. The frankness of your desire at that moment was so intense it's almost painful to recall. It strikes you that this was one of the few truly unguarded moments you've shared with another person in your whole life. There've been plenty of encounters with men since. But never without the sensation of watching, being watched, the character you perform for them and for yourself. You imagine how you looked to Louis at sixteen years old. The candour in your eyes. The longing there. But your gaze also extends further out, out towards somewhere beyond him. Just as now on the plane, you look out of the window to the horizon, with its promise of the unscripted, the always-possible. Even now, some bright future forming out of sight, coming into reach.

The Stranger

The town was up in the mountains, a tiny Ruritanian place of cobbled streets and timber-framed houses. It was market day and, in the main square, crowds of local people browsed stalls piled with fresh bread, cheese and cooked sausage. I drifted among them, passing unnoticed.

In the afternoon the sun slid behind the mountains. With the waning of the light, a madness seemed to infect the crowd. Uniformly they turned to me, evil intent in their eyes.

I left the square and hurried down a narrow street. The villagers came after me in a herd — there were too many of them to fit easily, but they were coming anyway. I ran and they followed, and I knew that if they caught me they would beat me to death. I slipped on the cobblestones. The crowd drew closer. A hand grabbed me and then another. I was pulled back into the mob. A hail of punches and kicks landed on me. I blacked out.

I woke up, my arms and legs jerking, still trying to fight them off. I felt no relief to discover myself at home. For the past year I'd been plagued by nightmares. Over and over, I'd returned to the Ruritanian town and its murderous citizens. There were other scenarios too, leaving me with flashes of falling through darkness, of being hunted by men or dogs.

Always, the hardest moment to bear was on waking. Consciousness could chase away the phantoms, but immediately afterwards nothing felt solid – it was as if everything around me might dissolve into the terrors of another dream.

I was twenty-seven but the frequency of the nightmares meant I went to sleep each night afraid of the dark, like a child. I kept a landing light on and the blinds open a crack so that the amber glow of the street lights seeped into the room. I even left the radio tuned to the World Service, knowing that if I woke before dawn after another nightmare, I'd be met with a news bulletin about some conflict across the globe, details impossible to follow at that hour and just the reporter's voice, speaking low from a far-distant place, drawing me back to sleep.

—

The earliest nightmare I can remember is from when I was eight. I was walking along a deserted jetty that stretched way out into the sea. A cold wind stirred the waves and sent them slapping against the wooden planks of the structure. Saltwater flecked my face. The jetty was old and rotting and the further out I went the more dilapidated it became. There was nothing secure to hold on to. In the gaps between its planks, I spied the choppy water. The sight terrified me. I was sure that at any moment the boards might split and send me plunging into the sea. I was too scared to keep walking yet I couldn't find the courage to go back. The jetty swayed as the wind blew. I felt completely vulnerable.

I can still picture that jetty today, and with it comes the same sense of vulnerability that I experienced then. It's only in looking back that I see how closely the mood of the dream matched the way I so often felt as a child.

I grew up in Queensbury, a quiet, 1930s London suburb on the northern tip of what is now the Jubilee Line. It was the 1970s and in the latter years of the decade the haberdasher's and the bakery on the high street had given way to Asian sweet shops. The cubes of vivid pink and yellow confectioneries stacked in the windows pointed to the area's changing complexion. A continent away, Idi Amin was expelling the Asians of Uganda. Some of them had re-settled in places like Queensbury. Their arrival meant a few more Asian kids at my primary school. Not that it made much difference. My class was still almost entirely white. Aged eight, I was still the only Black kid.

Mostly I didn't feel any distance between me and my best friends. Greg had affectionate, generous parents I secretly wished were mine. We acted out each Wednesday's *Six Million Dollar Man* epi-sode the next day and got excited about the arrival of Ossie Ardiles and Ricky Villa at Spurs after the 1978 World Cup. And when I was with my friends, I felt good.

There were also times I hated them. I remember them laughing along when someone made a joke about my 'rubber lips' and how you could always find me in a dark room by the whites of my eyes. I recall Spencer Wicks, who was nine and in the year above me, tell-ing me to go back home, back to the jungle. And Alan Taylor, who put his arm around my shoulder and explained that Enoch was right: you lot just can't help making trouble.

I remember their anthropological fascination with the colour of my skin and the texture of my hair; the kids stretching their arms out next to mine in the summer to compare tans, as they put it. In fact, their colour fascinated me as much as mine did them. White seemed such an inadequate description for the mottled flesh that could flush to ruby with excitement, skin so pale that sometimes you could see the veins through it, alternately red and blue, pulsing beneath the surface.

My racist friends. I envied the freedom their colour bestowed. Whiteness meant a lack of self-consciousness. No one pointed or laughed or sneered. No one made monkey noises or mimed the throwing of spears. It meant you could lose yourself in a game of war or British Bulldog in the playground without being yanked from fantasy by a shout of 'Wog!' or 'Kunta Kinte!' How normal, how everyday, the hostility around me felt. On TV, Jim Davidson cracked racist gags about Chalky White, his doltish, fictional black friend. Black footballers ran on to the pitch to monkey chants from their own supporters. My desk in school had the interlocked NF logo of the National Front scratched into the wood with a compass. A gang of six skinheads hung about outside the Chinese chip shop across the road from school. They'd left at fifteen but still remained prominent figures for us. That was how we'd end up if we didn't stop mucking about and get down to work, our teachers warned. The skinheads wore cherry-red, sixteen-hole Dr Martens and bleached jeans and I found them fantastically intimidating. Although they were too caught up in play-fighting and throwing chips at each other to notice me, I avoided crossing over to their side of the road. Their presence felt like a warning against presuming that I could ever fit in properly among the people I'd grown up with.

At home I watched *Spider-Man and His Amazing Friends* with my brother and sister, just the three of us in the house before our parents returned from work. No one mentioned the threat of being beaten up or the mortification of getting teased for having an African name. The hurt we carried didn't always express itself in words.

After school one afternoon, aged nine, I stood in front of the bathroom mirror. I had a Brillo pad in my hand and I started to scrub my face. My forehead reddened. The wire fibres of the pad tugged at my skin. It stung terribly but I continued. The skin began to tear and little beads of blood prickled their way to the surface. I went at it harder, until my forehead was grazed and red and raw to the touch. It was soon too painful to continue. But I also knew there was no point in carrying on. I wanted to scrub the blackness away. But I couldn't erase what I saw in the mirror.

I often felt unbearably visible. That sensation intensified as I grew older and saw my body become an object of apprehension and hostility. That afternoon parked outside the Express Dairy with my dad, debating the merits of *Capricorn One*, a conspiracy thriller about a faked NASA landing on Mars. The policeman called to investigate two suspicious Black men lurking in the neighbourhood. My amusement at the time, not realizing what it meant.

When I was eighteen, I left home for university. I was studying politics at the LSE. My siblings had already moved out and my parents decided that, once I'd gone, they'd also leave. They relocated to Northampton, where they could get a bigger house with a smaller mortgage. After their departure there was no reason for me to go back to Queensbury. I still had friends there, but once I'd left I couldn't face seeing them, or Queensbury, again. It wasn't just that I wanted to put the people and the place behind me. My aim was a larger, more final one: to eradicate the very memory of those years of shame. Photos, records, old exercise books, any memento of my childhood had to go. I gathered everything I could find, dumped it into a black bin bag and left it out with the rubbish. I would refuse to look back. In this way, I'd be free to be myself for the first time ever. That's what I told myself. And I think at the time I really believed it.

—

Much of what I was drawn to in adulthood came from the style magazine *The Face*. The magazine treated the apparently throwaway stuff of pop culture – fashion, music, film and clubbing – with a compelling gravity. Poring over each issue as a teenager in Queensbury, I had discovered Jim Jarmusch movies and Def Jam records, Detroit techno and Jean-Michel Basquiat. Its pages held out the promise that you could be who you wanted to be on your own terms, instead of being defined by the expectations or prejudices of others. I longed to be part of its world.

After I graduated from university in 1990, I managed to get a couple of stories published in the magazine, and over time I became a regular contributor. *The Face*'s offices were in a former textile factory in Clerkenwell: a big, open-plan place with bare, dark-wood floors and a bank of windows running along a wall. I relished going there, ostensibly to pitch feature ideas, but mostly just to hang out with the editorial staff, whose writing I'd followed for years. Like me, they seemed to be outsiders, a bit too cerebral or self-conscious to ever throw themselves wholeheartedly into a situation; more likely instead to look on from the sidelines. I felt at home among them. This was where I belonged, I told myself.

By this time I was out at gigs or clubs or film previews most nights. I flew to Iceland and Los Angeles and New York to interview Björk, Ice Cube, the Wu-Tang Clan. And when I was home there was always another deadline to meet. There was no time to dwell on the memory of skinheads or the so-called jokes from my best friends. I could continue to deny the past and, by so doing, convince myself I'd found a new pattern for my adult life. What I didn't realize was how much of myself I lost in that process.

I remember the moment when I began to see the consequences of my actions. It came at the end of a short, failed romance.

I met Léa in the summer of 1994. She was French, a photographer, short-haired, stylish and gamine, like Jean Seberg in *Breathless*, I thought. I'd had a few girlfriends in the past, but intimacy made me nervous. It felt too exposing. Being close to someone else meant also having to get in contact with myself, which was a prospect I couldn't abide. Léa was more comfortable in her opinions and feelings than anyone else I knew. She seemed to exist in a state of completeness that I was both drawn to and intimidated by.

We dated for a few months but then she left London for Paris. We decided to keep seeing each other, meeting up once or twice a month for long weekends in our respective cities, and at the end of the year we arranged a trip to Arles, a pretty town in southern France with a history that reached back to Roman times.

It was a disastrous holiday. Together for a whole week after months of shorter meetings, it was as though we were seeing each other properly for the first time. Léa was exactingly curious. I watched her wandering through the Old Town or out into fields with her eye to the viewfinder of her camera, searching, searching for the elusive sights – a footpath winding shyly into the woods or an old china tea set from the flea market, its floral patterning faded practically to invisibility by the wear of many hands – that would enable her to shoot the visual stories of light and darkness she aspired to create.

She brought the same acuteness to her own feelings, poring over her anxieties and desires and past love affairs with daunting honesty and directness. Threading through the town's cobbled streets after her, I wanted to be just as bold, just as open. But I'd become so used to hiding away inside myself that I couldn't respond to her with any spontaneity. I was stuck in the shallows of my emotions, with nothing meaningful to offer back.

The trip became a torture. Each day I felt her draw further away from me. I was frozen by shame. On our last morning together, Léa woke early to catch a flight back to Paris. I heard her moving round the hotel room, packing in the dark while I was still half-asleep. When she was done, she leaned over the bed, kissed me faintly on the lips and left for the airport. I travelled back to London that afternoon, feeling empty and miserable. We spoke by phone the next day.

'This isn't working,' she said. I didn't hear much else after that.

We agreed to stay friends. But there were no more weekends in Paris. And when we spoke, I could never bear to mention that trip again.

———

I was ashamed to admit how hurt and lonely I felt after Léa finished with me. There were still clubs and parties to go to, and more trips for *The Face* to Jamaica and Japan, but my sense of loss didn't dissipate. Around that time I left my room in a shared flat in Islington and went to live by myself. I see that move now as an act of deliberate self-isolation. My new flat was squeezed between two office blocks on the edge of the City of London. It was in a commercial area, so I had no neighbours other than the men and women bustling in and out of those offices. By evening, the streets were deserted.

It was in the solitude of the flat that I began having nightmares again. They came unpredictably – sometimes months apart or at dawn, after I'd made it unscathed through the earlier hours of darkness – and they were disturbingly vivid. On one occasion, I discovered myself in the back garden of my family home. The lawn was overgrown and unkempt, littered with rusting tools, an old rotary mower, a pair of shears and coils of dried-out dog faeces. I glimpsed movement in the grass; a snake sliding quickly out of sight, green and, I guessed, venomous. I saw now that the lawn was infested with them. I tiptoed forward, trying to cross the grass without stepping on them, knowing already it was an impossible task. I felt jaws clamp on my leg, fangs pierce the skin on my ankle, a jangle of pain as poison spread through my body.

As the dreams became more numerous, I noticed the same figure was always at their centre. I came to know him as the stranger. He appeared for the first time when I was scaling a cliff face. It was dark. The rocks were cold and sheer. I inched my way up, feeling for handholds with the tips of my fingers; hour after hour of effort while the ground below vanished into a black void. Near the top, I reached a small plateau where I could rest. But there was a man standing on the ledge blocking the way. He was dressed in black and I couldn't see his face.

I was exhausted. I reached up for help. He didn't move. Then, very deliberately, he began to kick my fingers away from the shelf. Each time I scrambled to catch hold again, he pushed me again. He showed no emotion and made no sound. With a final swipe of his foot, he shoved me free. I tipped backwards into nothingness, falling for forever.

From then on, the stranger became a regular presence, lurking at the edge of a crowd or driving beside me on the motorway. His appearance coincided with the point when a dream lurched into horror. The crowd would turn into a lynch mob; I'd lose control of my car at high speed – he seemed to hover over my nights so that I dreaded going to sleep for fear of seeing him.

To try to make sense of the dreams, I kept a notebook beside my bed, forcing myself to scribble down what I remembered before I was fully awake. Writing brought no consolation. I found I couldn't adequately capture the alien texture, the gearless slippage from calm to violence, that I'd experienced. I filled up half the book with notes but the sight of the accumulating pages depressed me: proof of my own powerlessness against the force of those visions.

———

In the autumn, I received a call from a friend, Sasha. She was in a hospital in Camden after having herself sectioned. Would I come to visit?

Sasha was a senior editor on a fashion magazine. She was quick, perceptive, well practised at spying out the conceits and vulnerabilities of strangers. We'd been friends for the past five years. During that time, I'd seen her break up with her husband, struggle with alcoholism and then sobriety – and now a psychotic episode. She'd smashed a mirror, wanted to cut herself into pieces with the shards, and become so scared at what she might do that she'd gone to her doctor and asked to be hospitalized.

Yet when I met her on the ward she was cheerful. We sat in a corner of the day room. A pale light percolated through the windows. Sasha tucked her knees up under her chin. She wore grey jogging bottoms and a blue hoodie. A large woman with thinning hair moaned softly to herself in an easy chair.

In Sasha's fortnight in hospital, her most frequent visitor had been her therapist. This was the woman who'd helped her confront her alcoholism. The breakdown was a setback, Sasha conceded, but at least therapy had given her enough perspective to see that she needed help. She looked up at me.

'Have you ever thought of seeing someone?'

The idea felt alarming and embarrassing. I wondered if she was judging me. Was I a failure or a fraud in her eyes? But the directness of her question captured my imagination. Until then I'd never admitted to myself how confused and unhappy the past few years had left me.

'Something's not right,' I said. 'I can feel it but I can't put it into words. It's like I've lost touch with myself.'

Sasha said that, if I was interested, she could help me find a therapist. Across the room a man in green pyjamas, thin and sallow in complexion, began to swear loudly and angrily. Outside the windows, traffic rumbled by, faintly audible, as if from a great distance. Sasha said she was going to take a nap. She'd been sleeping a lot since admitting herself.

'It's a relief being here,' she said. 'You don't have to hold everything in any more.'

—

I didn't take up Sasha's offer until the following February, after I'd returned from Minneapolis. Prince was releasing a new album after a long contractual dispute with his record label. The record was called *Emancipation* and the cover featured a pair of hands breaking free from a set of shackles. I was invited to Paisley Park, his home-cum-studio complex to interview him. The one condition on talking to him, a restriction he imposed on every journalist at the time, was that I wasn't allowed to write down or record our conversation. I said yes straight away. Prince was the artist I'd most loved growing up, and I still adored him. I was wildly excited about doing the story.

Perhaps it's partly that absence of record-keeping which gave the whole encounter a hallucinatory quality as I look back at it. The night I arrived, Prince played a small, invite-only gig at Paisley Park. It was thrilling enough to see him onstage up close, let alone across a table in a conference room the following day. In person, he was charming, elegant and good-humoured. But the interview was overshadowed for me by what I'd seen earlier in the day during a guided tour of Paisley Park. As well as the recording studios and rehearsal spaces in the complex, I was shown past a room decorated like a nursery. The walls were painted sky blue with white clouds and the floor was scattered with toys.

Earlier in the year, Prince had married Mayte Garcia, a dancer in his band. I knew before the interview that she'd given birth to their first baby, a son, just a few days earlier. The nursery was waiting ready for him to arrive from hospital. But what I also knew from reports was that the baby was desperately ill. He was suffering from Pfeiffer syndrome, a rare genetic disorder affecting the skull. Prince didn't mention his son during the interview, although it's hard to imagine the boy wasn't on his mind. He insisted, rather, that he felt great and was excited to be finally recording on his own terms again. As he talked, all I could do was picture the empty nursery and think about the gulf between his words and what must have been the true state of his emotions.

It was snowing as I left Paisley Park and by the time I landed in Britain Prince and Mayte's baby was dead. Of course I couldn't blame him for avoiding the subject when we talked. He was justified his privacy in what must have been a situation of extraordinary heartbreak. All the same, I felt somehow dispirited. I'd admired Prince as an artist of rare honesty and creative bravery for most of my life. But if he could continue to conduct interviews and promote his album in such distressing circumstances, how sincere could he ever have been? The gap between his words and emotions disturbed me. I sat down to write the story. Instead of assessing the album, all I wanted to do was describe the hollowness of my meeting. Yet, as I typed, I also realized that my disappointment at his lack of openness probably had more to do with me than with Prince.

Through Sasha, I contacted a therapist. Christina received patients in the front room of her house in Highgate. She was in her late fifties, silver-haired, elegantly dressed, and she listened attentively as I talked, perched opposite her on the edge of a daybed. Sometimes her cat Zoe, a beautiful blue-grey Persian, insinuated herself into the room. She'd curl up on the far end of the daybed, purring softly. Her presence was quite the compliment, insisted Christina. Apparently Zoe was very particular about which patients she took an interest in.

Despite winning the cat's approval, I dreaded therapy. I felt awkward and ashamed talking to Christina. How could I articulate the swirl of anxious thoughts in my head? Or let down my guard to reveal feelings I'd kept penned away for years? I spoke only in generalities, about how I didn't feel 'good' or 'whole', without addressing the emotions behind those words. I squirmed with embarrassment listening to myself wallow in blandness.

Even the journey to her house in Highgate was hard to bear. Ominous signs lined the way. To get there I caught the Tube to Archway, the carriage almost empty except for a few scattered passengers like me riding north against the flow of central London-bound morning travellers. Outside the Underground, Archway Tower, an enormous obsidian office block with blank windows, loomed over the station like a sentinel to the afterlife. I never saw anyone enter or leave the building and it was impossible to look up at it without a shudder of foreboding. Further up the hill that led to Christina's, a fussily ornate Victorian bridge ran high over the main road, offering a popular departure spot for the locally suicidal.

Sometimes I arrived at her house late. Despite my apologies, Christina would be annoyed. 'You have a choice. If you're late, it's a decision to not respect me or our sessions together.' She was right. Secretly I was glad to have her angry. It was a small rebellion against the stiltedness of our meetings. And the minor guilt of being late was a welcome distraction from the larger sense of shame and sadness that came over me with each session.

We struggled along uneasily like this for several months. I became more and more frustrated and worn out. What was the point of talking to someone when I couldn't find the words to communicate? I considered quitting the whole excruciating situation. And I might have done so if Christina hadn't asked a particular question towards the end of an especially halting session.

It was a drab morning in June. I'd spent most of the time grappling for something to say. I wanted to flee outside. Even the grey, damp weather felt preferable to the straitened atmosphere in the room.

Hours seemed to pass without a word between us. Eventually Christina broke the silence.

'What do you dream about, Ekow?'

Until then, I'd said nothing about my nightmares. Now, I described a dream from earlier that week in which a troll-like elderly woman, small and misshapen and dressed in a white doctor's coat, was clutching a whirring electric drill. She wanted to drill into my head and I was helpless to get away. I was repulsed by her ugliness, and scared by the drill which also had a probing, phallic quality.

I sat back on the daybed, flushing at the memory of the scene.

To my embarrassment, Christina broke into laughter. It was the first time I'd seen her abandon a guise of studied calm. I felt annoyed that she'd apparently done so only to mock me.

'Is that really how you see me?' she said, stifling her laughter.

I got it. The aged crone was her, or at least the version of her I'd manifested out of fear of being stripped bare or penetrated, in our sessions.

'You know it's not how I really see you,' I stammered.

Christina brushed my apologies away. She leaned forward. 'Is there more you want to say, Ekow?'

I told her how insistent and forceful my dreams had been over the past few years. In a recent instance, I was riding alone in an empty Tube carriage. As if compelled, I stuck out my left middle finger and plucked the upper joint free, revealing the empty socket, white with bone and wet with some clear viscous fluid. I woke up feeling queasy at the memory of my finger slipping apart and the residue of sticky liquid left in the stump.

Before I could continue, she interrupted me. Our session was over. For the first time since I'd been seeing her I wanted to carry on talking. I was more at ease discussing dreams than abstract emotions. We continued to explore them and, as we did so, I began to look forward to our sessions together. My hope was that in addressing them, the nightmares would go away, yet the opposite was true: they became more violent and unsettling. I was pitched back into the Ruritanian town. I was still running from a mob. And, increasingly, I felt the presence of the stranger. He hunted me assiduously.

On one occasion, I found myself running across a deserted town square. In a medieval tower overlooking the square, the stranger hefted a sniper's rifle to his shoulder. He peered through the telescopic lens. The perspective of the dream shifted. I saw myself running through the crosshairs of the rifle. He pulled the trigger. I woke with a start. How long could I keep running from him before he caught up with me?

Some months later, in October, just after the clocks had gone back, when the days felt hushed and gloomy, he came closer than ever before. My car had broken down at night on the motorway. I was parked on the hard shoulder, huddled in the front seat waiting for a recovery truck. Cars roared by, headlights glaring. To the side of the road was a field. A man walked towards me across the grass, intermittently illuminated by the lights of passing vehicles. Reaching my car, he tugged at the door handle. The car rocked back and forth. He scratched at the side windows and banged on the windscreen. I felt completely trapped and I knew he would break in and kill me. I woke shouting, trying to fight him off.

It was early morning and still dark outside. I felt a stinging pain in my mouth as if a pin was stuck in there. I went to the bathroom, clicked on the light and looked in the mirror. A sickle-shaped wound of about half an inch stretched along the tip of my tongue on the left side. The vertical face of the wound had a raw, livid complexion. There was little sign of blood, just a stain on my lower front teeth and a metallic taste at the back of my mouth. My tongue flickered oblivious in the mirror. I felt sick with horror at the sight of it. It was hard to believe what had happened, yet the evidence was right before my eyes. I had bitten off a piece of my tongue and swallowed it whole as I slept.

'You can't keep running. You have to go after him.'

Christina's response surprised me.

To escape the stranger's hold, she insisted, I needed to understand who he was and what he was after. Why was his face hidden?

How come he was hunting me? Until I confronted him, the dreams wouldn't end.

I lay back on the daybed. The room smelled of cat hair. I stared at an oil painting on the opposite wall, trying to fathom its thick swirls of murky red and burnt orange. How do you chase down a figure from your own nightmares?

I'd been seeing Christina for about a year. From stray comments I'd guessed she had a grown-up daughter. I even had an idea that the daughter was responsible for the oil painting. Beyond that, Christina's life was a mystery to me. Nevertheless I felt she was kind and patient and I thought of her as a fellow explorer, helping me to map a path through that hidden world. I trusted her. So we went forth together into the darkness, neither of us knowing the way.

This is how we hunted him: by not being afraid, and by leaving him with no place to hide. I revisited my memories from school and the years afterwards that I'd tried to excise. All those faces I couldn't bear to see again: Alan, Greg, Spencer. The failure of the trip with Léa. How much it hurt to look back. And how long it all took. I began seeing Christina three times a week. Even at that rate, it was an arduous climb. Eighteen months. Two years. Three years. Each morning, hating the Tube journey, the forbidding bulk of Archway Tower, the suicide bridge. Each morning, dreading the rawness of the session ahead, but going anyway and giving what I had.

Finally, I closed in on the stranger. April 2001. A cold spring. Long days of rain. I dreamed of him two nights in succession. On the first night, I found myself in the inner chamber of a stone temple. On the flagstones at the centre of the room was a wooden box, a foot square. The box was shut. It was waiting to be opened. I woke up, fell asleep again and returned to the same scene, but a few minutes earlier than before. Now I saw that it was the stranger who had left the container. I saw him set it on the floor and creep away. The box was glowing and I was sure it contained a bomb. The prospect terrified me but I felt in some way that I had no choice. I had to open it. The following night I returned to the temple. The stranger was holding the box before him. This time he didn't slink away. Light streamed from its seams. I knew that opening the lid would trigger an explosion. I could already feel the heat of the blast. I wanted to run away but I drew closer. His face was obscured by shadow as usual but I was close enough now to touch him. He held the box towards me. I was trembling. I opened the lid. Light sprayed from its interior. It vanished harmlessly in my hands. The stranger remained, standing opposite me. For the first time his face was uncovered. I recognized him all too well.

It wasn't yet morning when I woke up. A loud, insistent rain was falling on to the empty street. I gazed at the ceiling, trying to absorb the dream. I had met the stranger at last, and I understood now that I had always known him. I had looked into his face and seen myself staring back.

———

When I return in my mind to those sessions with Christina, I picture the oil painting on her wall, its swirling reds and oranges. At the time, I imagined my unconscious as a shadow realm of ghosts. I realize now that if it could be said to have any physical form, it was much more like the oil painting – mysterious and confounding, but bearing the evidence of a guiding intelligence.

I think of it too like the sentient planet Solaris, in the movie by Andrei Tarkovsky. A group of scientists in a space station orbit a mysterious giant planet. The surface of Solaris is blanketed in an ocean that swirls and shifts colour in constant, mesmerizing motion. And while the scientists look down from their spacecraft, trying to comprehend its secrets, Solaris is peering up into their minds. As they sleep, the planet taps their most intimate memories, presenting back to them fragments of buried trauma and desire.

This is as good an analogy for the unconscious mind as any I can summon. Throughout my twenties, when I felt so lost and isolated, my unconscious was reaching out to me. It spoke in images, not words, in dreams that were often baffling, even terrifying. But there was no hostile intent behind them. They were signals of the unresolved sorrow I'd carried with me since childhood. The longer I ignored them, the more desperate those signals grew. This was how the stranger came into being – he marked the vehemence with which I ran from pain and sadness. He was a mirror to my fears and he might have haunted me forever if I hadn't sought him out on my own terms.

I'd imagined him as a force of malice. In fact, I couldn't have been more wrong. He was a messenger with a single dispatch: look to yourself. Once that was delivered, he no longer had a purpose. My nightmares faded away and I never saw him again.

The stranger was never out to kill me. He was trying to save my life.

One last dream from that period stays with me. It occurred just a few days after my final encounter with the stranger. In the dream I was standing on a humpbacked stone bridge looking down at the river that ran placidly beneath it. The day was clear and calm. I felt deliciously light. Clambering on to the wall of the bridge, I stretched my arms out to either side. I knew for certain that I was inside a dream. The realization was glorious. It meant I could come to no harm. I pitched myself off the bridge towards the river. As I fell, I made the choice to rise, and felt myself ascend, haltingly, into the sky. For a moment, a flash of fear set my limbs flailing. And then I levelled out and regained a sense of serenity. I glided over woods of beech and chestnut. Moorland flecked with purple heather. The earth unfurled beneath me as I flew like a song waiting to be heard. A song many lifetimes in the making.

After his 1833 performance at the Theatre Royal, Ira Aldridge left London to continue touring the provinces and established himself as a major theatrical star. In the 1850s, he travelled to continental Europe, where he was met with widespread acclaim. Among multiple honours, he was awarded the Golden Cross of Leopold by the Tsar of Russia and received the Gold Medal for Arts and Sciences from Friedrich Wilhelm IV, King of Prussia. He never performed in Covent Garden again.

Having reached the North Pole in 1909, Matthew Henson spent the remainder of his career working in obscurity as a clerk at the US Customs House in New York. Belated recognition came after his death in 1955: Henson's body was reinterred at Arlington National Cemetery with full military honours in 1987, and in 2000 he was posthumously awarded the Hubbard Medal by the National Geographic Society. In 2021, a crater at the South Pole of the moon was given the name Henson in tribute to his achievements as an explorer.

Upon leaving Algeria, Frantz Fanon worked with the FLN in Tunisia, and in 1960 was appointed ambassador to Ghana by the FLN-led Provisional Government of the Algerian Republic. He died of leukaemia in 1961. During his lifetime, Fanon published two seminal books: *Black Skin, White Masks*, an analysis of the psychological effects of racism, and *The Wretched of the Earth*, a searing interrogation of race and revolutionary struggle that established him as the leading anti-colonialist thinker of the twentieth century. The Blida-Joinville Hospital where he worked in the 1950s was renamed the Frantz Fanon Hospital after his death.

Malcolm X was assassinated on 21 February 1965 while speaking at the Audubon Ballroom in New York, a week after his house was firebombed in Queens. Today, May 19th, his birthday, is honoured as Malcolm X Day in many cities across America. He remains an iconic figure, recognized internationally for his tireless pursuit of racial justice.

Justin Fashanu retired from professional football in 1997. He was working as a coach in Maryland, Georgia, when he was charged with sexually assaulting a teenage boy in April 1998. He denied all wrongdoing. Fashanu died on 3 May 1998, taking his own life. He was inducted into the National Football Museum's Hall of Fame in 2020. He remains England's first and only openly gay male professional footballer.

Acknowledgements

I am enormously grateful to Hermione Thompson, my editor, for her insight and astuteness in helping shape this book and her careful reading at each stage in its development. My thanks to David Godwin, my agent, for his guidance. To Simon Prosser for his continued support. And to Sarah-Jane Forder for her clear-sighted and thoughtful work as copy-editor. To Richard Benson – I am deeply appreciative of your friendship, encouragement and advice. My gratitude to Amoako Boafo and Mariane Ibrahim Gallery for allowing me to reproduce the painting *Steve Mekoudja,* 2019, on the cover. I also wish to express my thanks to the Whiting Foundation for its award of a Whiting Creative Nonfiction Grant, which I received at a pivotal stage in the development of this book.

A number of works have been helpful in the course of my writing. They include: Bernth Lindfors, *Ira Aldridge: The African Roscius*; Bernth Lindfors, *Ira Aldridge: The Early Years, 1807–1833*; Shane White, *Stories of Freedom in Black New York*; Gordon McMullan, *Shakespeare in Ten Acts*; Marvin McAllister, *White People Do Not Know How to Behave at Entertainments Designed for Ladies and Gentlemen of Colour: William Brown's African and American Theater*; Matthew A. Henson, *Matthew A. Henson's Historic Arctic Journey*; Bradley Robinson, *Dark Companion*; Lisa Bloom, *Gender on Ice: American Ideologies of Polar Expeditions*; Kenn Harper, *Give Me My Father's Body*; Bruce Henderson, *True North – Peary, Cook and the*

Race to the Pole; Fergus Fleming, *Ninety Degrees North: The Quest For the North Pole*; Wally Herbert, *The Noose of Laurels: Robert E. Peary and the Race to the North Pole*; Susan Kaplan and Genevieve LeMoine, *Peary's Arctic Quest: Untold Stories from Robert E. Peary's North Pole Expeditions*; Josephine Peary, *My Arctic Journal: A Year Among Ice-fields and Eskimos*; S. Allen Counter, *North Pole Legacy: Black, White and Eskimo*; Frantz Fanon, *The Wretched of the Earth*; Frantz Fanon, *Alienation and Freedom*; Jean Khalfa and Robert J. C. Young (eds.), *Frantz Fanon, Black Skin, White Masks*; David Macey, *Frantz Fanon: A Biography*; Leo Zeilig, *Frantz Fanon: A Political Biography*; Nigel C. Gibson and Roberto Beneduce, *Frantz Fanon, Psychiatry and Politics*; Richard C. Keller, *Colonial Madness: Psychiatry in French North Africa*; Alice Cherki, *Frantz Fanon: A Portrait*; Malcolm X, *The Autobiography of Malcolm X: As Told to Alex Haley*; Leslie Alexander Lacy, *The Rise and Fall of a Proper Negro*; Les Payne and Tamara Payne, *The Dead are Arising*; Manning Marable, *Malcolm X: A Life of Reinvention*; Herb Boyd and Ilyasah Al-Shabazz (eds.), *The Diary of Malcolm X: El-Hajj Malik El-Shabazz, 1964*; Maya Angelou, *All God's Children Need Travelling Shoes*; Jim Read, *Justin Fashanu: The Biography*; Nick Baker, *Forbidden Forward: The Justin Fashanu Story*; Brian Clough, *Clough: The Autobiography*; Duncan Hamilton, *Provided You Don't Kiss Me: 20 Years with Brian Clough*; Jonathan Wilson, *Brian Clough: Nobody Ever Says Thank You: The Biography;* Simon Garfield, *The End of Innocence: Britain in the Time of Aids.*

Publisher's Note

The Strangers is a work of creative non-fiction. Some of the characters, interactions and events it depicts have been drawn from the historical record and others are products of the author's imagination. The book was inspired by the lives of real people.

Permissions and Credits

The author and publisher gratefully acknowledge the permission granted to reproduce the copyright material in this book. Every effort has been made to trace copyright holders and to obtain their permission. The publisher apologises for any errors or omissions and, if notified of any corrections, will make suitable acknowledgement in future reprints or editions of this book.

Portrait of Ira Aldridge after James Northcote, private collection, on loan to the National Portrait Gallery, London; reproduced by kind permission of the rights owners. Image of Matthew Alexander Henson, head-and-shoulders portrait, facing front, wearing his fur suit, reproduced courtesy of Library of Congress, LC-USZ62-42993. Image of Frantz Fanon © Archives Frantz Fanon/IMEC. Image of Malcolm X at a press conference given by Martin Luther King at the U.S. Capitol about the Senate debate on the Civil Rights Act of 1964 by Marion S. Trikosko, reproduced courtesy of Library of Congress, LC-DIG-ppmsc-01274. Image of Justin Fashanu © PA Images/Alamy Stock Photo.

Extract from *Notes of a Native Son* by James Baldwin (Beacon Press, 1955). Extracts from *The Wretched of the Earth* by Frantz Fanon, reprinted by permission of HarperCollins Publishers Ltd © (1961) (Frantz Fanon). Extracts from Frantz Fanon's letters to Daniel Guerin and the Minister of Algiers, reprinted by kind permission of the Frantz Fanon Estate. Lyrics quoted from 'I Am Strange' by Sun Ra. Extracts from *Amsterdam News:* 'Malcolm X

Flees for Life; Muslim Factions at War' (20 June 1964); 'Muslim Factions at War; Clay's Ex-Secretary on Run' by Les Matthews (16 January 1965); 'Exclusive: Malcolm X Speaks' by James Booker (6 February 1965). Extracts from *The New York Times:* 'Malcolm X Calls for Muslim Peace' © 27 June 1964, The New York Times Company; 'Malcolm Rejects Racist Doctrine' © 4 October 1964, The New York Times Company; all rights reserved; used under license. Extract from the *Pittsburgh Courier* (7 November 1964), reprinted by permission of the *Pittsburgh Courier* archives. Lyrics quoted from 'Memory Lane (Sittin' in da Park)' by Nasir Jones, Christopher Martin, Reuben Wilson and Peg Barsella. Lyrics quoted from 'Shook Ones Part II' by Albert Johnson and Kejuan Muchita. Lyrics quoted from 'Dear Mama' by Tupac Shakur, Joe Sample and Tony Pizarro. Lyrics quoted from '4:44' by Shawn Carter, Dion Wilson and Kanan Keeney. Lucille Clifton, 'reply' from *The Collected Poems of Lucille Clifton*, copyright © 1991 by Lucille Clifton; reprinted with the permission of The Permissions Company, LLC on behalf of BOA Editions, Ltd., boaeditions.org. Extract from *The Bluest Eye* by Toni Morrison (Holt, Rinehart and Winston, 1970).